SUNSHINE, SIXES AND CIDER

The History of Somerset Cricket

The county ground with its much-praised new pavilion, as it looks today (*above*)

And how it used to look (*below*). Note the old familiar scoreboard, the tall hoardings and the distant Quantocks

SUNSHINE, SIXES AND CIDER

The History of Somerset Cricket

David Foot

DAVID & CHARLES
Newton Abbot   London   North Pomfret (Vt)

To Mark, my son, whose gentle persistence led to this book; to all the Somerset players in it – many I watched, though I pretended I saw all of them

Statistical Supplement by **Michael Hill**
Additional research by **Keith Ball**

British Library Cataloguing in Publication Data

Foot, David
  Sunshine sixes and cider : the history
  of Somerset Cricket.
  1. Somerset County Cricket Club – History
  I. Title
  796.35'863'094238   GV921.S6

  ISBN 0-7153-8890-8

Typeset by Typesetters (Birmingham) Ltd,
Smethwick, West Midlands
and printed in Somerset, Great Britain
by Butler and Tanner, Frome and London
for David & Charles Publishers plc
Brunel House   Newton Abbot   Devon

Published in the United States of America
by David & Charles Inc
North Pomfret   Vermont 05053   USA

Contents

Introduction

The title of this book is unashamedly romantic. For me to have hinted so early on at recurrent crises – mostly financial – and darker deeds would have been to betray a lifetime of misty-eyed affection for a county which, as doting schoolboy and supposedly impartial cricket writer, I have watched in all its endearing, infuriating, quirky, charming moods.

Somerset's variegated history sways with the sheer weight of mavericks: from Herbert Hewett to Ian Botham. There have been a few despots and committee rooms have reverberated with invective. One or two players, among them a captain, left in a huff when their authority was challenged. Another, I seem to remember, was banned from the game when cannabis got a trifle confused with cover drives.

This is a pot-pourri of fantasy – and frailty, in a way. So much about Somerset is fantastical: cricketers who kept wicket for both sides or played under an assumed name to fool the Inland Revenue. There were batsmen who wore their homburgs at the wicket or, in the case of an amateur from Wells, who insisted on wearing a beret all the time because he was bald. One, Seymour Clark, made nine ducks in a row and decided to terminate his brief, unproductive first-class career.

E. W. Swanton said that no county which had 'Crusoe' Robertson-Glasgow in its team could ever be remotely dull. Nor, surely, with the loquacious Bill Andrews around. He once kept his plus-fours on under his flannels because the weather was so cold; and to save on expenses before the war, he was known to pitch his little scout's tent on the ground at Clacton – next to the beer tent, of course.

Bill was apt to speak out of turn. So did Dar Lyon when he criticised Jardine's appointment as captain of England. So did the brilliant, tragic Harold Gimblett, usually in the hearing of the starchier members at Lord's. Andrews was sacked four times for his pains; Gimblett wilfully prejudiced his future as a Test player. In this book I have tried to explore the rather blurred pre-Lansdown days of Somerset cricket, gone on to dally over famous names like Woods, White and Wellard, and finally savoured – as have all the county's supporters – the triumphant era that came, after agonising disappointments and years of waiting, in the late seventies and early eighties.

Status has never been easily earned by Somerset. In the early years there were too many cheap jokes at the county's expense, though the lengthy cast list of eccentric part-time cricketers (on reflection, not only amateurs) encouraged the patronising chortles. Test match recognition did come, however grudgingly, with Len Braund and later Jack White. In 1924, four

Somerset men played for the Gents, which suggests the county was strong both on playing ability and social graces that summer. In 1980, for the fourth Test against the West Indians at Leeds, Somerset supplied four players, including the two captains – Botham and Richards, who was standing in for Lloyd – and both umpires, Bill Alley and Ken Palmer.

The book looks at the contentious balance between amateurs and professionals between the wars. One amateur from that period feels I have been rather less than fair in my judgement. I hope not. I carefully dusted off my own compounded memories and talked to the erstwhile occupants of the separate changing rooms, as it were, before making my reassessment. Somerset had some delightful amateurs, a number of whom were always prepared to share a beer and a railway carriage with the pros. The county's professionals, bronze-faced, wholehearted, with that tell-tale flicker of good natured cynicism in their eyes, were perhaps never quite as subservient as we imagined. That talented, taciturn all-rounder Ernie Robson, once given a silver cigar holder and brandy flask by Ranji who admired his bowling so much, stood up to Sammy Woods – and not many did that. The two were batting together and Woods suddenly said: 'Just make sure you keep your end up, Ernie.' It was a scorching day and the quiet pro had no doubt already been toiling away as a bowler. His reply was uncharacteristic. 'You look after your end, sir, and I'll look after mine.' Robson went on to make 104.

That admirable journalist, the late Ron Roberts – I took over his job on a Bristol evening paper – conscientiously charted the first sixty years of Somerset's history. This book was not intended as merely an up-dated version. I set myself a slightly more anecdotal brief and went to different interviewees. Maybe some of the interpretations and conclusions will also vary. Modern Somerset, resilient Somerset, has international cricketers of ageless magnificence, a new pavilion and an emotional wave of loyal support that, like the distant Quantocks in the mists, shows a reluctance to disappear when once again the wins become rather more elusive. The county club, for all its whims, flaws and caprices, remains a creature to be much loved.

Acknowledgements

A history like this demands a careful balance between statistic and anecdote, the bones and the flesh. Long ago, as a fledgling journalist, I learned the value of accuracy; but facts, when it comes to cricket, have not been from choice my forte. For that reason I have been apt to lean towards Keith Ball, a gentle and ever-helpful cricket historian, in my pursuit of elusive scores and scorers. He has kept a conscientious umpire's eye on me whenever, in an imaginative burst, I have threatened momentarily to lose length and line. I thank him in the same way that I thank Michael Hill, the county chairman and the most diligent and good-natured of cricket statisticians, for his excellent supplement at the rear of the book.

My gratitude goes to the Somerset County Club for their co-operation. There were fruitful, nostalgic hours spent with many – with Nigel Daniell, who reminisced about his father and the contemporaries who called at the family home; with Vic

Robson, who also talked about his father, Horace Hazell, Rt Hon Geoffrey Rippon, QC, MP, Reg Ingle, Mandy Mitchell-Innes, Micky Walford, Colin Atkinson, John Barnwell and Cecil Buttle. Eric Hill, who should really have been persuaded to write this book, helped me with specific points of post-war history.

To all those former players who gave willingly of their time – and in some cases their hospitality – I offer my thanks. The list of helpers is a long one and there is no attempt at batting order. They include Hugh Watts, Bill Andrews, Jake Seamer, the late Maurice Tremlett, Brian Langford, Fred Castle, Louis St Vincent Powell, Roy Kerslake and Andy Wilson. Len Creed was full of zestful memories; additional facts came from Jack Burrell, John Ruddick and Richard Walsh. Somerset have much for which to thank the Supporters' Club and the Wyverns. In turn, I'm grateful for the co-operation of Rex Frost and G. A. Stedall in the case of the former, and Royse Riddell and Edward Francis the latter; equally for the co-operation of the Somerset County Record Office and Bath Reference Library.

The photographs came from various sources, apart from my own collection. I thank especially Ken Kelly for his fine illustrations, Alain Lockyer, E. Pix, Vic Robson, George Baker, *Somerset County Gazette*, BUP and Sqn Ldr J. M. Warner (RAF, Rtd) and John King. I am also grateful for permission from the Lady Lever Art Gallery to reproduce Turner's water colour, 'Wells Cathedral with a Game of Cricket'. In conclusion I thank my wife. Her patience has been in the Frank Lee class.

Bibliography

Altham, H. S., *A History of Cricket, Vol 1*
Andrews, Bill, *The Hand that Bowled Bradman*
Arlott, John, *Jack Hobbs, Profile of 'The Master'*
Bradfield, Donald, *The Lansdown Story*
Broadribb, Gerald, *Next Man In*
Bush, Robin, *The Book of Taunton*
Frith, David, *The Slow Men*
Haygarth, Arthur, *MCC Cricket Scores and Biographies, Vol 6*
Hobbs, Sir Jack, *My Life Story*
Martin-Jenkins, Christopher, *Bedside Cricket*
Parker, Grahame, *Gloucestershire Road*
Pridham, C. H. B., *The Charm of Cricket Past and Present*
Roberts, Ron, *Sixty Years of Somerset Cricket*
Robertson-Glasgow, R. C., *Crusoe on Cricket*
Wisden Cricketers' Almanack 1880–1986
Bath Evening Chronicle
Bath Express
Somerset County Gazette
Somerset County Herald
The Times
Western Daily Press
Western Gazette

NINETEENTH CENTURY

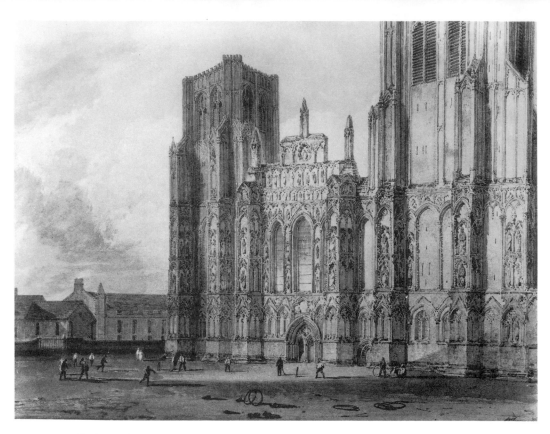

Early cricket: *Wells Cathedral* with a Game of Cricket (circa 1795) by J. M. W. Turner (Lady Lever Art Gallery, Port Sunlight)

Early days at Taunton – cricket at the county ground just after the turn of the century

Taunton, County Cricket Ground.

CHAPTER ONE
Port — and Poetry

It may be true that Lord Byron limped to the wicket at the original Lord's ground in Dorset Fields, a runner by his side to compensate for the inhibitions of a club foot, so that he could play for Harrow in their inaugural fixture with Eton. But, despite diligent research, I can find no evidence that Wordsworth and Coleridge tossed anything except radical and poetic thoughts into the air as they walked the Quantocks.

That's a pity. The history of Somerset county cricket has for ever been tinged with poetry: romantic notions and intense feelings and metaphors that mischievously leap from horror to hilarity.

Somerset men have rosy faces. They speak slowly, caressing and rolling their 'rs' with a rural relish. Their eyes sparkle with an engaging cunning. And indeed the subterfuge was there as early as the second — if not the first — county match, in 1798. All was fair, of course, in those fledgling days, just as long as the gentry passed the port and the bets were settled with civilised accord.

Nearly ninety years before that, Kent had played an unofficial match with Surrey. Cricket was becoming increasingly popular much earlier than the historic heathland contests on Broadhalfpenny Down, though Hambledon is usually taken as the convenient starting point. There were knots of enthusiasts all around the country. Gloucestershire had been experimenting, much of the cricket crude and convivial, since the 1720s. Royal approval came from Frederick, Prince of Wales, the son of King George II. He played badly, watched avidly and, it could be said, lived and died for the game. His death, in the middle of the eighteenth century, was attributed to a blow from a cricket ball.

Well-heeled young Somerset blades returned to their country seats with tales of this manly and emerging sport, and they talked it over with some of their chums on the Wiltshire side of the border. The decanter was flourished and emptied — and Somerset's first fixture was arranged. It was played on Roundway Down, Devizes, a pleasant strip of meadowland. The Eleven Gentlemen of Somerset, a composite of rather comic and unproven talents, were well beaten.

A return match was agreed for the following week, this time at Claverton Down, on the outskirts of Bath. It did not take place because several of the Somerset team were supposedly ill. 'But we'll play you later in the summer.' And they did, on their own devious terms.

I lean on that fine local historian, the late Donald Bradfield, for his account in *The Lansdown Story*. Those Eleven Gentlemen of Bath and

11

Somerset, he tells us darkly, wasted no time 'in hiring five players from the counties of Surrey, Middlesex and Hampshire'. The villainy was apparently compounded when they included a guest who they claimed was John Thomas, a basket-maker from Bath. There is something especially racy and versatile about the ageless uses of 'John Thomas'. None of these, as far as I know, had much to do with basket-making. His true name was revealed, amid the post-match jollity, as Scott. He was 'nearly the best player in England' and had been enticed to take part. Somerset won convincingly. It isn't recorded whether the Gentlemen of Wiltshire shared the joke.

For a superficially decorous city, Bath wasn't averse to pulling a trick or two. The flamboyant Beau Nash had come and gone by now. An occasional raffish and rather endearing cardsharper mentality could still be detected. When, forty years after the matches with Wiltshire, Clifton came to Bath, there was more unseemly behaviour.

Lansdown had been playing a man short. Then, well into the match, John Sainsbury, who happened to be a very good cricketer, arrived at the ground and prepared to play. 'Only if he goes in last', said Clifton, who had no intention of losing their apparent advantage because of some belated selection jiggery-pokery by the home team.

'Sainsbury's our missing player and we can decide where he goes in the batting order', they contested noisily.

The match was halted while the argument increased in rage and decibels. It was all too much for the umpires. They called 'Play' and were ignored; so they pulled up the stumps and marched off. In the early days of club cricket in Somerset – and no doubt everywhere else in the country – players flirted with the nebulous laws and resorted to the unorthodox, and at times unlawful, in pursuit of a win.

Lansdown are acknowledged as the oldest and first officially organised club in Somerset. They were formed in 1825, though there had been plenty of haphazard cricket in the county before that and a few country-house games were played. The result was never important and the shorthorns usually had to be driven off the parkland before the stumps could be stuck in the ground. Quarrymen and miners on the Mendips and shepherds on Exmoor had for a long time their own version, usually played with a stone and a club. By the mid-eighteenth century, children were beginning to improvise. Gradually players became more ambitious and their equipment improved.

Turner arrived in Wells with his sketch-pad five years before the turn of the century. His water colour, *Wells Cathedral* with a Game of Cricket, offers a gentle and revealing piece of social history. The youngsters are using long curved bats and two stumps. This evocative view of the west front of the Cathedral can be seen at the Lady Lever Art Gallery, Port Sunlight.

A Bath cricket club seems to have preceded Lansdown by a few years although there was clearly an interchange of enthusiasts. Captain Thornhill lent his meadow, Sydenham Field, near to Queens Square. It was a decidedly up-market club that went on its exclusive way from about 1817 to 1824. Then it was time for Lansdown.

Fixtures were a problem. There simply weren't enough reputable and established clubs to play. The journeys to Devon to take on either Sidmouth or Teignmouth, developed into affable social occasions. According to a Bath newspaper report of the time, when the Somerset men went to Bristol, they played on Clifton Downs: 'From an early hour the ground was thronged with multitudes of spectators, including all the beauty and fashion of Clifton and neighbourhood. Good food was provided afterwards in a marquee.'

Contemporary reports suggest that a good deal of betting went on when Clifton returned to Bath. Maybe the Bristol cricketers were inhibited by the proximity of Christchurch and other ecclesiastical restraints. Bath is smaller but it has a stronger gambling instinct.

The affluent William Keating had undeniable claims as the founder of Lansdown. But the Rev James Pycroft played for and, of course, wrote about the club and one should not carp about his tendency to bask in slightly dubious fame: 'I have as much as anyone alive the right to be called the founder of Lansdown.'

The trouble with Lansdown was that they almost got above themselves at one time. Someone called the club 'the MCC of the West'. Selection wasn't very democratic — in fact, it was often downright unfair. They were part of elitist Bath, where well-bred sportsmen vied for a place in the team.

Lansdown gave status to Somerset cricket. The county had been slow to reflect the growing interest in the game. In that first 1825 season there had been just one fixture but now they were catching up, playing MCC, Oxford University and, by 1865, a United All-England XI.

The XVIII of Lansdown contained three of the Graces — E.M., W.G. and Henry. It was both a Grace monopoly and a defeat for England. The Graces took all the wickets between them and, one assumes, never wanted to come off. 'E.M.' scored 121, one of his twelve hundreds for the Bath club. The Coroner was, throughout his eventful cricketing career, equally adept at compiling runs and ingeniously forsaking his legal duties.

From Lansdown, one could argue, indirectly came Somerset County Cricket Club. There has been a long tradition of notable 'groundsmen' and players. John Sparks, who had been a gamekeeper, was the first man hired to scythe the outfield and bowl to the members. They called him their 'pro' in 1830 and willingly subscribed to his wages provided he did all the manual work.

Years later Viv Richards cut the grass, too. The great West Indian spent a year playing for Lansdown and qualifying for Somerset. There were blisters from the mower, runs by the hundred and pleas from opponents that he should be discreetly left out. Lansdown also had briefly the delicate, talented Tom Young as pro (1910), and the Lee brothers, Jack and Frank, played there while they qualified after arriving from Middlesex in the 1920s.

The formation of Lansdown prodded other areas of Somerset to action. In 1829 the Taunton and West Somerset Club started, and over the next thirty years or so an increasing number of small clubs were formed. Some were village sides — far more classless, though the squire's sons were usually

13

invited to play (it was father's park, after all) and a remarkable number of country clergy joined in. It's hard to know when the summer sermons were prepared.

Bridgwater, Street, Weston-super-Mare, Crewkerne, Castle Cary, Somerton, Barrington and Ham Hill were among the early clubs. Railways were being used significantly now and perhaps that partly accounted for the formation of a cricket club at Templecombe. The Chinnocks were going strong, even if there were no discernible signs of any agricultural Markses (Vic's ancestors) in the batting order: 'Montacute played two games in a week with a Chinnock party and received a regular good licking.' Not quite Cardus-style journalism, but the competitive fervour is quite clearly conveyed. The weekly paper report goes on to introduce an intrepid social comment: 'It looks as if the Montacute team is chosen with regard to their respectability . . .'

One visit, decidedly unsuccessful, of the United All-England XI has already been mentioned. Two earlier journeys to Somerset by John Wisden's top-hatted ambassadors and the England XI were altogether more in keeping with that rather grandiose title of theirs. Wisden (compiler of the *Almanack*), a diminutive, quickish off-cutter, had founded the side and brought them to the Sydenham Field in Bath for two days in August, 1858.

Bath batted twenty-two, and opened with E. M. Grace and his uncle, Alfred Pocock. The pair made 1 run between them and the elongated side was out for 76. Pocock was run out by 'E.M.', doubtless a matter of family consternation. United England were dismissed for 57 in their second innings, and rain put an end to the match.

Two years later, on the same field, the 'England Eleven' played against 'Twenty-two of Lansdown (no professionals)'. Bath turned out for this one. The England team included Thomas Hayward, the finest professional batsman of his day, and Julius Caesar, whose name provoked chuckles and awe in Bath, just as it did on his tours of North America and Australia. It might be charitable to imply that the Sydenham wicket was particularly capricious. The XXII were all out for 28 (ten ducks, top score 7). Hayward must have been pleased with his bowling; in 120 balls, he took 13 wickets for 16 runs. Not that England excelled with their batting; they were out for 75 and 77. Bath was renowned for its hospitality in those days. Just as well it rained before the match could be finished.

This preamble, full of unofficial and VIP matches, is all very well. But how far back do we go to pinpoint the formation of Somerset?

There is a case to be made out for 1865. Yeovil were ready to seize the initiative from lofty Lansdown. Special committee meetings were held and it was agreed to form a Yeovil and County Cricket Club. At least the town members weren't too self-effacing; they were ready to look on themselves as a county club – just as long as the town's name took precedence.

They bought a piece of ground near Pen Mill station, conscious of the scope for future travel and anxious to be near home when their opponents arrived. They staged a rather grand musical concert to raise some much-needed money for the new pavilion fund. Mr Wadham, the secretary, proudly announced: 'We're busy levelling the ground and three county matches have been arranged – against Devon, Dorset and North Wiltshire.'

It was probably optimistic to expect to move straight on to the new ground. Nor did the playing strength look quite up to standard. Yeovil and the County did rather badly in an early match against Shaftesbury, prompting a stinging paragraph in the *Western Gazette*, the local paper: 'A professional from Oxford has been engaged for the Yeovil Club and we trust that members will come out to practice, as the professional is now on the ground and ready for bowling . . .'

Things weren't going too smoothly, despite the brave words and the bonhomie at the pre-season meetings. In the June, when the club went to play Montacute in a club fixture, they were three players short. It emerged that the missing cricketers had actually joined Montacute the day before. But it was time for a *county* fixture, and eleven Gentlemen of Devon piled out of the train at Pen Mill. Yes, it rained and was never completed.

As the match has a modest claim to be Somerset's inaugural county contest, the score has some historical importance: Somerset made 73 and 142; Devon made 46 and 28-1. Then came the downpour.

Quite apart from the rain, the amount of interest was minimal. If this was county cricket, the humbler elements of Yeovil's population preferred to get on with their gloving. A committee member of the club said succinctly: 'We are sorry so few bothered to turn up and watch.'

The 'county' team, if we are to give the players such exalted stature, was: C. Newman, the Rev C. Ainsley, E. F. Henley, H. Lang, S. C. Voules, J. P. Gundry, A. A. Henley, H. P. Dodington, G. B. Voules, C. Pendarves and H. Monk. There are a few familiar local names but not many readily associated with Somerset cricket. It had been a good and ambitious idea but even the officials of the Yeovil club were soon agreeing, with some reluctance, that their all-embracing concept lacked practicality. And, according to the results, it also lacked talent. Pen Mill was far more exciting for its steam locos than its batting.

In the next ten years the scope and the standard of the game improved across the county. Many villages now had their own side. Some strong-muscled labourers were even chosen on merit, just as long as there was no haymaking to be done. Local rivalry flared when neighbouring parishes took to the field, but it wasn't always intense by any means – at Wincanton, twenty-two Marrieds played twelve Singles.

There was a growing envy about the way other counties were becoming established. Those bewhiskered cricketers in Somerset who read *The Times* felt they were due for a mention in the paper's august sporting columns.

The steps taken following a leisurely match between the Gentlemen of Somerset and the like-minded of Devon, at Sidmouth in August 1875 suggested a *fait accompli*. Not too much is known about what happened on that bracing field, but the meeting that followed was of considerable interest.

Those Gentlemen of Somerset and their friends who had travelled down to Sidmouth with them sat, glasses in hand, and passed a resolution that Somerset should have its own county cricket club. It didn't bother them a jot that they had no ground: 'The matches shall be played on any ground in the county that may be selected by the committee.'

The acting secretary, Edward Western, recorded the decisions of the meeting in his best copperplate and sent a copy to as many potential supporters as he could list. Nominations for president, vice-president, treasurer and secretary were requested. There was to be a committee of nine – and matches initially against Dorset, Devon, the Civil Service and several other reputable and, in some cases, esoteric sides.

And, oh yes, it would cost half a guinea to become a subscriber.

Mr Western appealed to the conscience in his final paragraph: 'It is hoped that the result will be such as to prevent the great expense of county matches falling too heavily on the individual players. Otherwise, many good men are excluded and the county cannot do itself justice.'

He sat back in his Taunton office and waited uncertainly for the response. At least he felt certain of one thing: if Somerset were to have county cricket, Taunton, the county town, was the logical base. He didn't really approve of 'outposts' like Yeovil pre-empting them.

Taunton had a healthy sporting instinct. Just before the end of the eighteenth century, there had been horse racing on Bloomhay Common. Bridgwater took over for a time when the common was enclosed, then racing came back to Taunton, first on the site of the present King's College and afterwards on Trull Moor until 1855. The Taunton and West Somerset Cricket Club had now been going for forty-six years, and some of the players rather grandly imagined they were ready for greater challenges and acclaim. Organised rugby had started in the town, and athletics had an increasing appeal.

Mr Western foresaw no geographical problems now that Taunton was well served by the railway. Nor did he or the other committee members allow anything as insignificant as the lack of a ground to trouble them and cloud their optimism. There was always Fullands playing fields, where the existing club side spent their Saturday afternoons.

Fullands House had been a mental asylum early in the nineteenth century. The owner had apparently scarpered rather than face some scandalous allegations. Fullands became a private school instead in 1840 – and here it was, where once the hapless patients wandered, that Somerset played their early matches.

There was, of course, the question of the subscribers. The secretary's pleading letter met a pretty tardy response. In all, 112 people enthused sufficiently to produce the required 10s 6d. One or two civic dignitaries were also persuaded to put their hands, none too deeply, into their pockets. The sum total of £70 17s was hardly a reassuring financial starting point.

I'm not sure what method they had in those prim Victorian days for collecting the gate money but from their relatively few home fixtures in that

16

first season, the county benefited by £1 15s 8d. Fortunately the amateurs turned up with their own kit and bought their own tickets for the away journeys.

Nothing as trifling as a shaky balance sheet was going to dissuade Somerset. That was true in 1875 – and a dozen times afterwards. The history of the county is heavy with the sighs of despairing accountants. But self-indulgent amateurs, good-hearted benefactors and cautious businessmen have in turn kept the bailiff away.

When did Somerset become a first-class county? There have been various theories, some excessively influenced by native allegiance. *Wisden* gives 1882 as the year, and Lancashire as the opening opponents, at Old Trafford on 8, 9 and 10 June. Most other romantic claims can be quietly discounted.

In the years leading up to that, Somerset shunned insolvency and mostly enjoyed their unofficial county cricket. The fixtures varied in standing; some were arranged annually on an 'old-boy' basis. Some canvassing went on in a quiet way for elevation. Other counties weren't particularly interested. There was something of a disparaging sniff when the subject of Somerset's admission was broached, but it was a rather patronising reaction. Hadn't these other haughtier counties yet heard of Edward Sainsbury or William Nicholas Roe? They should have.

Ted Sainsbury, born at Bath, was renowned at Sherborne School for his slow, beguiling under-arm bowling. But he was a better bat, often at No 1. One of the earliest recorded Somerset centuries was his 105 against Hertfordshire at St Albans in 1878. Two years later he hit another hundred, this time against Sussex at Brighton.

His club cricket was played for Lansdown, where he had the social aplomb to fit into that formidable, if snooty, company. He captained Somerset in 1886 and a few years later he was defiantly striding across the border to play another eighteen matches for Gloucestershire. We'll never know whether it was the result of persuasive charm on someone's part or a fit of pique. It happened several times with Somerset players – and vice versa.

Roe, a schoolmaster, came from an ecclesiastical family. He first played for Somerset in 1879, when he was still at school. Young William used to spend his holidays at Closworth, near Yeovil, and stories of his batting exploits as a sixth former soon reached Taunton.

He was a stylish and forceful batsman. In 1878 he hit four hundreds for his school and completed 1,000 runs. In three seasons with the school team, he took almost 300 wickets off deceptive medium pace. 'We must have him up', said the Somerset secretary.

The story of Roe's first delivery in county cricket achieved a kind of arcane fame at Victorian men's sporting dinners. He was full of blithe, boyish enthusiasm as he hurled the ball approximately in the direction of the middle stump. Henry 'Stonewall' Jupp, of Surrey and England, was rather too casual with his usually impeccable defensive stroke against this fresh-cheeked youth. The ball thudded against Jupp's pads. 'Howzzat!' screamed Roe, more boy soprano still than thundering baritone.

17

Slowly the umpire shifted his gaze from the far wickets to the pleading schoolboy: 'Hold on a minute, son. Not so fast. Can't you see what you've done? You've bowled the bugger!'

The ball had gone on to the stumps from Stonewall's pads. All that required reading of the Good Book back at the Clergy School should have caused young Roe to blanch at the umpire's basic linguistics. But he was too full of joy to notice.

Cricket was summarily put into perspective in the next match for Somerset. Roe travelled to Clifton College to play against Gloucestershire. W. G. Grace and brother Fred were bowling and the schoolboy, watching from the boundary, saw no obvious terror from the representatives of the awesome Clan.

When it was his turn, he strode confidently to the wicket. The Close had the same atmosphere as he had known and relished in school games. He scrambled a lucky single off Fred Grace, and then 'W.G.' immediately knocked over the lad's wickets. Roe returned disconsolately to the pavilion.

On the way, 'W.G.' called across to him: 'Never mind, son, come into the nets with me in the morning.' The Old Man, not always remembered for his generosity of spirit, fulfilled his promise. He kept bowling at Roe and offering practical advice, which was no doubt slightly at variance with the more pedantic and theoretical counselling of the school coach. In the second innings, Roe made 23 not out. He had learned how to play 'W.G.'.

Roe won his Blue at Cambridge in 1883. By then, he had made sure of an indelible statistic. Playing for the Emmanuel Long Vacation XI against Caius Long Vacation Club (there were so many of these esoteric encounters) he scored 415 not out. The runs took him just on five hours, out of a total of 708-4. There is little evidence of the standard and penetrative qualities of the Caius bowling; there is much of Roe's prodigious memory. They always said at Taunton that he kept an infallible check on his score without ever needing to look at the board.

In the *Wisden* obituary of this notable West Country cricketer, it is claimed of that massive innings for Emmanuel: 'So close was his concentration on the game that he counted all the runs and challenged the scorer with having given him one less than his total.' I prefer to view that as an apocryphal postscript. My Somerset heroes don't niggle over stray runs like this. Not when they have scored 400 first.

Roe played sixty-six first-class matches for his county and was captain in the late 1880s. His best hundreds were scored at Taunton, against Middlesex, Sussex and Surrey, but the highest innings for Somerset was against Hampshire at Bath in 1884.

So, the county had Sainsbury and Roe, the schoolboy discovery; and there were others. In 1882 the game's establishment still had some qualifications but agreed that Somerset should become first class.

By now the noteheadings at Taunton were printed with an apposite flourish. The president was the Earl of Cork and Orrery. Such a title took up much of the page, though it did suggest that the leprechauns might in future be propping up the batting order. Mr Western was still the honorary secretary and there was a committee of eighteen, democratically spread around the county – the democracy being at least geographical, if not social.

CHAPTER TWO

Who Remembers Fothergill?

Somerset's debut among the first-class counties was disappointing. The words are not mine; I'd never presume at this distance. But it is worth quoting at greater length from the 1883 *Wisden* as it perceptively summarises, in its idiosyncratic way, the debut deeds of Somerset in the previous summer:

> It should not be discouraging . . . they had many good reasons to account for a disastrous season. Mr Evans was available for only two of the matches, and Mr Ramsay and Mr Roe for only four.
>
> In the coming season, it would seem the county will have a better chance of showing a more satisfactory table of results at the end of the year, as matches with Surrey will be substituted for those with Lancashire, and they will not have to meet the all-conquering Colonists.
>
> Perhaps the most valuable hand in the eleven was Mr W. H. Fowler, as this gentleman played in all the matches with the capital average of 23.3, and bowled with such success in three matches that, all told, he captured 12 wickets – seven bowled – at a cost of only 13.9 runs per wicket.
>
> Mr Ramsay did not bowl for Somerset with nearly half the success which attended his trundling for his University, but his spirited batting against Hampshire gives him a good average of 20.6. Mr C. Winter proved a very useful change bowler, but Fothergill, who had the lion's share with the ball, was terribly expensive, and it is curious that his best bowling for his county was against the Australians.

Poor Fothergill. And let me add: 'Who remembers Fothergill?'

Arnold James Fothergill was the first Somerset player to be capped for his country and should not be relegated to the small print. He was a Geordie who was taken on the Lord's staff and often played for MCC. Between 1882–4 he had sixteen first-class matches for Somerset. He bowled left-arm, fastish. In the late 1880s he toured South Africa with Major Warton and played in the first two Tests ever staged against South Africa. The team was led by C. Aubrey Smith, with not yet a thought in his head about sunshine and studio lights in Los Angeles.

But the sparingly praised Fothergill was punished as he bowled away in

1882. Somerset played eight matches, one of them against the Australians. Lancashire, Hampshire and MCC were played twice, Gloucestershire for some unknown reason once.

I can't imagine that Somerset ever got over the first game. They were bowled out by Lancashire in the first innings for 29, and they lost by an innings and 157 runs. That kind of form wasn't guaranteed to give the newcomers a psychological fillip. They could almost hear the sly I-told-you-so affected coughs that came from cricket's establishment figures. It wasn't a game anyone at Taunton had a wish to remember. As a historical point, the vanquished team was: W. H. Fowler, E. Sainsbury, H. G. Tate, F. T. Welman, A. J. Fothergill, H. F. Fox, F. J. Pothbury, H. Fox, W. Trask, H. Hall and H. Scott. There were two pros – Fothergill and Scott.

A Lancashire professional was the principal executioner. George Nash took 4 wickets with successive balls and finished in the first innings with 8-14. He bowled slow left-arm with an action that didn't satisfy every umpire. Somerset perhaps hoped in vain that he would be called during that day of batting disintegration at Old Trafford.

From the debris of that first season Somerset scratched their way to a single win. They beat Hampshire at Taunton in the August and there was much celebration afterwards. Somerset, ever unconventional, selected two wicket keepers – Fred Welman and Francis Terry changed roles intermittently. Maybe it confused the batsmen.

And of course there were other morsels of comfort: like the jaunty deeds of William Herbert Fowler, who played for Essex before coming to Somerset. He was a towering figure and weighed more than fourteen stone. He scored the county's only hundred in 1882 and was perhaps the earliest Somerset batsman to parade the fundamental skills of slogging. There was mischief in him and he could also bat with exaggerated style.

Those sturdy shoulders were his gimmick. At Lord's, playing against MCC, he leaned back and threatened to sky the ball to his native Tottenham. It actually went 157 yards, out of the ground, and contemporary statisticians paced the hit with solemn expressions that cloaked their admiration. That was one for the record books. Bill Fowler, in fact, had a thoroughly good match. In the first innings he took 4-8, and that included the hat-trick. He was always an amiable companion, even more so when things were going so well for him.

At the Spa Grounds in Gloucester the same summer he was apparently below his best. He braced himself and his mighty blow ended a mere 154 yards from the batting crease. W.G., the bowler was not noticeably amused. It was still another for the record books. When MCC came back to Taunton, he treated their bowling again with no more than token respect. The ball dislodged a few roof slates and described a succession of circular ripples in the Tone. He was out for 139, to the marked disappointment of his team-mates who had offered him jocular encouragement.

Some likened his beefy straight drive to the way he drove off from the tee at golf. That was in truth a rather flattering reflection on his cricket; he wasn't quite as straight as that, back over the bowler's head, all the time. Certainly he was a gifted golfer. He went on to play for England against Scotland in 1903 and the next two years. He also designed Walton Heath and a number of other golf courses here and in America. But he remained close to Somerset and the affection was ever in his voice.

The match with the Australians in this inaugural first-class season was a predictable failure for Somerset. 'Demon' Spofforth and Harry Boyle, the bearded spinner, bowled unchanged through both innings without even working up a serious sweat. Spofforth ended with 13-113, Boyle with 7-106. But then, the pair had bowled out MCC between them for 33 and 19 four years earlier.

The final word on 1882 belongs to Charles Winter, a bright-eyed Londoner. He made his debut for Somerset, at the age of fifteen years and 288 days, against Hampshire. Over the next thirteen years he played a modest twenty-five games for the county. He took 50 wickets and once cobbled a brave innings of 62; but a sheepish one-line entry to record his schoolboy arrival is really the limit of his fame.

Somerset retained so-called first-class recognition for four years. In that time the treasurer was apt to agonise over the hazardous art of balancing the books. Form was indeterminate; team selection was inclined to be determined with a nod and a wink over drinks; outsiders' reputations were consciously inflated as a prelude to inclusion. There were also good players – and good results.

Edward Bastard, born locally and educated at Sherborne and Oxford, was a slow left-arm bowler who met with most success at university. He didn't play often for Somerset but when he did, he was accurate enough to take 8-59 against Hampshire at Southampton in 1885. Somerset lost that match by 8 wickets but they did turn up with only nine players.

Not that the depleted and probably disgruntled team did at all badly. Quite apart from Bastard's unchanged spell of 35-15-59-8, that was the game when Winter hit his 62 ('capital stuff from him, not a chance given'). And there was also Octavius Goldney Radcliffe.

It may be the absolute grandeur of the name, but in moments of nostalgic journalism I have recurrently been drawn back to the mostly ignored deeds and, some might imply, the disloyalties, of Radcliffe. He started out with five games for Somerset and then – maybe he disapproved of counties who could rustle up only nine men for a first-class fixture – played 119 times for Gloucestershire. Born in Wiltshire, he had the advantage of some impartiality.

Radcliffe was a circumspect opening bat. He scored four centuries for Gloucestershire and ended up going on the Sheffield tour to Australia in 1891–2. In the days, later on, when he captained Wiltshire he had a ready answer to those who joked that he always played as if he were out for a stroll around the North Newnton lanes where he was born: 'I once hit E. M. Grace's lobs for four sixes and a four in an over.'

Somerset may have had acute trouble at times in finding eleven able-bodied men on the same day but there was never a problem in enlisting the active support of the Church. The Cloth and cricket at Taunton were interwoven. You could fill a score of pews with clerics who first received the call when idling in the nets.

The early 1880s made the point with an ecclesiastical flourish. If the little pavilion rumbled reverentially with the intonations of collective prayer, it's rather a pity there was no practical response from above. Quite often there were two parsons in the same Somerset side. They found neighbouring vicars to minister to the sick of the parish and officiate at inconveniently arranged weddings, while they slipped their cricket bags into the pony and trap and drove, without too much guilt, to the match.

The long roll-call might almost be that of a theological college.

The Rev Lyonel D'Arcy Hildyard, the Rev Francis Reed and the Rev Francis Terry came first. They all played in 1882. Hildyard would thrust out his gentle, healing hands at point and never, according to his colleagues, put down a catch. As a middle-order batsman he was talented enough to win his Blue all three years at Oxford. He played seven times for Somerset and eight for Lancashire.

Reed, a Devonian, fielded in the slips where he offered observations on the state of the game in Latin. He managed one half-century in ten first-class matches spread over three seasons.

Terry, previously mentioned as the unlikely joint wicket keeper in one fixture, could also bowl at medium pace. These dual talents were still usurped by his batting. In 1883 he hit a hundred off Hampshire. One should marvel at his versatility. He went to Canada and playing for Ontario Hospital against Forest Club scored an undefeated 130 out of a total of 149. There is indisputable evidence that in the same game he took 2 wickets, stumped one Forest batsman and caught another behind the stumps. No wonder that, on the day he arrived for his first game for Somerset and asked what he did best, the erstwhile Oxford man pulled at his dog collar and said: 'Whatever you require, my dear friends. I can bowl and I can stump for you. And if you wish, I can do both.'

The Rev Albert Lavington Porter switched livings and counties. He began briefly with Somerset, in 1883, and played equally briefly for Hampshire a decade later.

There were the Spurways. The Rev Edward Popham, rector of Heathfield, made just two well-spaced appearances for Somerset. Much later, in the 1920s, the Rev Francis Edward, of the same family, kept wicket for twenty-three matches.

Almost at random, like turning a bible at any page, we find the Rev Wilfred Young, an old Harrovian who had a top score of 13, all studiously compiled in one innings, the Rev Wilfred Noel Kempe, another wicket keeper, and the Rev George Wood.

For a little more about Wood (three matches in the early 1890s), we should turn to his near namesake, Sammy Woods. No one would list Sammy's *Reminiscences* as a literary compilation, but they are splendidly racy and carry much of the flavour of the Aussie anglophile, whether or not he got some help with the writing:

> I remember an occasion at Tonbridge. We were playing Kent. Lionel Palairet had appendicitis and could not play. I wired Bedminster for the Rev Wood. He was playing very well and had got over 50, when he hit a ball into the country where another reverend gentleman was fielding. A splendid bat but the worst fielder in Europe. He picked it up on the long hop and chucked it up. The umpire gave my Christian out. Worst decision I ever saw. 'Christians awake', said a man in the stand.

I have no idea how religious a man was big S. M. J. Woods, but it does look very much as if he believed clergymen were quite capable of cheating.

There were other clerics who played for Somerset, for the most part likeable, absent-minded and, as cricketers, undistinguished. I have deliberately ignored the Preb Archdale Palmer Wickham so far. There will be much to say about him – and his extraordinary wicket keeper's stance – in a little while.

In the meantime, let me redress any tendency to lampoon some of Somerset's more godly sportsmen. Bath and Wells, for instance, have always been strong and even competitive in cricketing matters. I have played against them, admiring the fresh crease in the flannels and the glint of battle in the striker's eye. They will tell you, with the fervour of a truth that should never be questioned, that yellowing records are preserved of a match in 1911 when the Clergy of Somerset took part in a one-day match and scored 453-9 in just over three and a half hours. Professor H. A. Harris writes of the occasion in *Sport in Britain*: 'Lest the parsons should be guilty of the mortal sin of pride, the Somerset Stragglers replied with 454-1 . . . in 122 minutes.'

High scoring had been an occupational hazard for the Somerset fielders in the 1880s. Some of the trauma was self-induced. The county had a disturbing talent for parading fieldsmen of singular ineptitude, who lacked mobility and sharp reflexes. Physical fitness was no prerequisite for a place in the team. It is true that some of the bumpy outfields didn't help.

In 1884 the Hampshire batsmen clinically took the Somerset bowling apart at Southampton to score 645. The next summer it was Surrey at the Oval; they stopped at 635. It wasn't good for Tauntonian livers, and those in charge of the first-class game were not very impressed.

From 1886 to 1890 Somerset lost their first-class status. There was some huffing, a few letters in the papers – second-class cricket lessened the interest and hurt the pride. Sainsbury and Roe got the occasional century but it wasn't the same. And a strapping lad, with a shock of unruly hair and a Digger accent, was in 1888 playing for the Gentlemen of England: two days later he was walking out with Australia in a Test match against England.

His name was Woods. 'Wouldn't mind getting hold of he. Do us, down

JUST SOME OF
THE CAPTAINS

Herbert Hewett (1891–3),

Sammy Woods (1894–1906),

R. J. O. Meyer (1947),
Harold Stephenson (1960–4),

N. S. Mitchell-Innes (1948)
Colin Atkinson (1965–7),

George Woodhouse (1948–9),
Roy Kerslake (1968),

Massey Poyntz (1913–14),

Jack White (1927–31),

R. A. Ingle (1932–7),

Stuart Rogers (1950–2),
Brian Langford (1969–71),

B. G. Brocklehurst (1953–4),
Brian Close (1972–7),

Maurice Tremlett (1956–9),
Brian Rose (1978–83),

hure, a bit o' good,' they were saying down on the Somerset farms – prophetic words.

Form may have been sluggish and brief prestige taken away again, but Somerset had made one highly significant move. They had found a ground of their own. No one was too happy with the way the club was meandering on, playing on grounds by the courtesy and good nature of other people and attempting to placate the more pressing creditors. A meeting of the more loyal members was called and everyone agreed there was need for some restructuring. In 1886 the club took a nineteen-year lease on the Athletic Ground at Taunton; the freehold was to be acquired ten years later for £2,000. This was the site of the county ground as we know it today. Then the turf looked rough and ill-nourished. The buildings were sparse and inadequate, and there was no obvious place for a wicket. But it was at least a green space in the centre of Taunton, and it was Somerset's own. The possibilities for it became a matter for excited and ambitious debate at a series of committee meetings.

News of what was about to happen stimulated membership. Subscriptions perked up, and the builders, assured that they would be paid, moved in. They put up stands, then a pavilion. The ground was levelled and laboriously rolled. But it wasn't ready for any decent cricket yet awhile. Somerset played home matches, in some cases, at Bath and Wellington.

Mr H. Murray-Anderdon was the new secretary. He had a commanding, aristocratic manner. His orders were incisive. He arrived at the ground in a chauffeur-driven Daimler in later years; initially there had always been someone to drive the pony-trap – Murray-Anderdon was a man of some style.

His family home was at Henlade, on the edge of Taunton. Cricket, along with fishing, was his passion. He enjoyed the local esteem in which he was held. He took pride in his dark, luxuriant beard. A relative told me that he had grown it originally because he had difficulty tying his bow or cravat following a serious accident when he was knocked down by a steamroller near his front gate and one arm was badly and permanently injured. He played occasionally for the Club and Ground, very much down the order and with minimal success. But he was a fine administrator and his job was to shake the place up.

The county ground, small and intimate, and gleaming in the sun with its licks of white paint, was soon looking an attractive asset. Trees were planted in a neat line. The River Tone ambled by, with barely a murmur of urbanity, a few yards from one boundary edge. 'Opponents will want to come here and play', the new secretary told the other officers.

He also reminded them that the team was not talented enough: 'We must go out and get some more players.'

'Wherever from?'

'From the universities.'

And in the years that followed, Oxford and Cambridge became regular sources. Eggheads took over from the clergy. No one would say Somerset were a team without brains.

It was all very well for the favoured Middlesex, Surrey, Lancashire, Yorkshire, Sussex, Kent, Nottinghamshire and Gloucestershire. But Somerset, tired of snide insults, wanted to be up there with them. 'There's only one way we'll do it', said Murray-Anderdon with analytical assertion. 'We must demonstrate that we are good enough'.

They did: in 1890.

There were thirteen fixtures. Somerset won twelve and the other, against Middlesex at Taunton, ended in a tie when Maurice Dauglish was run out off the final ball. The decidedly larger-than-life Tim O'Brien, not yet knighted, was bowled for 1 and 3.

Somerset were led by Herbert Hewett. Five of the games were won by an innings. Suddenly they had become quite lethal. Hampshire, Leicestershire, Stafford, Glamorgan, Warwickshire, Devon, and Middlesex – already beaten in the opening match of the summer – went away licking their wounds and showing grudging admiration for the all-round skills of their West Country opponents.

Inevitably, Somerset walked away with what was called the Second-class County Championship. It was a heady late August. The Mayor of Taunton, Alderman George Saunders, beamed as he dug into his social budget. He hosted a complimentary dinner at the Castle Hotel; the speeches were fulsome in their praise. All the players were there, the three pros, Tyler, Nichols and Clapp, in their best suits but, according to custom, without their initials.

Ted Tyler had taken 126 wickets from 669 overs. Next came George Nichols, with 79. The old Year Book records: 'Nichols bowled two no-balls in his 556.1 overs.' Such honest toil and accuracy could not be ignored.

Hewett topped the batting averages. His 203 not out against Staffordshire utterly dominated the match. It was no way to further demoralise the visitors who had already been bowled out for 43 in their first innings.

Pause to ponder some of the other names that followed his: Roe and the Palairets, Gerald Fowler, Hedley and Challen, Newton, Robinson and Vernon Hill. A team was taking shape.

Off the field there was a discernible rustle of expectancy. Members' subscriptions were up to £379. Middlesex's visit brought £53 15s 3d to the club through the gate; Hampshire were clearly less attractive (£20) and Leicestershire less so again (£11). At Bath, Glamorgan's arrival earned paltry gate receipts of £6 12s 9d.

The club sides were by now being persuaded to feel they were part of the county. Bath, Bedminster, Bridgwater, Lansdown, Shepton Mallet, Taunton and Wellington paid a guinea each for the privilege of affiliation. Bloomfield, East Harptree, Ilchester, King's College (Taunton), Wells and Wraxall, either more wary or less flushed, sent 10s 6d.

In that regenerated 1890 season, the professionals were paid a total of £132 for their appearances in county matches. There was also £72 for 'ground bowlers' wages'. I am reassured that 'horse fodder' came to no more than £8 14s 9d. The gate-keeper earned four guineas, the accountant £10.

27

A whole season without a defeat – and a civic dinner to round it off. Somerset could not possibly be snubbed again when it came to 1891.

The county secretaries met at Lord's in the December, with Somerset's record before them. The familiar cynicism, out of the corner of the mouth, had gone: 'Do we agree then, gentlemen, that Somerset be admitted to the first-class county cricket championship?' Hands went up; there wasn't a dissenting voice.

CHAPTER THREE

First-class Occasions

The 1891 competition comprised nine first-class counties: Gloucestershire, Kent, Lancashire, Middlesex, Nottinghamshire, Somerset, Surrey, Sussex and Yorkshire. In 1895, five more counties came in – Derbyshire, Essex, Hampshire, Leicestershire and Warwickshire. There were still to come Worcestershire (1899), Northamptonshire (1905) and Glamorgan (1921).

Somerset's amateurs arrived earlier than ever before for their pre-season nets. They knew the county was on trial and they went off at a gallop. The Club and Ground games were a thoroughly serious business: so much so that, at Glastonbury in an afternoon match, Nichols took 5 wickets and followed up with 311 not out. The ale was donated from all quarters at the old George and Pilgrim that evening.

A few days later they went down to Martock, where Archie Wickham was the vicar. He captained the village XVI and they did rather better than Glastonbury. Nichols took 7 wickets, all bowled, and was then run out for 27 by a stiff-jointed amateur. But Lodway and Flax Bourton and Martock, down among the Ham-stone cottages could be a dangerously deceptive prelude to Lord's and the Oval. Hewett, pugnacious chin jutting forward and eyes that didn't laugh easily, called his players together: 'Surrey will win the championship but don't let them frighten you.' At the same time he announced his team for the opening fixture, against Middlesex at Lord's (in batting order): H. T. Hewett, G. Fowler, J. B. Challen, Nichols, W. N. Roe, Tyler, Clapp, A. E. Newton, S. M. J. Woods, V. T. Hill, C. J. Robinson.

It rained and the match was never finished. The Whit Monday was a wash-out; more than 4,000 came to watch on the Tuesday and they saw enough of Somerset to agree with the verbose and influential cricket writers that here was a county worthy of its new station.

But cynicism could be detected a few days later: and not without cause. It was time to play the all-conquering Surrey at the Oval. Lionel Palairet had to put his tutorials first and couldn't play; nor could Roe, and nor could the infectiously enthusiastic Woods, troubled by an injury. It was no way to take on Surrey.

The sun shone as Surrey went out to bat. Somerset were left, in effect, with just two bowlers, Tyler and Nichols. It was a fearful responsibility for two honest pros, used to wheeling away with the sweat-stained shirts stuck to their bodies. Surrey made 449 and Bob Henderson, the Surrey professional whose career was blunted by ill health, hit 106, his highest score. Bill Brockwell and Henry Wood enjoyed some jaunty professional comradeship for the ninth wicket and scored 150 between them.

That was dispiriting enough. Then came some rain and a conniving, drying sun. It was also George Lohmann's birthday. He rolled up his sleeves and perfunctorily took 11 wickets – in no time at all, but over the two innings. Somerset were out for 37 . . . and 37.

Hewett had been in some despair as he surveyed his depleted team and tried to determine the batting order. He'd had no trouble over the No 11; that had to be Wickham, known to his friends as 'Snickham'. But he was left with about ten other options. In the end he decided to open with Crescens James Robinson, an amateur of unexceptional talents – though he was still Somerset's top scorer of that whole, wretched day with 11 – and Clapp, an amiable but undistinguished pro who would alternate for both Somerset and Shropshire some seasons.

The first innings lasted for just under 29 overs, the second for 19. The West Country batsmen sparred, missed and did nothing much more than exchange darting glances of anguish down 22 yards of the track. They were saying in their silent eloquence: 'So this is Lohmann, toying with us on his birthday!'

At the other end, John Sharpe, son of Nottinghamshire's Sammy, contributed even more economically to the rout:

Somerset   First Innings
  Lohmann 14.4-6-19-5
  Sharpe 14-6-15-5

Somerset   Second Innings
  Lohmann 10-3-21-6
  Sharpe 9-5-16-4

Defeat by an innings and 375 runs. Back around the Quantocks there was some spluttering and choking on the evening ale. 'See you again in August', said Bobby Abel, as he smiled sympathetically and shook hands with the departing West Country foes. Maybe Abel, 'The Guvnor' as they called him, was privately looking forward to some easy runs. They, in fact, didn't come till 1899 when he scored 357 not out against Somerset at the Oval. Only Archie MacLaren ever got more in a championship match. And yes, it was also against Somerset. That innings must wait, to take its turn in the absorbing catalogue of the county's disasters.

Meanwhile there's a sweet and stunning irony to cherish. Surrey returned to Taunton with an understandable swagger. They were widely expected to win a second time by an innings. They lost by 130 runs.

Herbie Hewett, a man of quite fiery temperament, was still smarting from what had happened at the Oval. He didn't approve of the cheap jokes about village-green cricketers. This time he made sure, by the intimidating rasp of his voice, that he had a decent team around him.

The Palairets, Lionel and Richard, were in, and so was Roe. John Bonamy Challen, a schoolmaster who recoiled from his nickname of 'Venus', was also around to bolster the batting from No 3. He was a neat, stylish figure at the wicket and a superb patroller of the covers. Perceval Graves, who watched Challen play, wrote in an article for the *Journal of the Cricket Society*: 'I should put him almost in the same class at cover point as Jack Hobbs.' So he was in against Surrey to save the runs as well as score them.

Woods was fit and available again. His much-needed role was to take the new ball with Nichols and, even before that, spirit away the furrowed brows in the dressing room: 'We were a bloody disgrace at the Oval, Sam. See if you can change things for us.'

The big, bronzed Aussie was twenty-four, old enough to know his worth. He took a manly swig at his hip-flask and nodded as he changed into his baggy flannels. The waist was still slim but the shoulders were broad; he needed them as a wing forward.

At various points in this book I shall nominate matches of romantic and imperishable appeal. This was one of them. Somerset won in the last over and indeed the hero was Woods. After two balls of appalling length, one an embarrassing beamer that had Sharpe demonstrating some of the mobility he had acquired as a Notts County footballer, the off-stump went careering halfway to the third-man boundary.

Hewett, both Palairets, Roe and 'Venus' Challen had all batted well and bravely at different times; Woods and Nichols had got the wickets. Surrey, jolted by the home county's improvement and competitive edge, had soon decided on the last day to settle for a draw. They still had 5 wickets left with half an hour to go, but Woods, always a fearsome sight as he pounded up to the wicket, threw up his hairy arms for a return catch from Lohmann and then bowled Read for 94. The old scorecard records with pride: 'Won — two minutes to time.'

Wisden adds: 'An arrangement had been made to draw stumps at 5.30pm. Sammy Woods got the last Surrey wicket almost on the stroke of time . . . There was a great display of enthusiasm at the finish and the victorious eleven were warmly congratulated on their brilliant and well deserved win.'

Woods used often to talk about that match. He once wrote: 'Our spectators went balmy, flung their hats in the air and hit each other about. And they varmers do talk about it to this day.'

That was Sammy going into the vernacular. In late years, over a dram, his friends used to ask him if he really did bowl the last man, Sharpe, with a full toss. 'No I didn't, me dear — it were a long hop!'

The tongue was frequently deep into the cheek when Woods reminisced with such joyful relish. And the twinkle in his blue eyes allowed him to be a trifle cavalier with his facts. 'We won with the last ball of the match', he wrote. As already mentioned, it was the third ball of the over. But who's ever counting when it comes to Sammy?

One tale of that remarkable game he insisted was true went like this:

The scorecard – quite apart from Sammy Woods' story of a one-eyed batsman – surely deserves some kind of immortality:

SOMERSET v SURREY

At Taunton. Thurs, Fri and Sat, 13, 14 and 15 Aug 1891
(Somerset won by 130 runs)·

SOMERSET

First Innings		Second Innings	
Mr L. C. H. Palairet c Wood b Lohmann	8	c Wood b Brockwell	60
Mr H. T. Hewett (capt) lbw b Lohmann	55	c Abel b Sharpe	42
Mr J. B. Challen c Sharpe b Lohmann	6	b Lockwood	89
Mr S. M. J. Woods b Lohmann	11	c Lohmann b Brockwell	14
Mr R. C. N. Palairet b Lockwood	33	b Brockwell	13
Nichols b Sharpe	9	run out	0
Mr W. N. Roe b Abel	29	c Lockwood b Lohmann	36
Mr W. A. R. Young b Lohmann	13	did not bat	
Mr V. T. Hill c Read(M) b Sharpe	18	b Lockwood	31
Mr A. E. Newton not out	5	b Lockwood	26
Tyler b Sharpe	2	not out	15
Extras	5	Extras	5
Total	194	Total (9 wkts)	331

SURREY

First Innings		Second Innings	
Abel b Nichols	11	c L. Palairet b Woods	29
Mr J. Shuter b Nichols	4	b Nichols	29
Read(M) b Nichols	25	b Woods	94
Mr W. W. Read b Tyler	12	c Tyler b Nichols	11
Lohmann b Woods	19	c and b Woods	58
Henderson b Tyler	0	b Nichols	1
Lockwood c Newton b Woods	8	b Woods	14
Mr K. J. Key c L. Palairet b Woods	25	c and b Tyler	0
Brockwell lbw b Nichols	0	c Hill b Tyler	0
Wood b Woods	29	not out	0
Sharpe not out	18	b Woods	4
Extras	3	Extras	1
Total	154	Total	241

BOWLING ANALYSIS

	First Innings				Second Innings
Lohmann	37 overs	10 maidens	84 runs	5 wkts	44-11-91-1
Sharpe	27	9	52	3	22-9-48-1
Lockwood	22	8	47	1	28.1-10-62-3
Abel	6	4	6	1	7-3-12-0
Mr W. W. Read					8-0-32-0
Brockwell					23-9-48-3
Henderson					16-7-33-0

	First Innings				Second Innings
Mr Woods	31.4 overs	11 maidens	70 runs	4 wkts	49.3-16-103-5
Nichols	41	22	52	4	47-22-82-3
Tyler	11	4	29	2	12-0-31-2
Mr Roe					4-2-9-0
Mr L. Palairet					8-3-15-0

With ten minutes to go, Sharpe joined Henry Wood. I was going to bowl in that last over when Wood said to me 'Keeps his end up well for a man with one eye, doesn't he?' 'Which eye?' 'Left one.' I bowled my first round-arm ball of my life and hit his off-stump. Had I not had that information, we wouldn't have won. Another case of *Silence is golden*.

That was it: still talked about nearly a hundred years later. Surrey finished up with the title, of course. Somerset shared fifth place with Kent. In addition to Surrey, they'd beaten Gloucestershire twice, Kent and Yorkshire once. Quite a recovery, in fact, after the indignity of the Oval. Spectators at Taunton had also seen a solid century from Lord Hawke, at the top of the order for Yorkshire, and Timothy O'Brien similarly, full of Irish blarney, for Middlesex.

In *A History of Cricket*, H. S. Altham wrote: 'Few more attractive sides have ever taken the field than Somerset in the Nineties.' Could there be anything more glowing for newcomers to the first-class cricketing coterie? But the Somerset secretary was rather more pragmatic in his annual report for 1891: 'We have not been able to collect all the money promised.'

What did please him was the way that county cricket was already stirring the imagination of the local public. Gate money was well up and even the flowers were blooming for Somerset:

> In the present year £554 11s 9d was taken at the gates, of which £233 14s 9d was taken in the Surrey match alone, for which unprecedented amount we have in a great measure to thank the Horticultural Society who kindly arranged for their flower show to fit in with the first day of the match, and also advertised it on their bills.

There was also some good-natured gloating at the annual meeting over the way that Gloucestershire had been beaten, by 10 wickets at Taunton and by an innings and 130 runs at Cheltenham.

'W.G.' hadn't been at his best in 1891. He was a good doctor but lacked the healing hands for his own strained knee. Yet he went on playing, too often and too actively. He liked to open the batting and the bowling for Gloucestershire – or for any other side who would provide generous expenses for the occasional match. The bearded champion batted at No 1 in the two games with Somerset that season. His scores were 2, 7, 4 and 12. He took just 2 wickets. W.G. looked a weary man for much of that summer; maybe there had been too many nocturnal confinements around the narrow streets of working-class East Bristol where, between his crowded cricket diary, he tended the sick with far more compassion than that gruff and avaricious exterior might have suggested.

In the second match with Somerset, Gloucestershire were all out for 25 in their first innings. Woods and Tyler, the amateur and the pro, hardly had time to work up a thirst. They routed a pathetic batting side in just over 14

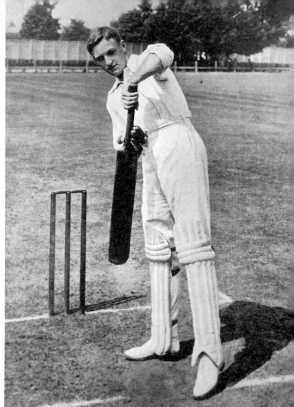

That's the way to do it . . . at least for the photographer. (*Above*) R. C. N. Palairet (1891–1902), C. A. Bernard (1896–1901), (*Below*) R. P. Spurway (1893–8) and V. T. Hill (1891–1912)

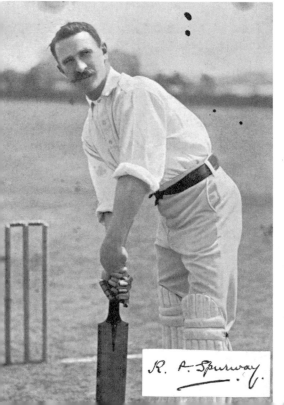

overs. Sammy (5-14) sent a pint of ale into the poky professionals' room afterwards to Ted Tyler (5-10).

It was to be Jack White who bowled out Gloucestershire for 22 at Bristol in 1922, and Tom Goddard who more or less bowled out Somerset on the Bristol sand dunes for 25 in 1947. Such nightmarish deeds must take their turn later in this account.

In the meantime, there is 1892. Some would argue that Somerset never had a better summer, though modern maestros like Botham and Richards would have every reason to contest the point.

I should unequivocally cite 1892 as the season of permanent attainment for the county. It was time at last for the haughty to stifle the last lingering jibes. Somerset, until now merely tolerated, and almost resented by some for the audacity of their upstart success, had finally unfastened the padlock of the game's freemasonry.

They were now admitted on merit. Murray-Anderdon tilted that bushy chin away from the wing collar with a justifiable gesture of exaggerated pride. The club president, the Hon Sir Spencer Ponsonby-Fane, KCB, beamed at the members on match days. The influential newspapers were becoming quite embarrassing in their praise. In the *Observer*, the cricket correspondent wrote: 'We know of nothing in the history of the game to equal the rise of Somerset.'

Hewett was in charge of the team and he was far less inclined than some of his predecessors to include a player on the strength of his social charm and ability to drink into the early hours. Nor was he much impressed by parental canvassing. He liked a good accent – but never as much as a good boundary.

There was now genuine competition for places, based on skill with a bat and ball. Colts matches were arranged all round the county. The Dodge brothers Bill and Herbert, Milborne, Holloway, Coleman, Maggs, Puddy, Laver and Hambling . . . a long, eager line of schoolboy players were all being encouraged for the first time.

The Colts, nineteen of them, captained by Walter Hale, one of Somerset's professionals, took on virtually a county side in a pre-season and made more than a game of it. Hale, who came from Bedminster, Bristol, scored 49 and 135 but his life as a Taunton pro was still limited to eight matches; he went on to play sixty times for Gloucestershire. Such impartiality, swayed by practical considerations, was evident when he turned to rugby. He was a fine player for Bristol, talented enough to represent both Somerset and Gloucestershire.

Back to the cricket. Somerset played sixteen fixtures in 1892 and won eight of them, finishing third to Surrey and Notts.

What do bare facts like that show? Certainly not that in August, before the rain came, Somerset often looked invincible. They were the best team in the country. That sheepish, self-effacing walk had gone and in a succession of matches they left oppositions bemused. The swaggering form was a revelation – and, of course, touched by unreality.

It wouldn't have done for the county to remain the best for too long. The peacock arrogance of such attainment isn't a West Country attribute. The Somerset temperament revels in heady peaks just as long as they don't threaten to take on any kind of permanency; there must always be a few troughs to restore perspective. The history of Somerset has always been a crazy graph.

The county met their 1892 come-uppance at Manchester. They lost by 8 wickets and it was all over in a day. 'Boy' Briggs, not much taller than the stumps, and Arthur Mold saw to that abrupt finish.

'Bloody disgrace!' rapped out Hewett, referred to as 'The Colonel' out of earshot. 'Now let's start winning again.'

That defeat at Old Trafford had come after four wins in a row. Who said Somerset were getting above themselves? Back in Bridgwater and Burnham, the county's supporters were feeling a little more comfortable in the perverse way people often have in reacting to the apparent relief of a let-down after alien success. 'No more than a Lancashire lapse, me dear', Woods assured his captain, vowels already a compromise of Sydney and Shepton Mallet.

Notts were by this time feeling understandably pleased with themselves. They (at least, the amateurs) booked in at the Castle Hotel on 18 August. The county had not yet been beaten and appeared a hot tip for the championship. They had a Shrewsbury, senior and junior, at No 1 and 10, a Gunn at No 3 and a Daft at 6. Notts indeed were a decidedly useful, well-rounded side.

They lost in two days by an innings and 122 runs. Two Somerset men had every right to bask in the Taunton triumph: Vernon Hill and Ted Tyler.

Hill had caused quite a stir in the University match that year. He backed himself to make a hundred and ended up with 114. He's always remembered for both his fiery batting and his self-confidence as a punter. The runs for Oxford were scored in a hundred minutes.

Hill was a left-hander with an extrovert nature who rather enjoyed being compared to Jessop. In truth, the philosophy was similar – not the technical skills. But Hill was a big hitter, at times imprudent in the extreme. He played mostly off the front foot and could drive magnificently. Old men used to tell of watching him in the nets before the start of play; pros bowled to him and promptly got out of the way. He tried quite indiscriminately to cart every ball. Bystanders surveyed his early-morning aggression from a distance. In the middle, he was never noticeably inhibited by a good-length ball. He must be included when we compile our definitive list of Somerset smiters.

When he went to Winchester, Hill was a better bowler. He hardly ever turned his arm over for the county. Yet do we slight him? 'Got brought on once against Notts in 1894 as seventh change, my good man. And took the wickets of William Gunn, Dixon and Wright in nine balls. Only gave away one run. How about that?' The record book bears it out.

After the Varsity match in 1892, he went off to Taunton a richer man. Against Notts in that memorable match, he batted fourth wicket down and was caught off a flailing bat for 93, then Notts were hustled out for 118 and

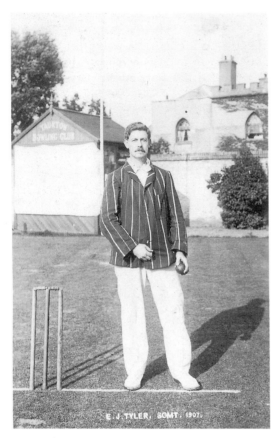

(*Left*) E. J. Tyler, slow left-arm bowler renowned for flight and stamina, later to be
J. C. White's tutor

(*Right*) H. Murray-Anderdon, an outstanding early administrator

69. And that brings us to Tyler, who used to open the bowling with his
flighted left-arm slows. He took 15 wickets for 96 runs in the game – and he
needed only 38 overs to do it.

Somerset have much to thank him for. He teased away on a length; then,
as coach at Taunton School, he taught Jack White the rudiments of flight.
Later, I shall evaluate the collective value of Tyler and his fellow pro and
buddy Nichols. The handbook for 1892 reminds us that they were already
jointly in business in North Street as cricket, tennis and football outfitters;
the balance sheet also reveals that they paid £2 14s for the advertisement.

A muted Nottinghamshire team took the train out of town. Somerset
immediately beat Middlesex and then entertained Yorkshire at the match
when Hewett and Palairet put on 346 for the first wicket, still a county
record.

In the famous picture, as they pose in front of the scoreboard, Hewett is
wearing his shoes, as if rushed back by an opportunist photographer (Mr
Chaffin, of Taunton) at the close of play, to capture the historic moment.

From the age of five or six, I could memorise almost every feature of that sepia print: the normal stylised pose of the two batsmen, legs nonchalantly crossed over with toes digging into the hard turf, begrimed and eloquent bats, ties knotted around the waist, expressions of stern, manly virtue and caps that waver neither in angle nor jauntiness. Behind them are the white railings and the tall stone barn. But it is the figures on the scoreboard that still dominate and convey the sheer drama of this piece of encapsulated history.

Hewett and Palairet had little overtly in common – and, like the best contrasts, they complemented each other with an indelible charm and skill. Charm, the more perceptive might argue, was not one of Herbie Hewett's more obvious attributes. In tandem with Palairet, however, the batting took on a mesmeric beauty. Somerset could never ask for a finer pair of openers.

The partnership of 346 against Yorkshire, on 26 August 1892, took just over three and a half hours. Then Hewett was bowled by Bobby Peel as the tired arms swung in the direction of mid-wicket. The left-hander had scored 201 and was ready for a drink. So, knowing the extent of his thirst, must have been Peel. Lord Hawke was inclined to find fault with the slow bowler's human frailties. No one would have questioned his resolve for Yorkshire that steamy day as Somerset amassed 592 and Peel completed sixty overs during which he took 7 wickets. He was one of eight bowlers who tried in vain for so long to terminate the playful supremacy of two great opening batsmen.

As a boy I listened to graphic accounts from ancient supporters who claimed they saw it. Most of them probably only pretended they did. It doesn't matter – the facts were fundamentally correct.

They told of how Palairet, handsome and ever decorous at the wicket, never seemed to hurry; they told of the cover drives and the way he occasionally lifted his harlequin cap to wipe his brow; and they told of Hewett, pulling and driving as if it were a cardinal sin to let a ball go by without scoring.

I am convinced that Lionel Charles Hamilton Palairet was the most stylish batsman ever to play for Somerset. In 1975, when the county were celebrating their generally accepted centenary and the mighty I. V. A. Richards was only just emerging, I edited a special brochure in which we tried to nominate Somerset's greatest batsman over all those years. In the end I settled for a rather cowardly compromise and bracketed Palairet with Harold Gimblett.

In truth I felt unqualified to compare cricketers from different eras. My choice of Gimblett was based on some wonderful innings I had seen, and the sheer impudence of his stroke play; it was also partly emotional. I only *imagined* that I'd seen Palairet.

Palairet was born in Lancashire and schooled for a time at Clevedon, then in Somerset. He was tall and upright and looked the all-round sportsman. And indeed he was: a middle-distance runner of some note and a soccer player worth his place for the Corinthians. But cricket was his passion, which he indulged with plenty of shots and not too many words.

It wasn't just that Plum Warner, C. B. Fry and Ranji were lyrical in their praise, making him sound more like the sublime creation of a poet than a functional cricketer. I had long ago come to the firm conclusion – and I don't think it was partisan exaggeration – that 'LCH' was one of the most unwaveringly *stylish* batsmen ever to play the game in this country.

He was captain at Repton and at Oxford, where he won his Blue all four years. In 222 matches for Somerset, he scored nearly 16,000 runs and twenty-seven hundreds. Most of the day's pundits felt he should have played more than twice for his country. Perhaps his manner wasn't flamboyant enough – he got his runs with the minimum of extrovert flourish and had no quaint mannerisms to amuse or intrigue the spectators. His stance was perfect, and motionless. Everything about him epitomised grace; there was never a superfluous movement. One obvious point of comparison with Viv Richards, in fact, was his absolute *stillness* at the crease. The back lift, the quiet and assertive advance of the front foot, the overall co-ordination were near perfection. He played mostly off the front foot and a few were uncharitable enough to suggest that brother Richard was more reliable when playing back.

'L.C.H.' recoiled from improvisation. He refused to stray from the orthodox, and some might see this even as a flaw, reflecting lack of imagination. The fact is that he made the orthodox beautiful. Batting was always an aesthetic exercise for him; he vehemently rejected the uglier strokes that encroached with the fresh challenges of improvisation. He carried his bat at least four times for his county.

Palairet had most of the shots, though he's always remembered for his off-drives. They were gems of delicate elegance. The power came from the timing, not the muscle.

Yet, Gilbert Jessop used to tell of one match between Somerset and Gloucestershire when a new and naïve Bristol amateur was put back on the long-off boundary as soon as Palairet got to the wicket. The first time the ball came in the novice fielder's direction he put out a hand in casual anticipation. He was completely unprepared as the shot scorched towards him, skimmed his hand and hit him in the face. Play was held up while the boundary man was helped from the field. He was replaced by a substitute who was similarly injured by the next ball.

Palairet was later to have one season as Somerset's captain. He lacked the driving personality for the job, preferring to take orders from Herbert or Sammy – or just be left to get on with his batting.

In passing, we shouldn't forget either his bowling or his brother. He took 143 wickets at useful medium pace. Brother Richard made eighty-five appearances and scored two centuries for Somerset. He, too, was a fine cricketer but his mobility was impaired after he broke his kneecap playing soccer. Richard was both secretary of Surrey and later president of Somerset. And, in the context of recently evoked cricketing history, he helped to manage the eventful MCC tour of Australia in 1932–3.

Lionel Palairet was also president of Somerset, in 1929. His roots were by then solidly West Country, so much so that for a time he was honorary secretary of the Taunton Vale Foxhounds. He was a land agent who liked to create a free afternoon for an unostentatious return to the county ground. He didn't much care to talk about that bountiful stand with 'The Colonel'.

Herbert Tremenheere Hewett played, astonishingly, only fifty times for the county. He was gruff, direct and, as befits a man who trained as a lawyer, analytical. He harboured grievances, looked you in the eye as he spoke his mind, and made a few enemies. Against that, he was a fine cricketer, at times an inspiring captain and a valued influence in the shaping of Somerset as a county to be taken seriously.

He has long fascinated me, not just for the way he left and the rows he had. No doubt he was exasperated by the stubborn opinions of some committee members; he hated both opposing bowlers and cant.

Hewett was a left-handed batsman with an attacking inclination which he usually manifested from the opening over. He admired but didn't bother himself too much with the orthodoxy of Palairet. He pulled; he cross-batted; he took a long look at where the fielders were placed and then tried to hammer the ball between them. Of course he was fallible. But he was also possessed of an eagle eye, considerable meat and the ability to make his forcing shots highly attractive.

He went to Harrow and got a Blue at Oxford. Contemporaries claimed he was always picking his teeth. Perhaps that helped the mental processes. He had an unrelenting tactical sense to complement the strength of his personality: hallmarks of notable captaincy. I think he would be in my all-time Somerset side. The only reservation is his suspect temperament. How well would he integrate in a Taunton dressing room along with the more recent superstars?

He went with Hawke to North America in 1891 and to South Africa on an unofficial tour four years later. In different circumstances he'd have walked into an England team – and demoralised much-vaunted opposing new-ball attacks. Reputations didn't mean too much to him. For a West Countryman – he was born at Norton Manor near Taunton – he was a competitive and belligerent batsman. People began to appreciate him when it was too late.

By the end of 1893, Hewett was dramatically packing his bags and bidding a curt goodbye to the county club. But first we must take a final look at the Yorkshire fixture when Hewett and Palairet almost contemptuously broke the previous best opening stand, made twenty-three years earlier at the Oval by W.G. and B. B. Cooper.

The historic Somerset partnership is apt to obscure another exceptionally well-made innings in that match. It came from Walter Coote Hedley who in his time, the record books remind us, was entitled to the prefixes 'Sir' and 'Colonel'.

He was a professional soldier, so his cricket was sporadic, with eighty-four games ranging over thirteen seasons. He had started off with a few appearances for Kent and ended with three for Hampshire. He scored two hundreds for Somerset, and one of those was against Yorkshire; he carried on

BOWLING ACTIONS (*Above, left to right*) Senior pro Tom Young at net session; Bertie Buse in his 1953 benefit year, (*Below, left to right*) Horace Hazell, comfortable and accurate; Johnny Lawrence – gentle cunning; George Nichols – working out his next play?

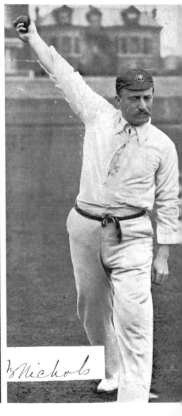

Sammy Woods – the famous pose

Joel Garner – 'tall as the pavilion'

Tom Cartwright – superb technician

Brian Langford – his first fine season

when Hewett had left off. But he was of more value – and rather more interest – as a bowler. His medium pace was straight and penetrative enough for him to take 254 wickets at a time when the county frequently needed another bowler. The trouble, unfortunately, was his action.

His more carping opponents had never really been happy with it. This was a time when a number of bowlers were being maligned for supposedly suspect actions. No doubt there were a few disparaging comments from the Yorkshire batsmen in 1895 when he ended with 14-70 against them.

There was an odd pettiness about the cricketing grapevine in those Victorian days. At the turn of the century the county captains called a special meeting to decide just how legitimate was the delivery of Hedley and a few other alleged deviants. Hedley, off on a posting in South Africa at the time, snorted when he heard of the meeting, held at a moment when he couldn't answer back. That was no way to treat an officer and a gentleman. 'No nonsense like that in the army', he used to say: and he didn't play so much after that.

In 1892 he had come third in the batting and second in the bowling averages. Hewett had been one of the leading run-getters in the country, and Sammy Woods, with his healthy digger lungs, had once bowled 91 overs in a match. 'Something to think about during the winter evenings', he later wrote. Something for modern bowlers to ponder over.

CHAPTER FOUR

Search Party for the Aussies

The summer of 1893 was anti-climactic. The Palairets were busy sorting out their careers and couldn't play regularly till late in the season. Hewett sustained his left-handed aggression, hit two more centuries and looked in vain for support at the wicket. Some of the last-minute team selection mocked the wise recruitment of recent years.

There were nine counties in the first-class table, and Somerset came eighth. When it was a matter of assessing the scoring rate of runs, Somerset were second. 'The Colonel' saw to that – and now, sadly, he was on his way.

That brings us to the visit of the Australians to Taunton in the July: it holds the key segment of the acerbic script.

I have read and reread the accounts of what happened. As a boy I listened, enthralled, amused and horrified, to those who remembered from personal experience. Austere Victorian newspapers weren't averse to the occasional outbreak of sensationalism; they encouraged feelings to run high, even if they sanctimoniously kept the headlines small.

The arrival of the Tourists in the West Country was a matter of considerable interest. Taunton had silenced the prejudices and become established as one of the new centres of cricket. The Australians had been here once before, in 1882, when 'Demon' Spofforth had done his worst. This time, everyone sensed that Somerset had a chance.

There was heavy rain overnight. It didn't apparently deter local enthusiasts who were out under their umbrellas or standing excitedly in shop doorways when the Australian party arrived 'on the mail' at half-past one in the morning. Play was not due to start till midday and the cricketers were hurried to the Castle Hotel for a good night's sleep. The sun was shining by the morning but when at 11am the umpires, Lillywhite and Atkinson, went out to have a look at the soaked wicket they were in absolutely no doubt – cricket would be quite impossible for the day.

By now the streets of Taunton were thronged with people. Spectators had come from all over the West Country. There were Welsh and Midland accents; some supporters had arrived in single-minded determination from East Anglia. The early-morning humour had been good as the potential spectators swapped stories of how they had got to the market town. Some had come by rail, some had walked miles, right through the night. It was the one match they were intent on seeing.

When news of the umpires' decision began to filter through, the reactions were first of disbelief and then of anger. They pointed to the sun and found it hard to envisage a squelchy county ground. There were by now thousands in St James's Street and the road leading up from the station. The good-natured banter had given way to a crescendo of protest.

'We've been up all night and you owe us a game of cricket. At least have another look at the wicket.'

Inside the county ground, the committee sat around with glum faces. Some of them felt with increasing passion that the umpires' inspection and decision had been premature. Sammy Woods, who had taken over from Tom Spencer in assisting Murray-Anderdon with the secretarial duties, was silent for once. Sam was never much of a businessman but he could imagine the extent of the financial loss if the match didn't start.

The touring team had been forewarned and stayed in their hotel. Alternative plans were soon being made. Assured that there would be no play that day, the Australians set off in a large brake at one o'clock. It had been agreed that they would have a picnic on the Quantocks instead. The idea appealed to them; the brake was stacked with crates of ale.

They had difficulty getting through the crowds. Their complexions reddened and their ears burned as the abuse intensified. It wasn't personally directed at them, more at those who'd called play off for the day. The Aussies, rough-hewn in a few cases and adept themselves at verbal excesses, widened their linguistic education.

A contemporary report says: 'The party were loudly hooted as they proceeded through North Street. The mood was very ugly . . . The crowds felt betrayed.'

The gatemen at the county ground, not all of them intrepid by nature, made regular sorties into the improvised committee room to convey just what was happening in the surrounding streets: 'They're pleading with you to think again.' By now the impassioned words weren't confined to the frustrated spectators. Captain and officials were caught up in the acrimony. Fists were being thumped on the table.

'Let's take another look – the sun's been shining most of the morning.'

'What, and turn ourselves into a bloody laughing stock? An official decision's been made. You can't go back on it. Just think what they'll say in London – they'll say we allowed ourselves to be swayed by a mob.'

But just before 2pm, the umpires, Lillywhite and Atkinson, went out again. They prodded the wicket with their fingers and walked ruminatively across the outfield where earlier there had been pools of water. They tried to decide whether there was going to be any more rain. And they stayed out there, two perplexed umpires who must have felt they were being manipulated, for ten minutes of intense discussion. Then they solemnly walked back towards the knot of Somerset officials standing in front of the pavilion: 'All right, then.'

They said it without too much conviction. But the sun had helped and some play, not in the best of conditions, would be possible in a couple of hours. Hewett scowled; organisation seemed chaotic. How would the Australians be contacted and brought back to the ground in time? A messenger was sent off on horseback. 'Yes, we know the Quantocks picnic party could be anywhere. Just ride around until you find 'em.'

The unreliable telegraph between Taunton and Bishop's Lydeard was set creakily in motion, and the cricketers were found. Relishing both the red-earthed hills and the West Country ale, they spluttered on the froth when the harassed horseman rode up and told them that they were needed.

Play started at 4.20. Not long before that, the 'sixpenny visitors' were let into the ground. It wasn't a very clever way to placate a vast crowd and an absurd bottleneck built up. Then they all surged in, some without paying. Some spectators were injured in the collective shoving and had to be taken to hospital. It was an especially cruel postscript for them.

Hewett walked out to open the innings with Palairet. His mind wasn't on the game. He spooned an early catch to mid-off and Coningham, the sun in his eyes, put it down. 'The Colonel', more grim-faced than usual, swung his bat for another four and was then caught in the slips for 12. He hurried with a preoccupied stride back to the pavilion and threw down his bat. Somerset, he argued, would be held up to the nation as the team who couldn't make up their mind: and he'd be the scapegoat.

It rained again on the second day. There was never going to be any play but the umpires had by then painfully acquired the art of diplomacy; they didn't make any announcement till late afternoon. On the third day, a Saturday, it was wet and miserable but they played an eventful game. Twenty-four wickets fell for 249 runs. Somerset gained a first innings lead but eventually lost by 6 wickets. Woods bowled magnificently to take 6-26 and 3-31; and he matched his fellow countrymen, dram for dram, in between.

Herbert Hewett was bitterly hurt by what had happened on the first day of the match. His authority had been undermined; he looked in vain for more support from some of the committee: 'If a captain can't lead at Taunton, this is no place for him.'

He may have been over-sensitive, but he was a dogmatic and proud man. He was only irritated by the sycophants who loudly applauded his skills as they asked him to stay. Rumours of his pending resignation mounted.

The next match was against Lancashire and Hewett stood down. 'Herbert is unfit', said the club manfully. Who were they kidding? Later in the week he went off and played for Harrow Wanderers and scored 124. He would never forgive. And he would never escape from controversy.

Though he left Somerset at the end of that season, he was asked to lead an England XI against Yorkshire during the Scarborough Festival in 1895. It was a compliment to him and he looked forward to the match. But it rained, and the start was delayed. Hewett, in the spirit of the festival, was this time prepared to ignore the minor puddles in the outfield and to play at the appointed hour. The umpires were far more reluctant. A holiday crowd, impatient for some cricket, assumed the former Somerset man was responsible for the delay. They turned on him, releasing a salvo of earthy North Country insults when at last he led the England team on to the field.

Yorkshire's captain, Lord Hawke, was acutely embarrassed. 'Keep quiet or I'll think about calling the game off', he thundered. Hewett, resenting the crowd's attitude and their ignorance of what had happened, didn't bother with any mere threats. He turned on his heels, walked off the field, changed and left the ground. He refused to take any more part in the match. F. R. Spofforth, than living in England, was asked to take over.

Hewett was a major loss to the game and particularly to Somerset, for whom he scored centuries before lunch and sorted out the hypocrites afterwards.

Over the next few years, *Wisden* had a pertinent comment or two to make. For example: 'Somerset cricketers are apparently of a mercurial disposition. Their history of recent years has been a record of brilliant victories and disheartening reverses. But the variability of their play has made it none the less attractive.'

In 1894 Somerset lost by an innings in a day against Lancashire at Old Trafford – just as they had two years before – and by an innings in a day against Yorkshire at Huddersfield. In the Manchester match, the visiting county were all out for 31 in just over 18 overs. At least Lionel Palairet was around with a top score of 8; he opened with Percy Ebdon, the England rugby player. It was one of Ebdon's few matches for Somerset and he scratched 7 runs, the second highest score. He made a duck in the second innings and bade an abrupt farewell to the county game.

The South Africans came to Taunton in the late June of 1894 and lost by 9 wickets. Most of the runs against them were compiled by Palairet, Clapp the professional, Gerald Fowler and Henry Stanley, an Old Etonian who was killed while fighting in the Boer War six years later. As the convivial skipper, Woods didn't have much of a match. He at least handled his bowlers democratically, using nine of them. The amateurs included Gerald Fowler, brother of W.H., who started with Essex and ended up as the honorary treasurer of Somerset for twenty years; the professionals included Frank Bolus, who had only ten games for Somerset over two seasons.

The county may have called on nine bowlers on occasions; it also seemed once or twice as though they needed nine wicket keepers. They had exceptionally capable keepers like Archdale Wickham and A. E. Newton, but neither was available for the Kent fixture at Canterbury; nor was Leslie Hewitt Gay, who made four appearances for Somerset, nine for Hampshire and, rather surprisingly, one for England.

Lionel Palairet could keep wicket and did so for part of the Canterbury match, as did one or two of his team-mates. At Bristol, when Wickham was kept away conducting funerals at Martock, and Newton and Gay couldn't play, Teddy Compton, an amateur from Frome, was rushed to the ground. He batted last man but was much praised for the way he stumped Sidney Kitcat, perhaps better known as a hockey international.

Wisden was in really generous mood when it offered the comment: 'With its increased accommodation the Taunton press box is perhaps the most comfortable in the country.' It is, in fact, small, claustrophobic and perilously vulnerable. The Dickensian inkwells have gone but not so the mythical manual for self-preservation.

I have no idea whether mighty hitters like W. H. Fowler, Vernon Hill or Sam Woods ever shattered the glass in the lofty Taunton press box during the 1890s. It seems very likely, though none of them as far as I know had reason to assault the Fourth Estate in this insensitive way. Certainly in 1926, when Lancashire came, the local glazier was kept in full employment.

Guy Earle, who saw no serious sin in hitting across the line just as long as the ball was whacked out of the ground, drove straighter than usual when he smote over long-on and through the window of the press box. Such mischief must have appealed to Ernest Tyldesley who did the same later in the game.

Occupants of this age-old elevated literary establishment take their eyes off the play only at their peril. We have all seen Ian Botham throw out a challenging look in our direction and then aim at our typewriters. We've all ducked and dived for cover, most recently at the uncharitable behest of Rodney Ontong. Splinters of glass covered every corner of the box. We withdrew gingerly from beneath our barricades, shared a wan smile and took our time throwing back the ball which had taken up residence in the carriage of one of the typewriters.

The most comfortable in the country, did *Wisden* say?

When we come to 1895, it's hard to know where to begin — or with whom. It was the year of W.G., of Archie MacLaren and of Sammy Woods. The county's cricket was triumphant and, more often, traumatic. Mighty names monopolised the centre of the stage but half a dozen or so bit players shouldn't be ignored.

May comes early. So that summer did the illustrious Grace, nearly forty-eight, and ready to make a growing number of detractors bite their tongues.

He hadn't relished his catalogue of relative failures against Somerset, or indeed those of Gloucestershire.

By the time Somerset turned up at the county ground in Bristol in mid-May, W.G. had hit two hundreds and needed one more for his 'century of centuries'. The crowd was larger than usual. The Grace entourage was well in evidence, but they were all inconsiderately kept waiting while Gerald Fowler scored his only first-class hundred and the visitors reached 303. W.G. wasn't holding himself back; he bowled 45 overs and took 5 of the wickets. No one, of course, ever implied that he might like a rest.

The 'Old Man', as the Ashley Down devotees those days referred to him, was 38 not out overnight. He went on to score 288, supported by the sensationally successful schoolboy all-rounder Charlie Townsend (95).

W.G. reached his famous hundred off a thoroughly bad ball by Woods. It was almost certainly intentional. That was the man. Sammy used to say that the delivery he bowled to W.G. for that landmark gave him the happiest moment of his whole cricketing life, and he meant it. Never a selfish or vain player, he could share and savour the successes and joys of others.

As soon as the languid full toss had been hit for 4, E. M. Grace brought out the bubbly for his brother. There were extra glasses on the salver; everyone wanted to participate in the toast. W.G. had been playing the game at first-class level for more than thirty years and the old vigour and sparkle were back in 1895. He drained his glass, wiped his beard on the back of his hand and showed his impish gratitude by going on to a second hundred, and nearly a third. Hardly anything got past the bat. 'Might as well have stayed at home and prepared my sermon', said the admiring Wickham. The faded old scorecards assure us that in Gloucestershire's total of 474 there were only six extras.

Let's forget the precise chronology of this eventful summer and bound forward to the middle of July. The matches against Essex and Lancashire were lost by an innings and 317 runs and by an innings and 452 runs.

Essex came to Taunton with a strong batting side – and not a bad bowling side either, considering that Charles Kortright, perhaps the fastest of them all, didn't even open the attack. He still took four cheap wickets and knocked Sammy's middle stump halfway to the tavern.

The Essex total came to 692, which remains their highest score in county championship cricket. Somerset were without the persevering Nichols. Woods, often near despair, used eight bowlers and contemplated eleven including the wicket keeper, the Taunton amateur Fred Welman. There were three hundreds, one of them by C. P. McGahey, who had played cricket for England and soccer at full back for Spurs and Arsenal and whose West Country claim to fame was the fact that he gave Robertson-Glasgow the name 'Crusoe'. In any case, the Somerset players more frequently called him 'Glasgie'. He loved the game's eccentricities and found kindly mirth in the sweat-engrained faces of unfulfilled bowlers, himself included. What would he have made of the Essex fixture and the one that immediately followed, against Lancashire?

CHAPTER FIVE
Oh Dear, Archie's Match!

The fixture against Lancashire in July 1895 was Archie's match, of course. It wasn't simply and demoralisingly that Lancashire scored 801. Mr A. C. MacLaren, one of only two amateurs in his side (Somerset had nine) made 424. Such a first-class innings is never likely to be bettered in this country, although Viv Richards appeared to be in hot pursuit of it one sunny day in 1985.

MacLaren won the toss, and Woods scratched his head. Somerset's hapless captain was bereft of support bowlers, not a reassuring prospect on a summer's day when the sun shone and the placid wicket embraced only the batsmen. Sammy turned to the Palairet brothers: 'Well, me dears, I'm going to need both of you – and a few more besides.'

The big Aussie would open the bowling himself along with Ted Tyler, fast and slow. He looked with wary pessimism down the team sheet. 'Young Gamlin won't forget this dreadful week in a hurry', he forecast.

Poor young Herbert Temlett Gamlin, a lad from Wellington, was busily and modestly building a reputation for himself as a rugby full back. He would have been happy to stick to rugby – there was never a more fearless tackler. By 1899 he was making his debut for England, against Wales. He played for Wellington, Devonport Services and Blackheath, and fifteen times for his country.

But there he was in 1895, a seventeen-year-old suddenly plucked from village and colts cricket, probably on the impulsive recommendation of Lionel Palairet whom he had dismissed in a Club and Ground trial, coming in to make up the numbers for the games with Essex and Lancashire. Against Essex, he made two ducks and took 0-82. Against Lancashire, he made two more ducks . . . and took the wicket of MacLaren. What matter that the elusive success came off a long hop and that Gerald Fowler, fielding in the outfield, held on to the catch at the second attempt?

Gamlin's career as a professional cricketer was exceedingly brief and no one outside Wellington or a few schoolboy rugby friends had heard of him. But he went into the history books as the nice, naïve young man who got rid of Archie.

My reproduction of the scorecard shows that MacLaren's name was spelt wrongly; it also reveals that Lionel Palairet actually bowled 44 five-ball overs. The supplemented attack included Ezra Bartlett, a Yorkshire-born amateur who fancied himself more as a wicket keeper, Robert Porch, a schoolmaster from Weston-super-Mare who bowled amiable leg-breaks, and Dr John Trask, from Yeovil, who was decidedly better as a middle-order batsman with a penchant for slogging. Not the attack that dreams are made of. Sammy had tried eight of them by lunch. Bowlers, not dreams.

Their virtues had nothing too much to do with technical skill, rather more with stamina and sportsmanship. They kept going, while the perspiration dripped and the scorers frenetically scribbled, at the rate of 27 five-ball overs an hour. There was no new ball to await as a psychological gleam of hope, and no tea interval.

Archibald MacLaren was not only a fine captain. He liked to attack from the top of the order in the way, though arguably with more refinements, of Somerset's Hewett. Archie held his bat high as he waited for the ball to be released. His stance brought tut-tuts; none questioned his ability, paraded in turn for Harrow, Lancashire and England.

He found the short Taunton boundary, like the nondescript bowling, very much to his liking. Lancashire were 141 without loss at lunch. Then Arthur Paull took over from Albert Ward and for a long time the cricket turned into, if you were a West Country spectator, an embarrassing exhibition of batsmanship.

Stiff-jointed and unfit fielders exchanged shrugs as they retrieved the battered ball. Archie had passed his 200 in 260 minutes and when those drinks came out in late afternoon the score was 437-1. Palairet had by then gone over from medium pace to lobs, maybe as a realistic piece of energy-conserving. Paull was on 177 when once more he pulled at one of those enticing lobs. Young, confused, wholehearted Gamlin held on to a difficult catch.

Lancashire were 555 for 3 at the close of play; and just before lunch on the second day, MacLaren had cracked W.G.'s record 344. He was then 404 and looking tired. Just 20 more and Fowler juggled with and held the catch, almost apologetically, at long-off. Archie had batted for 470 minutes; the total was then 792-7. There wasn't a large crowd. But those who were at the county ground cheered him all the way back to the pavilion. Sammy led the prolonged applause among the players. 'Thought the old beggar would be out there till Christmas, me dear.'

No innings of that content could be quite flawless. Archie was dropped at mid-on when he had scored 262. Wickham, of all people, put him down early on the second day and no doubt went into clerical retreat on the spot. And after he had reached 400 he offered a venomous return to Palairet. As one of the papers noted quaintly: 'Lionel did not think it advisable to attempt the catch.' It was a magnificent innings. There was one six (remember how difficult they were to record in those days), 64 fours, 10 threes, 26 twos and 80 singles.

But the 1895 season wasn't all statistical gloom; we can find some marvellous gems to counter visiting batsmen's ungracious savagery.

Somerset had gone to Lord's in early June. The Palairet brothers, batting at Nos 1 and 3, both scored a hundred. It was the only time they did it together in a county match. Lionel compounded his delight by dismissing the stylish and ultimately tragic Stoddard when he'd scored a beautiful 150. Whatever the vicissitudes of his county that summer, the older Palairet looked a player of timeless stature. He finished fourth in the batting averages, only behind W.G., MacLaren and Ranji.

Two superb individual feats during the season must also be praised: the batting of Sammy Woods and the bowling of Ted Tyler.

Woods came off the field at Brighton and said to no one in particular: 'You can't beat the air down here. Nice and bracing. Good for runs.'

He'd just scored 215. It was his only double century and it took him two and a half hours. Sam had done some of his schooling at Brighton when he first arrived in England from Sydney. He liked the place, especially the cricket fields. His second hundred came within the hour.

The Somerset captain had already sent down 29 overs and allowed himself a sly smile when he bowled Ranji for 95. He knew he'd lost some of his earlier pace, but there was absolutely nothing wrong with the lungs and the heart, and, as he reminded everyone at Brighton, the muscle.

Several years ago in a book about my West Country heroes, *From Grace to Botham*, I said:

> There is really nothing more to write about Sammy Woods. The stories tumble over each other – and most of them are true, or at least in the spirit of this immensely lovable and outsized Australian. Everything about him was bountiful: his shoulders, his smile, the thrust of his bowling arm, the playful swing of his bat, his drinking capacity, and the warmth of his heart.

I repeat it here because the paragraph sums up the man and there is no point in changing it. My great regret is that I didn't see him play. Nor did I see him roll a skittle ball, play billiards as well as anyone in Bridgwater or Taunton, shove at the flank of a rugby scrum, sing at a harvest home or exchange impish blows in a boxing booth. I'd have settled for any cameo.

Samuel Moses James Woods came over with his father from Sydney when he was fourteen. His father had a good friend at Bridgwater, and Sammy's link with Somerset started. He was sent to Brighton College and did his studies under sufferance, as a way of breaking up the sport. Holidays were spent in the West Country. He had a splendid build and a mop of hair that was seldom combed. His guardian, a Mr Burrington, took him along to the county ground: 'Perhaps you can join them one day, young Sam.'

Sam got into Cambridge, although no one quite knew how. He was there from 1888 to 1891 and got a Blue four times. 'There are better things to do at Cambridge than study', he used to say. He made the point at Fenner's in 1890 when he took all 10 wickets in an innings for 69 runs, against C. I. Thornton's XI. He was very fast in those days and a bit wild when he wasn't concentrating; he frightened the life out of a few of the Thornton batsmen.

Not just a cricketer, he was a surprisingly nimble athlete for a big man (and it was all the more sad to see him limping so badly from an arthritic hip after the First World War). He played soccer at full back for Sussex. As a rugby player he appeared for Cambridge, Somerset and England. Maybe he represented his county – if not his country – at half a dozen other sports.

'Give me a ball and a glass of whisky and I'm a contented man', he'd say. Certainly in his later years, when the girth had broadened and he went around the Somerset and Devon villages with his Farmers' XI, he was quite capable of handling a cricket ball and a tumbler of Scotch simultaneously.

He was the greatest character in the history of Somerset cricket, as big a celebrity, around the Blackdown Hills, the Quantocks, the Mendips and Poldens, as Grace himself. Everyone wanted him to attend harvest suppers, social evenings, even whist drives.

Woods turned few invitations down. He was a bachelor with a freewheeling lifestyle and no domestic commitments. His favourite homes – he had several – were well-established pubs like the George, where the landlords adopted a liberal attitude to closing hours. There were times when he walked from Bridgwater to Taunton before a match.

Sammy actually had a Victorian sportsman's asexuality. He was happiest in a bar, spinning sporting yarns in interminable jest, not a single story touched by malice. He was noisy, even boisterous, enjoying attention and still ready to break into song when others were ready to stagger home.

One suspects that he also needed company. Like many beaming extroverts, he probably had a lonely side and he feared being left, the last man, at the barside. Some said he hated those winter evenings, when his friends had gone home to their wives and there was no skittle match to prevent a solitary evening. Mostly, however, he was never at a loss for a companion and shared laughter. Like most Australians, he was a classless man. He hunted and went beagling; he was a prized guest at country-house weekends and equally at ease in a Taunton side street where, according to Robertson-Glasgow, Sam knew everyone. He loved country folk, the carters and blacksmiths, as well as the gentlemen farmers.

He was of independent means, though only to the extent of never seeming to do a job of work – there was not too much evidence of affluence. He bought his round and his doting friends looked after him for the rest of the evening. No one quite knew, but he probably lived on family investments and the material rewards of a universal friendship.

Like the best of story-tellers, Sammy had a careless regard for facts. His printed memoir was readable, evocative, gossipy, and wayward when it came to dates and details. Jack MacBryan told me of the evening he was standing in the bar with Woods when George Geary walked past. He'd recently taken all 10 wickets in an innings for Leicestershire. 'Is that really the best you can do, George?'

Geary, taken aback, blurted out: 'Well, yes, I suppose it is, Mr Woods.'

'I once did better than you, George. Got 200 wickets in an afternoon.' And then, as an afterthought: 'Me brother got another 107.'

The big Australian watched and chuckled at Geary's reaction. Then he slapped him on the back. 'We'd rounded up several hundred aborigines and bowled them out one after the other.'

My own favourite Sammy Woods story is of the village match at Orchard Portman, in Somerset, where he was the umpire. Again MacBryan was involved. He had a very correct style and kept the ball on the ground. Suddenly his mentor, the umpire, said: 'You've been in long enough, Jack –

hit up a catch to Eddie [Lord Portman].'

Against his nature, MacBryan did, and the aristocratic host dropped it. 'Eddie should have held it. So you're out!'

The dapper and deflated Mac returned to the little pavilion. 'How were you out?' the villagers asked with puzzled expressions.

'Because Sam said so.' Everyone just accepted it.

When the Australians came over in 1888 they claimed Woods as one of theirs and he played in three Tests for them – without much success. He also played three times for England in 1895–6. He was happiest of all walking out with Somerset; the last of his 299 matches for the county was in 1910. By the 1920s he was limping badly and pretending he wasn't in pain. The injury emanated from an accident while he was serving in the Camel Corps in Egypt during the war. 'Riding a camel one day, me dear, and it set off towards some very dangerous-looking cactus shrubs. Had to take evasive action. Threw myself off – and broke me leg. Never quite got over it.'

In all first-class matches he scored 15,345 runs and took 1,040 wickets. He was always in a hurry when he batted, and could drive most handsomely.

As a bowler he never shirked a long, tiring stint. He was a captain who refused to hide or save himself. In the earlier years he was very fast and hostile, though the smile down the wicket was too genuine to imply anything more than a fleeting belligerence. He took 153 wickets in 1892, his best year as a bowler. In the field no one saw him flinch; he held on to nearly three hundred catches, many of them at silly point where he was a large, vulnerable target.

He captained Somerset from 1894 to 1906 with varying success. Perhaps at times he was too easy-going, lacking the competitive fibre of Hewett. He never noticeably grieved too much about a defeat; a rebuke to a pro (or amateur) was tactfully handled. The committee liked him, even if they shook their heads at a tactical lapse. Everyone liked him.

Sammy hit nineteen hundreds and one shouldn't try to devalue his batting in any way. The batting got better as the bowling tailed away. Fast bowlers don't keep going for ever, yet we suspect it was the wickets that he cherished even more than the runs. Didn't he strike with his very first ball for Somerset against Warwickshire? The Tasmanian, Claude Rock, who had been at Cambridge and had had some games for Warwickshire before they became first class, knew all about Woods' ability to whip the ball down and was rather surprised to find the wicket keeper, A. E. Newton, standing up. Perhaps, he thought, Sam was concentrating on length and not pace. It was a reckless surmise on the part of Rock. He was well beaten for speed and, to the astonishment of the batsman, the intrepid Newton had the bails off. It was a magnificent piece of stumping.

'Most bowlers start with a nice, gentle range-finder, Sam. I didn't know you were going to blast one down straightaway', said Newton.

'Don't like to waste too much time, me dear. But I'd stand back a little if I were you.'

Woods' opening delivery for Somerset was recorded as a fierce, fast yorker on the leg side. W. N. Roe, who played in that match, was in no doubt at all about it: 'The finest example of stumping I ever saw.'

The yorker brought Sam many of his wickets; the concealed slower ball also brought generous reward. But he was essentially a bowler who refused to trouble himself too much with subtleties, either on the cricket field or in life. As a person he had the uncomplicated characteristics of W.G. Both of them were probably philistines and they got on well together as they exchanged sporting stories. Sammy was still the more rounded man. He had an inexhaustible circle of friends and socialised with less discrimination. And W.G. would never, at any half excuse, have gone into a baritone rendition.

S. M. J. Woods was secretary of the county until 1923. He couldn't keep away from the ground. Gimblett, Richards and Botham have all, in their different styles, been cult figures at the county ground. In a bar or a Taunton side street none of them gathered so many doting eavesdroppers as Woods. His funeral in the April of 1931 was an extraordinary reflection of adulation.

But, as mentioned earlier, there was also the mighty achievement of Tyler in 1895. Edwin (Ted) James Tyler took all 10 for 49 runs against Surrey in the first innings. A collection on the Taunton ground brought him £35. It should have been more.

Ted was the best of the early pros, followed in merit by George Nichols. The two are inextricably linked in my mind, like a reliable, underpraised double act which never missed a cue. They gave everything for their audience, at times self-effacingly carrying the show when the rest of the bill was pretty banal.

Tyler was a slow left-arm bowler who hardly ever spun the ball but flighted it with an innate craftsman's skill. He could gather some deceptive pace off the wicket. He could vary the delivery without giving a flicker of a clue either in facial expression or the grip of the ball. Above all, he kept pitching on a spot. Somerset used him to open the bowling, with Nichols or Woods, and he just kept going, wiping the sweat from his eyes, until someone else took over – at times there was no one and he continued through the innings.

This six-footer from Kidderminster had a quiet, fairly phlegmatic manner and the distinctive vowels of Worcestershire. It was with his native county that he took 9-96 against Warwickshire – and it was surprising that Somerset wooed him away. He played for Taunton and a few village sides while he was qualifying.

As Somerset went first class, so Ted Tyler tied up one end. He had soon taken 9-33 against Notts; then in 1895 he ran through Surrey on his own. When the two teams had met earlier in the summer, he hadn't taken a wicket. Surrey won the first fixture and lost the second. They had a strong batting side and none of them could make anything of Tyler. His figures were: 34.3-15-49-10. Woods, Nichols and 'Captain' Hedley got nowhere at all; 'Scrimp' Leveson-Gower was among Ted's victims. Two of the batsmen were bowled. Mostly they were picked up at slip and short gully.

Ted had the perfect temperament for a slow bowler. He appeared to be impervious to punishment, though in fact there wasn't too much of that.

As a bowler, J. C. White modelled himself unashamedly on Tyler; he went to Taunton School at a time when Ted was the coach. White, too, was a flight bowler and not a spinner; he, too, wheeled away with impeccable length and kept the variations under his cap till the last second; he, too, had the dour, unruffled temperament that infuriated batsmen intent on disturbing an adversary's equanimity.

Tyler played just once for England. In all he took 895 first-class wickets and no one in the West Country was too pleased when, in 1900, a zealous umpire started no-balling him for throwing. It was the same umpire who made Arthur Mold's life a misery at Old Trafford the following year.

Ted was more surprised than hurt; no one had really complained before. He shrugged off umpire Phillips' indictment and went on playing for another seven years. I cannot help making the comparison with another slow left-arm Somerset bowler, Eric Bryant, from Weston-super-Mare. At Bath in the match against Gloucestershire in 1960 he was called four times in one over. It destroyed him and I felt desperately sorry for an enthusiastic young spinner whose undoubted talent was blunted by what some saw as a jerky action. He had just twenty-two matches for Somerset and went home a demoralised and finished professional cricketer.

Alongside Tyler, one places George Benjamin Nichols, Taunton's maestro of melodrama. Most cricketers played cards between innings. George pulled out a stub of pencil and tried to write plays. He had a soft Bristol voice and an honest, artisan face; and he was more literate and creative than most of the amateurs of his day. His spelling may have been suspect, but there was nothing lacking in his sense of theatre. He wrote about villains and pretty damsels, several of his plays were produced locally, at least one appearing, though briefly, on the London stage. Team-mates teased him about his playwrighting. 'Your mind's on the first act and not the first wicket', they would say, never unkindly.

Few spoke unkindly about him. He was a popular member of the team and a thoroughly useful pro who, off whippy medium pace, took 299 wickets in 134 games for Somerset. He came from Fishponds in Bristol and had five matches as an amateur for Gloucestershire before crossing the Mendips to make a new home and living.

W.G. was said to have been unimpressed with Nichols and he made the mistake of letting him go. But then the Doctor had little time for the English stage. He may have caught George working out his latest cast when he should have been giving his bearded superior some pre-match batting practice. At Somerset, Nichols, like Tyler, was an amiable team-man. For these two friends, the workload was heavy. They weren't the kind who complained, not even at negligible benefits. Ted Tyler picked up a mere £75 through the gate from the Surrey fixture he'd chosen. It was just as well the pair had heads for business. Ted for a time ran a pub. The two jointly and then separately had their own shops, selling everything from sports equipment and tobacco, to walking sticks and cycles.

Nichols gave up the game in 1899. At the age of forty-eight he died of pneumonia. His contribution to Somerset cricket – and even to the British stage – shouldn't be forgotten.

There is one final margin note. Playing against Gloucestershire at Bristol in 1896, Nichols was given out for hitting the ball twice. Versions of what happened vary a trifle. Was he being typically playful and demonstrating that theatrical sense of levity and diversion? Was there a Gloucestershire amateur, too rigidly obsessed with what was legitimate, who appealed and then wished he hadn't? Was it just an umpire doing his job?

The last four seasons of the nineteenth century were undistinguished for Somerset. Twice they finished eleventh in the table, twice thirteenth. They cobbled together a mere nine victories over that period; in 1898 there was a single win. All this reflects inept play, problems over team selection and too many passengers. The sneers from 'superior' counties were coming back.

Yet Somerset, cussed as ever, could still do the unexpected. Lionel Palairet, with a resilient flourish of dignity, hit four centuries in 1896. Southampton had seen some poetic stroke play over the generations, but not much was better than Palairet's 292. It took W.G. to top that (301).

Up to now all the county's home first-class fixtures had been played at Taunton. Significantly, a July match against the Philadelphians in 1897 was staged at Bath. The area, where arguably serious cricket in Somerset had started, was now ready for a county game – and the vociferous claimants were to be placated in twelve months' time.

The 1897 balance sheet shows that the book-keeping had a tight, prudent look about it. The purchase of 'talent caps', covering 1893 to the past year, had set the county back only £1 19s 3d. Not that there was too much emergent talent to be recognised.

A whole page in the Year Book was rather proudly given over to what was headed 'The 1897 Deficit'. In large, well-spaced type, the statement read:

> The Committee have much pleasure in reporting that the debt of £124 0s 5d has since been wiped out. Mr J. S. Donne very generously offered £25 towards clearing off the debt, provided the rest of the money was raised before Christmas. Subscription cards were issued and thanks to the exertions of our supporters, the balance was raised. The Committee take this opportunity of tendering their best thanks to all those who worked so hard towards attaining so desirable a result.

Not many wins, then, but books that balanced . . .

There were a few new names. George Gill was a professional who came from Leicestershire and eventually ended up back with that county. He bowled fast and hit the ball hard. Francis Ashley Phillips had roughly the same approach as an amateur. He played for Essex and Oxford University before coming to Somerset, where, though his bowling wasn't taken seriously, as a batsman he was well worth his four hundreds. Charles Bernard came in from Bohemians, the Bristol club side. He was more cautious and disciplined than some of the amateurs who had a transitory relationship with the county. Bernard made thirty-three appearances, scored two centuries and batted with gritty zeal for 94 against the Australians in 1899. The trouble was that he was such a poor fielder.

So much has happened on Bath's Recreation Ground, where games have been over in a day, beneficiaries have wept in public and the Aussies have been beaten, that I mustn't skip carelessly past the first county fixture there. It was played in May 1898. And a twenty-year-old with a slightly dour demeanour and a Kirkheaton accent made his championship debut for Yorkshire.

His name was Wilfred Rhodes. He only came in because another slow left-arm bowler, Bobby Peel, had gone out – for good – because of his unconventional view of water sprinkling on a cricket field.

Wilfred had played once for Yorkshire against the MCC at Lord's. Now he was summoned to see what he could do at Bath. It has to be said he did very well indeed. Yorkshire won by 198 runs and Rhodes' figures in the two innings were: 13.4-4-24-7; 13-6-21-6.

It was a game for the bowlers and the wicket was never remotely conducive to stroke-making. Ernie Robson (of whom much more in later pages) and even Gerald Fowler took cheap wickets. But the match belonged to the debutant. Somerset sparred, prodded and mostly missed as they were dismissed for 35 in the second innings.

The county have, of course, often been maddeningly adept at self-imposed disintegration. In 1899 they were bowled out by Middlesex at Lord's for 35 and 44; of the 35, Woods swung 20 with an engaging air of fatalism. There were twelve ducks over the two innings.

It was not simply that Somerset lost by an innings against Surrey at the Oval at the end of May – it was the way Bobby Abel carried his bat. The home county made 811 and Bobby, small, badly balanced and forced to squint because of a recurrent eye infection, seemed under no physical handicap at all as he scored 357. Nine bowlers tried in vain to ensnare him. Tom Hayward, the pro, and Mr V. F. S. Crawford added their centuries to the statistical orgy.

Less than two months later, this time at Taunton, Hampshire sympathetically declared at 672 for 7. Major Robert Montagu Poore, on his way to becoming a Brigadier-General, was a cricketing sensation that summer. It

Sammy Woods, as usual, rejected headgear. This 1897 Somerset team is: (*Back, left to right*) V. T. Hill, G. Gill, E. J. Tyler, R. C. N. Palairet. (*Centre*) L. C. H. Palairet, A. E. Newton, S. M. J. Woods (capt), G. Fowler, Capt W. C. Hedley. (*Front*) E. Robson and F. A. Phillips

This 1892 photograph shows L. C. H. Palairet (*left*) and H. T. Hewett (*right*) standing on either side of W. G. Grace. Their opening stand against Yorkshire had beaten the previous record, held by W. G. Grace and B. B. Cooper

Len Braund – 23 times an England player

L.C. BRAUND (Somersetshire)

was in effect his only regular season of first-class cricket and the free-hitting Dubliner ended with an average of more than 90.

'We did our best to give him that kind of average', said a few of the Somerset committee in measured and sardonic tones. He tore into the West Country bowling for an unlikely 304, before Archie Wickham stumped him and then led the applause.

'They do say he's an even better swordsman. And better still as a polo player.'

'Then why the devil does he have to come to Taunton and torment us with a cricket bat?'

The county loyalist does well to survey the records of the late 1890s with an unseeing eye. Some cynics claimed that dropped catches were the norm and physical fitness the exception. When it came to choosing the team, Sammy Woods was too steadfast in friendship. Somerset were once more a decidedly soft touch. But suddenly Woods would bring back sublime joy by an assault, as full of laughter as of fire, on the Sussex bowling. He hit 143 out of 173 that day in 1898 and everyone was saying once more that there was never a more entertaining side. It was a pleasant notion that kept subsiding and surfacing again. It still does.

Almost the end of the century: time to take stock; time, overdue, for a new vigour and purpose on the field; time to weed out well-fleshed amateurs and jokey public-school attitudes that lacked the competitive instinct; time once more to recruit.

The signs were good. Robson had arrived from Yorkshire and would be staying for nearly thirty years. He was to be Somerset's finest yeoman cricketer. He had little, socially or physically, in common with Sam Woods: but they were both all-rounders, both loved the game (and both could sing remarkably well).

Apart from 'Robbie', there were Beaumont 'Cranny' Cranfield, and Len Braund, who played his opening match for Somerset against the Australians in 1899. He went in first and scored 82. We'll never be quite sure why Surrey let him go. In first-class cricket he scored 17,801 runs and took 1,114 wickets; he was the best slip fielder Somerset ever had.

And there was a self-possessed young man from Cambridge, formerly from Clifton College. His life was cricket and rugby football. 'Wouldn't mind playing regularly for Somerset when I've got these boring studies out of the way', he said.

He did play regularly for the county. He captained them, and became their president. For years John Daniell was to be the Voice of Somerset cricket. That voice earned him the satirical title of 'The Lion of Judah' by a few of the cowed professionals. Most of them agreed he was good for the game in the West Country.

It is a reassuring thought on which to welcome the twentieth century.

UP TO 1939

Was cricket really so much more relaxed before the war? This faded snapshot of four amateurs, H. D. Burrough, R. A. Ingle, G. M. Bennett and N. S. Mitchell-Innes, enjoying themselves at a fairground gallery is in rather sharp contrast with the intense expressions of waiting batsmen Vic Marks, Ian Botham, Peter Roebuck and Phil Slocombe (*below*)

CHAPTER SIX
Fishing for Runs

Ranjitsinhji, the glamorous young prince, kept late hours. He liked frivolous parties, an occasional visit to the bawdy music hall and bridge-playing till dawn. His life was shallow and full of fun in the mood of unleashed Edwardian indulgence. He had yet to assume, with such conscientious regard, the awesome responsibilities of political office at home.

In the years up to and after the turn of the century he was one of the most discussed and admired adornments of cricket's Golden Age. He had immense natural gifts, all of them elegant, as a batsman. And he was an Indian aristocrat, heir to the throne of Nawanagar, of indisputable and gentle charm.

Older, supposedly wiser, men in the Sussex dressing room pondered his playful pursuits and the self-induced congestion of his social diary. They even offered discreet advice on the virtues of a good night's sleep.

'What is wrong, pray, with a rubber or two – or maybe a game of billiards after dinner? They are so very civilised', he would say with an expression of mock pain. He never seemed noticeably tired next morning.

Ranji especially liked coming to the West Country. It wasn't simply that, in season, Sammy would take him shooting around the Blackdown coverts – or that he could take a few bob off the equally nocturnal Australian at cards.

'I know why you look forward to coming down here . . .'

'Well then, tell me, my good friend Sam.'

'You don't come for the cricket – it's because of the fishing.'

It was their little joke. In 1901, five years after his first appearance for England, Ranji was in princely form at Taunton. He paraded the trappings and finery of genius as he made 285 not out, his highest score. The genius came from the wrists and the eyes and the majestic stillness that preceded the panther strike. Nearly 300 beautifully co-ordinated runs – and he hadn't gone to bed the night before. He'd gone fishing instead.

C. B. Fry, a great friend, used to dine out on the story but got one or two details wrong. It wasn't burly Billy Murdoch who spoke out with the voice of authority and told Ranji, in unequivocal language, to behave himself and get some sleep. Nor was it Somerset's Ted Tyler who helped to set up the rather audacious practical joke. Fry may have confused him with the left-arm slow bowler who was playing in that match, Beaumont 'Cranny' Cranfield, who had, apart from a nervous manner and a lugubrious face, a quiet sense of humour. They used to say of Cranny: 'He had £200 in one of the local banks but he never touched it. Always afraid he'd bump into the manager, Gerald Fowler, the Somerset amateur!'

But back to the joke played on Ranji. All the home players knew of his passion for fishing and the hours he had willingly spent in the past on the banks of the Tone and the Parrett. In a succession of confidential asides, they told him of a local mill-pond teeming with perch. The secret was to go by night.

The temptation was irresistible. He retired to bed early at the Castle Hotel and compounded the deception by putting his shoes outside the bedroom door for early-morning polishing. Then he slipped into spare boots and made a stealthy exit. He stayed at the mill-pond all night. There's no record of his catch or his demeanour when he rumbled the ruse. We can imagine his marvellous innings next day carried a vengeful joy.

Woods used to say in later life as he sat alongside the practice nets, a bottle of Scotch in his lap and nostalgia glazing his eyes, that Ranji claimed Somerset were second to Sussex in his affection. If he did, it was probably a romantic and fleeting thought influenced by a brace of pheasants and, who knows, even a few pockets full of perch.

There's a discernible Asian connection, of course. In the years leading up to the First World War, the Somerset team sheet was inclined to have a decidedly exotic look. Need we go beyond Prince Kumar Hitendra Narayan Singh and Manek Pallon Bajana? The scorers struggled for both space and spelling acumen. The locals settled for 'Prince' and 'Pyjamas'.

However did they reach Taunton? You could ask the same question a few hundred times when you look at the names, princely and prosaic, that make up the county's history. Just as well to chuckle and not explore. Few other first-class sides could remotely challenge Somerset's sheer, impudent, ingenious, illogical and, at times futile range.

Prince Narayan, the son of the Maharajah of Cooch Behar, played some cricket and made some West County friends at Eton. He made little impact at Cambridge and not much during his four matches for the county. He never looked strong and had died of influenza by the age of thirty.

Bajana was a better bet. He came over on tour with India in 1911, receptive to any suggestion that he might stay awhile and play some county cricket. 'Pyjamas' was a smallish, solidly built opening bat who went on to score two centuries in more than fifty matches for Somerset. The late Jack MacBryan, who played with him, remembered him as a useful addition to the staff. 'Came to us after making a hundred for the Indians at Taunton. No one had heard of him before.'

The Asian link was renewed in the fifties and sixties. There was the Pakistan all-rounder Khan Mohammad (one match only for Somerset), Yawar Saeed, who later became a Test selector for Pakistan, and the small, attractive Abbas Ali Baig, who as an Oxford undergraduate much impressed Somerset by getting co-opted into the India touring side and scoring a century on his debut at Old Trafford.

Let's admit it: the county were for ever too easily impressed. They were susceptible to exotic grandeur and haughty lineage. If the young man with the long name and the fancy cap could also play, it was a bonus to cherish.

They liked the sound of the Hon Mervyn Robert Howard Molyneux Herbert, not least for the way he'd knocked up 201 in a house match at Eton. 'Feel like a match or two with us, old chap?' he was asked at a weekend house party. It was the way it was done. He had already played half a dozen times for Nottinghamshire; now he stayed for thirty-one with Somerset, spread over twenty-one years.

First-class cricket was at that time full of itinerants. The pros moved in search of wages; some of the amateurs moved with the amiable unconcern of healthy, vacuous young men killing time before going off to manage a tea-plantation or having to take over from father in the City.

Cricket was a richer game because of the amateurs. Their talent was often indeterminate but their presence – the ostentatious spectrum of their headgear, the undisciplined waistline, the cheerful banter – added interest. Somerset, with little money, would never have raised a side at all without this apparently interminable supply of human curiosities.

There was nothing curious about Len Braund. He was an honest pro who put his cap on straight and arrived at the county ground in 1899 with the nondescript look of the bronze-faced journeyman as he unpacked his bags. Len was always an unassuming man. He was also canny enough, privately, to know his worth. He didn't often speak out of turn but one or two of the amateurs could tell by the glance he gave them that he had seen through them. He was companionable, occasionally stubborn. And in a very short time he became one of the greatest all-rounders in the world.

The mystery is why Surrey ever let him go. But he didn't do a great deal during his twenty-one matches for them. Perhaps one or two of the committee found him just a trifle too self-confident, even precocious in the way he twisted his fingers round the ball as he spun away at the nets. They couldn't decide if he was really a batsman or a bowler – or whether he was good enough at either. Len sniffed and on his own initiative joined Somerset. His pedigree appeared to be unexceptional. He was put in for the first time against the Australians in the late August of 1899. 'Going to let you open with Mr Bernard, Braund. See what you can do.'

He made 82, very well indeed. There was a tight, disciplined defence and a promising range of attacking shots. But his bowling, leg-spinners off near medium pace, was treated as batting practice by the tourists. He took 1-81 and said to no one in particular: 'The Oval's bad enough for leggers. Taunton could be worse.'

In 1900 he had other frustrations. This time it was the bureaucrats – they muttered out loud about his registration. Complaints had been received at Lord's and soon the MCC were ruling that he was playing county cricket illegally, before his qualification for Somerset had been completed.

It isn't clear whether Somerset were aware of the residential qualifications. They should have been. Maybe Murray-Anderdon, Gerald Fowler and Sammy, now the joint secretaries, were ready for a little mischief – to test the rigidity at headquarters. In any case, they brought Braund in for the third match of the season, against Middlesex. The fixture was at Lord's; you couldn't be more challenging than that. Woods, always pertinent and pithy on the subject, never could stand red tape.

Braund made 38 and 1. He took 2 wickets at some expense, mainly because Mr Stoddart (221) chose to make such a wonderful and theatrical exit from the county game. This fine opening batsman did a great service to the game's beneficiary, J. T. Hearne, a marked disservice to Braund, who rubbed his fingers sore without getting much spin.

The letters were flying after that. 'You should know that this professional is not eligible for another season', said the official note of rebuke.

'Sorry, Braund. Now go off and get some decent cricket before we can call on you again.'

He did, with the London County side at the Crystal Palace. His value as a batsman, in particular, was very evident to W.G. If the Old Man hadn't by now turned his back on Gloucestershire, he'd almost certainly have had Len Braund, by some means or other, looking for digs in Bristol.

By 1901, Len was legitimately embraced by Somerset. And there he stayed for a long time. No one was surer of his county place; seldom was there a better county cricketer, in the craftsman sense. He played twenty-three times for his country, often with distinction. He hit twenty-five hundreds. He could be obdurate or forceful, according to the needs of the team, but he preferred hitting to blocking.

As the county's fortunes are catalogued over the first twenty years of the new century, there will be much of Braund. For a long time he liked bowling as much as batting, his fingers were supple and the turn could be prodigious. But he knew the value of variation and pace off the pitch. Many slow bowlers have, for some inexplicable reason, suddenly lost the prized art of spinning the ball. It happened to Len Braund and for a time it demoralised him. Yet he wasn't a man to mope. Batsmen went on punishing him – and he gradually gave up bowling. There were still many runs to be scored after all.

And, of course, there was his superb fielding in the slips. Many of his contemporaries were emphatic that he was the best slip in the world. He wasn't flashy. But the anticipation was intuitive and the ball always seemed to come clean to his fingers. No one remembered a juggle, a showy dive. What spectators did remember was the way he could effortlessly stretch his body to the left to pick up almost impossible catches that had gone down the leg side, wide of the wicket keeper.

His England colleagues said he had the perfect temperament for the big occasion. He never looked nervous, at least never betrayed private fears to the opposition. He was a sound professional in that he never wantonly sacrificed his wicket in either leisure or levity; he disapproved of those around him at Somerset who did.

He liked a sing-song on tour and was proud, according to Robertson-Glasgow, of his bowler hat. His good nature was often evident: as early as that 1900 match with Middlesex when he was no-balled. He hadn't even let go of the ball – and he held on triumphantly, looking with impish challenge at the umpire. It didn't help him; in those days the umpire's call couldn't be rescinded and Middlesex got an extra run. 'Well, I'm damned', said Len in a voice always more Berkshire than Surrey.

Braund liked the horses and he liked his ale. Ernie Robson's son Vic told me how both Braund and Harry Chidgey, one of Somerset's wicket keepers, used to stay at his father's house and he called them Uncle Len and Uncle Harry. 'First thing in the morning, Uncle Len would send me off to buy a paper. I've a suspicion he was more interested in the racing than the cricket!'

As for the drinking, he'd deserved it. He toiled more and, in the end, suffered more than most cricketers. Both legs were amputated and still he turned out at Lord's, pushed there in a wheelchair by a friend, to see the cricket and pretend that he was still mobile.

From the moment he'd scored a hundred for W.G.'s team against the Australians while still qualifying for Somerset, Surrey knew they'd made a terrible mistake in letting him go.

After he gave up playing he became an umpire and also did some coaching at Cambridge. He'd always been an incorrigible conversationalist in the slips, his talk mostly centred on esoteric information about the likely runners in tomorrow's 3.45. As an umpire, he liked to chat with the fielders — between deliveries or back in the bar afterwards.

Len Braund didn't do very well with his benefit. In 1948 a fund was launched by Herbert Sutcliffe for Len and Phil Mead and it raised about £7,000. The following year, Braund was one of twenty-six former professionals given honorary membership of the MCC.

I'm apt to dwell more on the players than the playing record; the mundane data has rarely conveyed the spirit of the county's cricket. For instance, in 1900 Somerset finished eleventh in the table. But how much does that really tell us?

They were still spilling their catches with embarrassing and comic regularity and had few serious rivals as the worst fielding side in the country. They were still struggling to find and field a settled team. The elusive quality of reliability refers to their approach to punctuality as much as their ability in flannels. Yet they beat both Hampshire and Surrey twice.

The Boer War had depleted the playing membership of Somerset. Walter Hedley, Francis Phillips and Henry Stanley were out there fighting as officers and gentlemen. Stanley never came back. There is a lengthy and poignant list of Somerset players who became wartime casualties.

In the summer of 1900, the county's four wins have a pale look when compared to Yorkshire's sixteen. Yet it was at Dewsbury that little Beaumont Cranfield, the left-arm spinner brought to the county with the intention of taking over in time from Tyler, took 13 wickets. He tweaked away, po-faced as ever. He twisted and contorted his finger joints, never his facial muscles. Unlike Tyler, 'Cranny' could turn the ball; he lacked Ted's flighty guile and accuracy. The Yorkshire batsmen didn't know much about him. The nine professionals in their side rashly jettisoned their more customary traits of dourness as he kept tossing the ball up to them. Over the two innings, eleven batsmen snicked or gave simple catches.

SOMETIMES CALLED
'THE LEAGUE OF NATIONS'

Prince Narayan, son of the Maharajah
of Cooch Behar (Somerset 1909–10)

Bill Alley (1957–68)

Greg Chappell (1968–9)

Peter Wight (1953–65)

John McMahon (1954–7)

Colin McCool (1956–60)

Abbas Ali Baig (1960–2)

Kerry O'Keeffe (1971–2)

Beaumont Cranfield had a relatively short career of 125 matches for the county. He was dead from pneumonia at the age of thirty-five. Twice he took a hundred wickets in a season; in tandem with Braund, he gave opposing batsmen a thoroughly bewildering time. The pair of them spent some marvellous and mischievous hours for the MCC at Scarborough. Who's going to be churlish enough to remember the afternoons when the ball didn't turn at all at Taunton – and little Cranny was left shuddering and looking at the ground?

While we talk of bowlers, there is Albert Trott to consider. He has long rustled my journalistic instincts. There are various reasons for this: his enormous talents as an all-rounder, the slogging and record breaking, the unloving relationship with his native Australia, the single-handed conquests against Somerset, the whiffs of scandal, the self-destruction.

At Taunton in the early August of 1900 he took all 10 wickets in the first innings. The first four batsmen were bowled – and two more later on. His 10-42 in just over 14 overs was a triumph of variation. He peddled a hotch-potch of instinctive wizardry. 'Alberto' could swerve the ball, he could spin it; he manifested his personalised magic off deceptive medium pace.

Seven years later, Middlesex granted him a benefit at Lord's against Somerset. He was in decline as a player and he needed the money. The match never ran its allocated span. Trott simply bowled too well. He mesmerised Somerset, bowling Talbot Lewis, Massey Poyntz, Sammy Woods and Ernie Robson with successive balls in the second innings. As a memorable, though misplaced, encore, he ended the game with a hat-trick.

'Everything went *too* well for me. I've bowled myself to the bloody workhouse', he said with a laconic eloquence.

Here was one of the most unfulfilled careers in the whole history of county cricket. He started by playing for Australia but for a reason we'll never know got left out of the 1896 tour of this country. Brother Harry was the captain; perhaps he knew too much of the human weaknesses. Albert, with understandable petulance, packed his cricket bag and made his own way to England. He joined the Lord's groundstaff and went on to play for England twice and Middlesex 223 times.

Everyone quotes his historic hit off Monty Noble over the Lord's pavilion for the MCC in 1899. There must have been gut motivation; he did it against the Australians.

For some years his all-round talents were massive, maybe unequalled at that time. His huge hands gripped the bat, the ball or the stinging close-in catch – and the statistics multiplied. Then came the tragic decline. He put on weight, he drank too much, he was indiscriminate in his need and regard for women. Whenever he came to Taunton, he contacted the same pretty and amoral local girl. Her reputation was scarlet in this rather prissy town. It was generally believed that he paid for her services. She later died brutally. Alberto was of course wholly innocent but the gossips tittered with malice about his association with the girl.

Where once he'd been popular and convivial, in the dressing room and around the boundary, he withdrew more. He was morose and lonely. Severe dropsy caused him to limp. A day or two before the outbreak of the First World War he was found in his dingy little one-room digs at Willesden. Albert Trott, aged forty-one, had shot himself. The room was littered with empty bottles of cheap ale. He left his wardrobe and £4 in cash to his landlady.

We must return to happier things. Back in 1900, Lionel Palairet was fit and well again after appendicitis. Charles Bernard compiled a neat hundred at Southampton and Ernie Robson, the pleasant, taciturn Yorkshireman, scored the first of his five for Somerset, at the Oval.

MacLaren took two more centuries off them. 'Come on, Archie, give us a rest', they chorused at Taunton. He obliged by spooning a catch to Palairet as soon as he'd reached a hundred. Jack Board was less accommodating. In the Whit Bank Holiday match at Bristol, the Bristol gardener went in at No 6 and completed his best innings of 214. Jack, a modest professional, was perhaps the finest wicket keeper Gloucestershire ever had. In that same match, he held five catches and magnificently stumped Lewis as Somerset tried in vain to stave off an innings defeat. Back with the pros of both sides at the close of play, he was just as happy to advise on how to grow runner beans or how much horse manure to spread on the rose border.

Among the less familiar names in the Somerset teams those days were Charlie Dunlop, a young Scottish amateur played mainly for his enthusiastic fielding, two slow bowlers, William Trask and Ted Grant, and the hurricane hitter from Radstock, Billy Hyman.

We'll take Hyman first. People remember the deed, if not the name. In the evening sunshine of a July day in 1902, during a hurriedly arranged second innings, he thrashed and scythed his astonishing way to 359 not out for Bath against Thornbury. Some say it took him 110 minutes, others that it was a good deal less. The Gloucestershire bowlers included the county pair, Teddy Spry and Arthur Paish. There are no preserved pages from the scorebook to authenticate the bowling figures. But all thirty-two sixes, sent far out of the ground, were off the lobs of Dr E. M. Grace. Like his brother, he seldom had any inclination to take himself off.

The first time I wrote of Hyman's evening assault on the then decorous Thornbury landscape – today the A38 traffic thunders along the boundary of the ground – I was accused of making the whole thing up. But Billy was a down-to-earth Somerset lad from a mining community, and he had no truck with fanciful fiction.

He played on and off, both as an amateur and a professional, for the county up to the war. Once he scored a first-class hundred but his approach, even when he was hunting hungrily for runs from the middle order, was never as unconventional again.

Ted Grant, an occasional Somerset spinner at the turn of the century, played with Hyman in that match at Thornbury. He verified that eventide of indignity for 'The Coroner'. Ted once played against W.G. in a club match at Bath and thought he'd got the Old Man caught at the wicket.

When the batsmen crossed for a single, W.G. put his arm round Grant's neck and said, as confidentially as that high-pitched voice would ever allow: 'If I'd hit it, young man, it would have gone for four!'

I mustn't ignore two more amateurs from this period, though their sum total of achievement was singularly unexceptional. Alf Bowerman, for instance, made 8 runs from four innings. Montague Toller, a well-built Devonian, wasn't much better. But in truth they had other things to think about in 1900. They went off to play cricket for their country (or rather Devon Wanderers) against France (or rather, Paris) in the Olympic Games. It is a bizarre and non-recurrent piece of sporting history and I have the Somerset Wyverns to thank for resurrecting this strand of surrealism.

I'm not aware whether either of those Blundells old boys joined the Somerset Stragglers Cricket Club. So many of the county's amateurs did. The club was formed in 1900, with Murray-Anderdon as the president and the Rev E. P. Spurway as the honorary secretary. Lionel Palairet, Sammy Woods, Arthur Newton and Gerald Fowler were all on the inaugural committee. It was never too easy to join. You needed the right background and members had to be proposed and seconded by two members; then came long discussion at committee level. A former Straggler told me: 'They were dreadfully snobbish — you can't imagine how exclusive they liked to be.' Over the years, the rules were relaxed a little and democracy encroached. The Stragglers always had an outstanding fixture list, the standard was consistently high and their formidable history and progress were interwoven with that of the county club.

But, well, it was tough on tradesmen. Nigel Daniell, son of John and himself once Somerset's secretary, said in retrospective amusement and not complete approval: 'There was a chap I knew who went to Queen's College, Taunton. The trouble was that his parents ran a local café. He tried for ages to get admitted to the Stragglers and eventually I was able to help him.'

Wait a moment, what about Harold Gimblett, whose father was a Bicknoller farmer? He played a few matches for the Stragglers before he became a professional. 'His school, West Buckland, must have qualified!'

Harry Chidgey would never have been proposed. He was a village lad from Flax Bourton. His rural vowels were accentuated when he appealed for a catch behind the wicket.

The county had plenty of amateur wicket keepers — three of them superbly efficient — but they had jobs to think about and sermons to write. Chidgey came in and had ninety-eight matches, mostly in the seasons from 1900 up to the war. His merits shouldn't be obscured.

CHAPTER SEVEN
Clerical Keeping

Let's stay with the theme of wicket keepers. Henry Martyn, a Devonian, was already an Oxford Blue when he arrived at the county ground in 1901. For the next seven summers he was to complement the exceptional skills of Newton and Wickham. They must have been three wonderful keepers and I have a feeling, based on neither first-hand evidence nor statistics, that Martyn was the best of the lot — by a whisker. Certainly he could bat better than the others. That wasn't too difficult. Behind the stumps he refused to stand back, whatever the pace or hostility of the bowler. He was agile; his reflexes were as sharp as a Devon stag. Very little got past him.

By now, Sammy was bowling off half his run if at all. George Gill was nippy though predictable. Robson was medium pace, only troubling to the stumper because of the late swerve.

Perhaps Martyn would have played for England if he'd been available more often. His extrovert style pleased the crowd, especially because he was so tidy. He crouched at the batsman's shoulder; yet he never had to snatch. The clear-eyed vigilance never let him down.

By 1906 he was scoring 1,000 runs. The season before that he'd swung his bat to the consternation of the Australians to hit 130 at Bath. He toyed with the fielders, eluding their boundary patrols or lofting cheekily over them in the middle distance.

Arthur Newton, by comparison, was far more sedate. He was still at Eton, stiff and perhaps a little priggish, when he first played for Somerset in their non-first-class days. The other amateurs always called him 'A.E.'. He was terse and proper, with a no-nonsense look in those authoritative eyes. He was the Victorian concept of what an Old Etonian should be.

We suspect he didn't always condone Woods' boisterous approach to after-match recreation. They still got on well together; Sammy remembered with gratitude how 'A.E.' had contributed so spectacularly to his first wicket.

Newton had courage as a wicket keeper; so had he, they said, in the hunting field. He rode with the Taunton Vale into his late seventies. But then, he was still playing some club cricket when past eighty. I'm always meeting people who say they saw him make his last appearance at Taunton. He was seventy-four and turned out behind the stumps for the Somerset Stragglers. 'And he stumped five batsmen!' I'm not sure of the quality of the bowling or the batting that day. Is that being ungracious in the case of a marvellously resilient old man?

Arthur Newton played thirty-five years for the county, taking in the years before they were officially first class. Only Harold Stephenson, Wally Luckes and Derek Taylor could claim more dismissals. In 1901 at Lord's he caught six and stumped three Middlesex batsmen — and that remains a county record.

Yet the Rev Archdale Palmer Wickham remains my favourite. He lacked Harry Martyn's dashing qualities and A.E.'s sheer longevity in terms of cricketing prowess; but when it came to ecclesiastical style and eccentricity, he was a Somerset immortal.

They called him many things: Wickers, or, as I have already hinted as a grudging reference to his negligible batsmanship, Snickham. Back in the vicarage, relatives and friends called him Archie. The amateurs at Taunton preferred The Bishop, a title they bestowed with a sly wink and affected deference. They manufactured good-natured stories about his supposed ambivalence: about his Machiavellian approach to billiards or a game of cards.

Members of the family, inordinately proud of him, cherished and perhaps embroidered the tales about him, as they were affectionately passed down to succeeding generations. A great-nephew, Gordon Strong, told me of the time that Archie wagered the ducks that roamed his vicarage lawn — during cards. He lost the hand and the ducks were driven along the main street of Martock, in the early hours of the morning, to the home of the new owner.

It was probably true: just like those shadowy rumours that at billiards he surreptitiously put butter on his opponent's cue ball and at cricket confused the batsman by muttering Greek and Latin verse from behind the stumps. The Bishop wasn't averse to rumours, amusing reports and apocryphal stories about himself. In his rather proper, clerical way, he encouraged and cultivated them.

His stance as a wicket keeper was unique. He stood with feet absurdly wide apart, stretching almost from point to the square-leg umpire. He didn't crouch in the approved way. He kept his gloves on his pads, in what seemed like nonchalance, till the last second. His pads were distinctively topped with black binding. He was known, according to Mr Strong, to favour grey flannels and a black cummerbund.

No one should imply he wasn't God-fearing. He was born in a vicarage and he never contemplated any career except the Church. As a young curate at St Stephen's, Norwich, he found time to play for Norfolk with notable success. At the fine parish church in Martock, he was much liked and doubtless earned added respect because of his skills for Somerset. The sermons were said to be full of cricketing imagery. The county's fortunes in the current match would be adeptly woven into the weekly message from the pulpit at Matins.

'My dear man, I enjoy serving God at the wicket', he'd say.

He was appointed Rural Dean of Ilchester from 1900 and Prebendary of Wells Cathedral four years later. He had finished playing by the time he took

The Rev Archdale Wickham — 'The Bishop' — in that famous and distinctive legs-apart wicket keeper's stance of his, and (below) in contemplative old age

the living at East Brent. Here again the parishioners loved him. Cricket buffs are known to visit the church especially to see the set of cricket stumps discreetly represented in the stained-glass window which was put up to commemorate his stay in the parish.

What of Wickham's cricket? We mustn't let the fun and frivolity hide the considerable ability of the wicket keeper.

He played eighty-two times for Somerset, by the grace of neighbouring clergy if not God, and had a top score of 28 of which he was rather proud. Behind the wickets, despite the abnormality of his poised body − trunk to neck parallel with the ground, head and bushy moustache almost over the bails − he missed very little.

C. B. Fry marvelled at Wickham's agility when the ball came down the leg side. The wicket keeper, like Martyn, stood up for all the bowlers. Yet the game's historians will always recall him for the minimal number of byes he conceded. When Hampshire scored 672-7 declared in 1899, Wickham didn't give away a bye. There were other innings, less statistically spectacular, when he gave absolutely nothing away.

'The Bishop never dropped a thing', they used to say. Not quite accurate, but almost. He put down MacLaren on his way to 424. 'Archie should have been given out in the first over', he would tell his friends, just as he would remind them how redundant he was on the day W.G. reached his one hundredth hundred and went on to score 288. 'Wonderful innings − I might as well have stayed at home in the vicarage.'

Wickham went to Oxford like both Martyn and Newton. He loved and knew the records of Somerset cricket nearly as well as the scriptures. His appearances for the county were far more intermittent than he would have liked; at times Newton, local nuptials and interments had prior claims on him. Many said he was skilled enough to play for England. The same was said, not simply by partisans, about Martyn and Newton. Lucky, privileged Somerset to have had three such exceptional wicket keepers − more or less at the same time.

As a junior reporter on a weekly paper in South Somerset I used to cycle to Martock in the late 1940s to collect the village news. Elderly parishioners would tell me about Archie Wickham.

What a card he were. Bit of a lord of the manor with his tennis parties and all his servants. But he'd stop anytime for a chat − particularly if it were about cricket. Can still remember him setting off from Martock by horse and trap for the county ground. Quite a performance it was. His relations used to wave him off and wish him luck.

He was fifty-one when he last played for Somerset. After that, in the 1920s, he became the club president. He continued to play cards and billiards with Sammy, the abstainer and the boozer, into the early hours. There was more time for his great hobby of butterfly and moth collecting.

Robertson-Glasgow was a relative by marriage. We can only imagine that some of the gentle vicarage humour rubbed off on him.

To return to 1901, and the season when Wickham kept wicket for both sides. Somerset went to Oxford to play the University in early June. For a reason we'll never fathom – probably sentimental and obliquely theological – Archie went in first with Robson. But soon after he was out, William Findlay, the Oxford wicket keeper, was injured. This led to some intense discussion because the fresh-faced and embarrassed young undergraduates had no one capable of taking over the pads.

'I will', volunteered Wickham, keen that his return to the Parks should be as active as possible. So, for the only documented time in the history of the first-class game, a cricketer kept wicket for *both* sides. He gave away three byes when keeping for Somerset, eighteen in the second innings when keeping for Oxford. Any man who can grease the opponent's cue ball at billiards owes it to his county to let a few extras slip through at the right moment, surely . . .

It was the season when little Cranfield took 102 wickets; when Palairet came third to Fry and Ranji in the batting averages; when Braund was being written about as one of *Wisden*'s Cricketers of the Year. The Surrey exile was chosen for the Players against the Gents at Lord's. Very soon he'd be off to Australia under MacLaren for five Test appearances, one at Adelaide bringing him an undefeated 103.

Five times Palairet scored a century before lunch. And he was out for 98 at Portsmouth. His 194 against Sussex at Taunton was the innings they said was 'made for the poets'. Mr Fry and Ranji enthusiastically led the applause when at last Palairet was bowled by the toiling Joe Bean (1-130). The 182 against Lancashire at Bath must have been almost as dominant. Yet dominance was the least apposite quality to associate with the lean, handsome Lionel. His bountiful talents were often so effortlessly used that they were inclined to go almost unnoticed.

It was a summer of high scores – and Palairet found willing and varied partners. He figured in formidable stands with Lewis, Braund and Phillips. The sun shone and Somerset made 630 at Leeds, 561 at Bath against Lancashire and 560-8 at Taunton against Sussex. Yes, and Hampshire stopped at 642-9 at Taunton.

Woods got into the swing, though not strictly in the service of his county. He agreed to play alongside his good friend, Gilbert Jessop, in a match at Bristol. What a daunting prospect for a humble club bowler to see the two outrageous hitters walking out to bat together. Only a few dozen spectators were there to see it. They were kept busy climbing into back gardens retrieving the ball. Woods and Jessop took sixteen minutes over their hundred partnership. Then Jessop, maybe even taking the occasional liberty by then, was out. They had put on 142 – in twenty-two minutes.

The South Africans came and were beaten at Taunton by 341 runs. Fred Welman went in No 11 for Somerset. Welman, an amateur who played for the MCC in 1874, had nineteen games for Somerset over nineteen seasons. He was fifty-two years and three months at the time of the South African visit. One can imagine him saying to Sammy: 'How about it, then? Just one last match . . .' The captain was easily persuaded, especially if the request came late at night.

It doesn't even look as though Welman was included as a wicket keeper, his primary claim for a place in the county side. A. E. Newton was playing, so one assumes the susceptible skipper found a discreet hiding place in the field for his surprise choice.

'Surprise, me dear? The spectators were used to it. Never knew till I got to the bloody ground who was available', we can almost hear the big Aussie saying. There were certainly occasions, on his oath, when he sent up to fifty telegrams in search of players who might make up the numbers for a specific match.

For all their wicket keepers, Somerset couldn't find one for the visit of Yorkshire that year. In the end they pulled in Bill Price, a Tauntonian, for his only county game. He was nervous and gave away 35 extras in the first innings. It was still a marvellous match.

Palairet batted beautifully for his hundred and Woods belligerently for his 90. Cranfield and Braund, crafty and unruffled, took wickets and punishment. Rhodes was even more crafty – and less expensive. There were 12 wickets for him and nearly the winning run. Instead it was thrillingly pilfered by David Hunter. Yorkshire had squeezed through by a single wicket, with less than two minutes left.

Yorkshire were the champions in 1901 with twenty wins. But Somerset, destined again to be near the bottom of the table, assured Lord Hawke as he packed his bag after that tense match at Taunton: 'We'll even things out at Leeds.'

There was no comparison between the teams on paper that season and the idea of revenge, however tight and competitive the first meeting, seemed preposterous to most North Country devotees.

But Somerset took the train to Yorkshire with an uncharacteristic glint of battle in their eyes. Arthur Newton was back to keep wicket. The only 'stranger' this time was George Burrington, an amateur from Tiverton who was coming up for one of only three games for the county.

The defeat of Yorkshire by 279 runs was quite ruthless in its execution. West Country sport has often been disparaged and mocked for its soft belly. At Leeds in the July of 1901 the fighting ribs showed through.

Not at first, it should be said. Rhodes, still a slim, diffident lad, was baffling them again. Somerset were all out for 87, more than half of those coming from Woods' flailing bat. Yorkshire replied with 325. Disheartening reports were filtering back to the Mendips – with every reason. Schofield Haigh had been allowed to slog 96 at No 9, and Rhodes 44 at No 10. The result now, surely, was a formality.

Somerset went back to their hotels and digs in a mood that conveyed acute self-criticism. Sammy puffed aggressively on his cigar and said to Palairet: 'I'm relying on you and Len tomorrow.' The openers had both failed to score in the first innings.

Lionel Palairet walked out, upright and grim-faced. He scored 173. Len Braund, who could be loquacious, also had little to say – at least, not till the runs started to flow. Then they came in a surging burst. Seldom has batting from openers not given to flashy power carried a more vengeful eloquence.

A match was suddenly turned around. A Yorkshire crowd was suddenly silent. A succession of fine bowlers – Rhodes excepted – was made to look comically inadequate.

After Palairet and Braund came the underrated Monmouthshire amateur F. A. Phillips (122). Then Woods (66) and Vernon Hill (53), flexing their muscles and mutilating bowling averages. Then Ernie Robson, himself a Yorkshireman, adding his own sturdy blows. The total was 630. Hirst (1-189) had every reason to leave the ground in tears.

By now Sammy was grinning hugely and planning a celebration, albeit prematurely. 'Let's get it over quickly – I'm ready for a few drinks.' He gave Gill a few overs and then left it to the spinners. Cranfield and Braund both took 4 wickets. After Tunnicliffe, Yorkshire crumbled and were all out for 113.

Wisden was to call it 'the sensational match of the whole season and the only county fixture in which Yorkshire suffered defeat . . . to the wonderful victory gained by Somerset, cricket history can furnish few parallels.'

It was a notable and historic win, clinical and unsparing in the way the blade eventually went in. Somerset didn't play like a bunch of country-house amateurs on that occasion. The sporting prints were full of it. The volume of the compliments heaped on the West Country side affected the Hawke demeanour – and liver. Back at Taunton station the loyal supporters were waiting to cheer their heroes. Nothing wrong with the Somerset players' livers, unless it could be attributed to the democratic passing of the Scotch on the train. Surprising how a win like this would ease the social divisions, if only for a fleeting evening on the homeward run.

In 1902 the county won seven matches and stretched to seventh in the table, their best since 1894. They owed it substantially to Cranfield and Braund who took 209 wickets between them: the nervous, canny pro and small-framed West Countryman with his wary, staccato voice, and the Surrey reject who knew his worth and never quite forgave the county who didn't think he would ever be good enough.

Cranfield, whose spin rarely lessened though his line may have wavered, had his most productive summer with 115 wickets. He and Braund enjoyed themselves at Scarborough where between them they gobbled up 19 wickets. Cranny also played for the Players against the Gents at the Festival.

The match with the Australians at Taunton was drawn. George Gill was apt to earn rather tardy praise for some persevering pace bowling. Let's put that right. He wrote a modest, though indelible, footnote in cricket's colourful history in that game against the Tourists. He dismissed Victor Trumper twice.

'I got a real thunderbolt from Gill in the first innings and was out for five', the great Trumper wrote.

Fred Hardy held on to the catch in the slips. Then Trumper was out again for 5, this time lbw to Gill.

There are imperishable memories of Trumper as a superb batsman and a generous man. He was quick to praise the underpraised Gill and his own team-mate, Reg Duff, whose delightful 183 was composed without a chance. Back in the smoking room at the Castle, Victor made for the piano and vamped some of the popular songs of the day. The general conversation was about the county ground itself. A succession of touring sides were emphatic in their regard for it, the wicket as well as the intimate atmosphere. Years later, Don Bradman and his colleagues were basking in the run-getting and comparing the wicket with ones they knew at home.

Peter Randall Johnson had come in to make his debut against the South Africans in his only match of the previous season. Now against the Australians he scored 62 in a crisp innings of undeniable style. He was also the best-dressed man on the ground.

'Who's this young dandy?' the Aussies wanted to know.

'Comes from New Zealand, as a matter of fact. And we think he's going to make a lot of runs for us.'

The less sartorially conscious Australians eyed the well-cut clothes that Johnson wore. They'd already seen him go out to bat with a cravat and the hints of a swagger. 'Looks more like one of those Old Etonians that you counties seem to produce all the time.'

'He is.'

They were left to work out the conundrum of what a fellow from Wellington, New Zealand, was doing at Eton. Somerset were left to work out how often they could persuade this highly attractive young batsman, just away from Cambridge and about to become a stockbroker, to play for them.

We can't allow 1902 to slip away without a mischievous mention of Bramall Lane. The Sheffield wicket favoured the bowlers. Schofield Haigh was virtually unplayable (6-19). And Yorkshire lost – to Somerset, of course.

Never in his lengthy, lustrous career did Braund more dominate a game. In this low-scoring match he was his county's most successful batsman in each innings. The shots were assertive, yet disciplined. While others, with the exception of Palairet, sparred and missed, Braund intently accepted the challenge of first Jackson and then Haigh. The battle with Haigh was especially absorbing: here were two amiable pros playing for their bread and butter and still able to offer glances of mutual admiration down 22 yards of battleground.

In the end it was Len's bowling that brought Somerset such a creditable win by 34 runs. Never did he twist his gnarled fingers more. Never did he keep a more undeviating length. Never was there more Berkshire cunning. The triumph of Haigh was now superseded by that of Braund.

The partisan ecstasy of Bramall Lane, temporarily stilled as he took 6-30 in the first innings, was summarily stifled as he destroyed Yorkshire in the second. Cranfield took 1 wicket; Braund devoured the rest. His 9-41 was his best. It was Yorkshire's only defeat of the summer and Braund had magnificently taken 15 of their wickets. Not to be upstaged, little Cranny took 14 at Old Trafford.

These two slow bowlers, right- and left-arm, liked to open the bowling together – and so they often did unless Braund was perspiring from a long innings. Cranfield may have had a fragile build but his stamina was not to be questioned. When in a moment of tactlessness it was, he wasn't pleased.

At Gloucester in 1903, the pair bowled unchanged right through two completed innings. Braund (7-77) was the more economical, Cranfield (13-102) the more penetrative. They earned their ale, just as Robson and White were to, for bowling similarly unchanged at Derby in 1919.

Cranfield would accept the limitations of his batting. His shots were sparse and usually odd. So there was surprise and amusement when against Middlesex that year he figured in a last-wicket stand of 91 with John Daniell. Cranfield was in a mood for some selective slogging. He finished with 42, his best and his proudest.

But it was mostly a miserable summer. There was too much rain. Bath suffered particularly; the adjacent Avon overflowed and large sections of the ground were seriously flooded. It reminds us of what happened at Taunton during the floods of 1960.

Oswald Samson, a local amateur with an Oxford Blue in that 1903 season, celebrated with his only hundred for the county. He was a left-hand bat who liked to crack the ball firmly from the middle of the order. His century came at Gloucester. He had his final game for the county in 1913. Then came the war; he died of wounds, in France.

It's time discreetly to leap over undistinguished seasons. Who has any reason to recall 1904 – apart from Palairet's double century at Worcester? By the following year, he'd be having only two or three matches and concentrating more on his career as a land agent.

Cranfield's spinning fingers were losing their guile, while length and line were rarely a dependable last resort for him. It was sad to see Braund clobbered. Jessop hit him for 28 in an over at Bristol; but then, The Croucher was capable of doing that to any bowler.

Sadder still to see Woods' captaincy. The good nature was as evident as ever. Out on the pitch, the verve had gone. His leadership qualities were always questionable. Cricketers played their hearts out for him because they loved him. 'Had enough of it, me old dear. Ready to let someone else take over.' In truth he was running out of steam. The roistering lifestyle was just beginning to wane as he approached forty. The enthusiasm for sport and especially Somerset sport would never disappear. But all that big-hearted fast bowling, that prodigious hitting, that rollicking story-telling into the bachelor early hours were having their cumulative effect. He now liked to put his feet up when he had his dram at the close of play.

Some of the county's cricket in 1905 was appalling. No more than a token attack was agonisingly assembled for some matches. Albert Bailey, without any great pretensions as a left-arm spinner, headed the averages with 29 wickets. Braund took 60, but expensively.

Sammy kept sending the telegrams off – and spreading wide his bronzed, muscled arms in despair. He used twenty-three different bowlers during the season. In addition to his faithful core of regulars – their own figures suffering through lack of support – he called up relatively unfamiliar names like Ernie Shorrocks, a North Country pro also killed in action during the First World War, Albert North, a pro from Bedminster, Bristol, John Bucknell from the local parks in Taunton, John Harcombe, a South African slow bowler who settled in the West Country, Fred Lee, who came by way of Kent, and Arthur Sellick, by way of Gloucestershire.

You've heard nothing yet. No sooner did a newcomer nervously pull on his flannels in the changing rooms than the skipper's booming, ever optimistic voice would be heard in the doorway. 'D'you bowl a bit as well, then?'

He always assumed that they could bat – as it happened, a thoroughly unwise assumption. Many could neither bat *nor* bowl.

The scorers ran out of space and patience as Somerset paraded its motley crew of nominal bowlers. Johnson and Palairet were cajoled into overs of genuine emergency. Harry Martyn was asked, and agreed, to take off his pads and send down 4 overs.

And then there were Osbert Mordaunt, Montague Sturt, Gilbert Vassall, Colin Brown, Fred Coyle, Charlie Alison and Humphrey Burrington. Do I go on? They took hardly a wicket between them. Somerset won a single fixture. They were at one of their lowest points of morale. Gates were down; worse, the old cynicism was creeping back.

In the committee room a few voices were raised. The overall sense of failure and dejection resulted in frayed tempers. There was acrimony between the county and Surrey and, at this distance, we'll never know for sure whether there was a breach of ethics on Somerset's part or a case of well-intentioned misunderstanding.

The trouble was over Bill Montgomery, who had played fourteen matches as a professional for Surrey up to 1904. Then, it seems to the surprise and displeasure of that county, he packed his bags and came to Somerset. He was an all-rounder of modest ability. He hit one half-century and took just 3 wickets during well-spaced appearances over three seasons.

Surrey were outraged by the whole incident. Somerset were aggrieved by the venom of the reaction to what they saw as an innocent transaction. Fixtures between the two counties were broken off for several seasons. Committees on both sides acted, it would appear, with a juvenile petulance. Then sanity returned. They shook hands and got on with their matches.

Talking of committee rows brings me to Walter Brearley. His brimstone was equally directed at opposing batsmen and the Lancashire officials. At Old Trafford in 1905 his attention to the game in hand was undistracted. This fine and fiery fast bowler took 17-137 against Somerset who lost by an innings.

A peep at the battered scorecard makes embarrassing reading. It really looks as though Somerset went into the match with three bowlers. And

Cranfield was taken off after 5 overs which conceded 40 runs. Braund simply sweated it out (5-227).

There was, of course, the visit of the Australians to Bath. You'll remember it well enough: the time that Warwick Armstrong kept belting the ball into Great Pulteney Street while scoring 303 not out . . . the time that Tom Richardson made his unlikely and unhappy return.

Richardson, first. By now he was almost thirty-five and putting on weight. That superb fast bowler's physique was less evident. He had left Surrey the previous season, having lost both his place in the side and much of his natural pace. But it seemed a good idea, pre-empting the brash and canny world of public relations, to offer him the inducements to come down to Bath. He briefly took over a local pub as part of the arrangement.

Tom Richardson had taken more than 2,000 first-class wickets. He had a wonderful action and had been feared by the Australians. At Bath, in the July of 1905, he was embarrassingly ordinary. He went on at second change, after Braund, Robson and a very occasional county amateur, John Thomas. Everyone on the Recreation Ground was willing the rather portly figure to do what he might have done ten years before. Instead they saw him bowl 13 overs of innocuous medium pace. He gave away 65 runs in two gentle spells and came off for good.

It was all so ill advised. A great pace bowler, of envied reputation and classic style, could have done without that kind of shabby postscript. Six years later, his body was found at St Jean d'Arvey. For a long time it was assumed that he had taken his life. We are reassured by more recent evidence that he died, however tragically and prematurely, from natural causes.

As for the match at Bath against the Tourists, it was drawn – but not before three days of joyful batsmanship. The Australians understandably showed little regard for the county's rag-bag of bowling talents. Apart from Armstrong, massive in build and batting intent off the front foot, there was a hundred from Monty Noble and a comparatively delicate gem of an innings of 86 from Trumper.

The Somerset batsmen, it should be said, weren't overawed. Braund demonstrated his Test class as an opener with 117 and 62; and, as already mentioned, Martyn blazed his way to 130 not out, with the insolent air of a club game back in his native Devon.

When it came to 1906, Johnson topped the batting averages for the first time. The style was as silky as his neckwear. But there was very little to cheer. The county made a loss of £926 in the year, partly because of the poor support for home matches.

Those who went to watch at Bath were rewarded with a jewelled performance – provided they weren't blinded by the restrictions of partisanship. They saw the monopolistic grandeur of George Hirst.

He had every reason to remember past encounters with Somerset. They'd treated him with some unsubtle levity. His bowling figures were savaged and, as he confided to his team-mates and elated opponents, he had ended up 'with blisters on me feet and nothing more for me pains'.

Hirst carried some of the visible characteristics of the terrain where he was bred. But he had a ready, warm smile and bore no grudges. It was just that he adjusted the balance when Yorkshire came to Bath in 1906.

Yorkshire had already shaken off the indignity of regular, unseemly failure against Somerset. They had twice beaten the West Country side by an innings the previous season. Hirst, the punchy, middle-order batsman, had hit a career-best 341 against Leicestershire and was in vibrant form when it came to 1906.

It was the season when he scored 2,385 runs and took 208 wickets, an all-rounder's record which is unlikely ever to be surpassed. The runs were sturdily made, many from the adventurous pull shot. The wickets came from deliveries of a full length. He had command of swing and seam like very few of his contemporaries. His late swerve was as famous as it was feared. At Bath, he scored a hundred in each innings. That was bad enough for Somerset. But he also took 6-70 and 5-45. The match wholly belonged to him. Afterwards he pulled on his pipe and turned the conversation to the deeds of others. He was both a generous and modest man. The boys he coached at Yorkshire and Eton were indeed lucky.

I once met a man who claimed he didn't miss a ball during that fixture at Bath. 'George Hirst was one of the greatest cricketers of all times and we were privileged to see him trifling with Somerset. By the end we were cheering him. He was a player you always warmed to.'

It can also reasonably be concluded that there was precious little to cheer in the case of Somerset. Palairet stuck the captaincy for a year and had had enough. Ears burned as he spoke out at the annual meeting late in 1907. Where was the old team spirit? What had happened to the county? No one contested his indictment. No one could.

The balance sheet again made depressing reading. A resolution was passed that after 1908 the county would have to cut down drastically on the fixtures or go out of business for ever. Members also agreed with some reluctance that they would have to rely more on the amateurs; there should be three professionals at the most.

It wasn't a comforting thought as John Daniell took over as the new captain. There'd been three in three years. Woods was tired out and Palairet dispirited. Daniell was coming up to thirty and feared no man, as you'd expect from a rugby international hooker. The courage was verbal as well as physical. He was prepared to run Somerset in his own way, on his own terms. Somehow or other, he would find new players.

The county team of 1907. (*Back row left to right*) C. G. Deane, H. E. Murray-Anderdon, B. L. Bisgood, Lewis, P. R. Johnson, Montgomery, Robson, Bailey. (*Front row*) Tyler, S. M. J. Woods, L. C. H. Palairet, A. E. Newton, Braund (professionals denoted by lack of initials)

Somerset in 1912. (*Back row*) Robson, Bridges, Lewis, Chidgey, Braund, M. P. Bajana. (*Front row*) L. C. L. Sutton, E. S. M. Poyntz, J. Daniell, W. T. Greswell, J. C. W. MacBryan

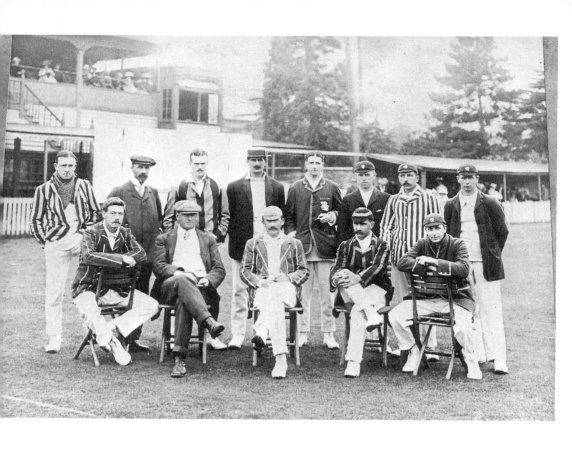

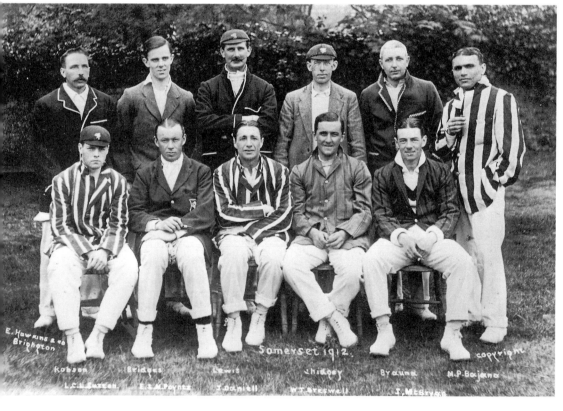

E. Hawkins & co.
Brighton

Somerset 1912.

copyright

Robson   Bridges   Lewis   Chidgey   Braund   M.P.Bajana

L.C.H.Sutton   E.S.M.Poyntz   J.Daniell   W.T.Greswell   J.McBryan

Looking back, it isn't difficult to see why Palairet, by nature sparing in words and emotions, should have spoken out with such force at the annual meeting.

At one stage in 1907 the bowling had looked so lamentably weak that Ted Tyler had been rushed back into service. He got someone else to pull the pints at the Fleur-de-Lis in North Street and to look after his varied business interests in the town, which now incorporated bookings 'to Australia, South Africa, India, New Zealand, West Indies, China, Japan and all other parts of the world, by quickest routes, and all leading lines of steamships'. Tyler was out of practice and, though he had given up county cricket for good, he had one good match against Sussex. Umpires with long, unsentimental memories, began no-balling him again. Ted, after 177 matches for Somerset and one for England, put his flannels away for good.

One hopes that Palairet wasn't too hard on Bert Bisgood, an amateur from Glastonbury who fancied his wicket keeping almost as much as his middle-order batting. His friends had advocated his claims and Palairet, agonising in efforts to find enough players for the visit to Worcester, risked the inclusion of the untried Bisgood.

He suffered neither from nerves nor inhibitions on his debut. In the first innings he scored 82 and in the second 116 not out. He went on to play nearly seventy times for the county, up to 1921; but it must be admitted that the drama of his arrival was never sustained.

Bisgood was the first Somerset player to score a century on his debut. The most famous instance was Gimblett, in 1935. Micky Walford did it against the Indians in 1946, Peter Wight against the Australians in 1953, and Brian Close against Leicestershire in 1971. By then, of course, Close was forty.

Braund topped the batting with a modest 709 runs. Three times that season he gritted his teeth and carried his bat, twice against Middlesex and once against Yorkshire. The most praiseworthy defiance was at Lord's. Somerset were all out on a difficult wicket for 97. Braund dug in for 28. Once more, in 1914 at home to Worcestershire, he carried his bat. He could be very stubborn and this adaptability of his considerable technique was an envied virtue.

Gloucestershire were bowled out for 37. They, too, were struggling frantically to balance the books. Such distractions were bad for performance on the field. The conquest for Somerset, against their neighbours, was nothing more than a fleeting consolation.

Daniell's first year as skipper brought no spectacular improvement. In fact, Somerset dropped two places to sixteenth in the table. Rightly there was no criticism. The new captain's eyes spelt out an aggressive message: 'What do you expect with this lot, for heaven's sake – give me more time!'

They were hammered for 601 by Kent; they were bowled out for 33 at Liverpool. The fielding was too often ragged, though Daniell crouched fearlessly himself at silly point and other positions uncomfortably close to the bat.

He had no fault to find with those yeomen bowlers, Talbot Lewis and

Ernie Robson; nor with Braund – by now no longer a dependable spin bowler – who compiled 946 runs and deserved better than the rain which ruined his benefit game with Surrey at Bath. Nor could he hide his enthusiasm when it came to the county's newest arrival, an eighteen-year-old all-rounder. He only hoped the rumours that young Bill Greswell would shortly be going off to Ceylon to work in the family tea business were inaccurate.

'When we find a bloody good player, then he has other things on his mind', said Daniell, who had himself shown a marked disinclination to stay in India and devote his life to the cultivation of tea. Apart from Greswell, the captain was thinking of Johnson. And with good cause.

Johnson played in four matches only in 1908 – and scored four centuries. On the strength of that, he finished with an average of 75.37, well ahead of the next man, Braund (25.56). Johnson played on and off for the county from 1901 to 1927. But he had a living to think about and managed only 229 matches, when Somerset would have liked it to be twice as many. He hit eighteen first-class hundreds. In 1908 he scored a century in each innings against Middlesex at Taunton; two years later, he made 98 not out and 96 not out against Sussex at Bath. That wouldn't have bothered him too much. He was a bit of a swank but never a braggart. He was a swank in the way he wore his clothes, an endearing trait. The late Christopher Hollis, an incorrigible cricketing romantic, would take me into the beer tent at Bath and talk nostalgically of Johnson. In his book *Oxford in the Twenties* he wrote: 'Always faultlessly dressed, it was his habit to drive up to a match arrayed in top hat and spotless morning coat. He would say to his fellow players "Just been doing a spot of work" as he changed into his flannels.' Hollis also claimed that when Johnson was playing in a match which started on the Saturday, he spent his Sunday in bed reading Dickens.

I grew up believing that P. R. Johnson was a magnificently stylish player in the direct tradition of Lionel Palairet. Maybe I was influenced by the admiring words from Robertson-Glasgow. Johnson was the kind of batsman whose cover drive caused opposing fielders to stop and applaud before returning the ball.

He had gone on tour – when still a young man not yet embroiled in the whims of the Stock Exchange – with Bosanquet to North America in 1901, and with Hawke to Australia and New Zealand in 1902–3. Three years later he went with the MCC to New Zealand. It's well known that he was invited to go to Australia with the Warner-Douglas team. He thought hard about it, tried in vain to revise his business schedules and said no to likely fame. With more spare time to play cricket, he would have walked into the England side – and adorned it with that touch of elegance inseparable from his tall, distinctive presence.

At Eton he fancied his bowling. Some were less than flattering about the sum total of control. Daniell clearly preferred him to stick to his batting; Johnson's progressively less hostile bowling brought him only 3 wickets for his county.

His final century, against Surrey in 1926, was arguably his best. He was forty-six then. The off-drives were as clean as ever; he was still hitting back past the bowler with the advantages of innate timing and footwork, the flamboyant silk handkerchief fluttering at the neck. Afterwards he used to play for Devon. Severe arthritis eventually confined him to a wheelchair. He died at Sidmouth in 1959.

Fellow Etonian Gerald Hodgkinson played alongside Johnson a few times in the years running up to 1911. His bitter disappointment was that his highest score was 99 not out. About this time, too, Stanley Amor, a fine club wicket keeper, had the first of his twenty-six games for the county. He captained Bath for thirty-five years, then became chairman and president.

CHAPTER EIGHT

Bill's Late Swerve

One of the privileges for the writer of an episodic book like this is that he can linger over his unlikely heroes, which brings me now to William Territt Greswell, a gentle, kindly man I briefly met when he was president of Somerset in the 1960s.

His instant impact as an eighteen-year-old from Repton has already been mentioned. The following summer he went in at No 9 and scored exactly a hundred at Lord's. It took him no more than eighty minutes. 'You didn't tell us you could bat as well, Billy', the older amateurs said.

He was primarily a bowler, deceptively languid medium pace. The sting was in the late swerve. Cricket's *cognoscenti* talked and wrote about him in the context of innovative in-swing. Some didn't know how to describe him. There were mutterings about his so-called quickish off-breaks. We even read of his apparent ability to bowl the googly in the early days. No doubt he chuckled away to himself.

Greswell was born in Madras but his roots belonged to West Somerset. He was happy to die at Bicknoller, where the soil is red and the conversation is often about cricket. This was the countryside that begat Jack White and Harold Gimblett; where the farmers stacked the bats with the hay forks.

Off that leisurely run, he could swing the ball wickedly. He could exploit the element of surprise without appearing to try. He could knock over leg stumps and orchestrate dolly catches to short leg. There was no malice in the man, only in the manner he made the ball swing in so late. Gerald Broadribb conveys in *Next Man In*, that splendid compendium of technical and human revelations, what he was really like.

There was the fixture with Hampshire at Bath in 1912. Greswell dropped the ball as he was about to deliver it. Jim Stone, like the good, alert pro he was, saw what had happened and, as the batsman, chased down the wicket in pursuit of a bonus with a free hit. In blissful ignorance of the unfolding drama Bowell, the non-striker, picked up the ball and handed it to Greswell.

'Quick, down this end', shouted the wicket keeper. The easy-going bowler did nothing and Stone was able to turn and scurry back. It was absolutely unthinkable to Greswell that he should run out an opponent in that way.

I turn to the same author for further evidence. Somerset were playing Oxford University in 1922. Bill's swing beat G. T. S. Stevens and hit him on the pads. He appealed for lbw, contemplated the movement of the ball and knew that he was wrong. He turned to the umpire in apology; he asked for his appeal to be ignored. But it wasn't as easy as that. The umpire had given Stevens out and he had no intention at all of changing his mind. The good-looking undergraduate, for his part, had no intention of surrendering his residency of the crease. He liked it there – for long periods. Three years earlier he'd gone into the record books for his 466 in a House match and had already played for the Gentlemen at Lord's. Now here was a bowler giving him the benefit of the doubt and the umpire was proving tiresome. Stevens refused to go. He added another 31 to his score. When the MCC learned what had happened, a firm letter was circulated, containing a strong rebuke for the batsman who wouldn't walk – all of which rather embarrassed Greswell. How he wished he hadn't appealed. He frequently didn't, if he was in some doubt.

Tea-planting, unfortunately, got in the way of Greswell's cricket. The seasons he was fully available, like 1909, his support for Robson and Lewis made so much difference.

In all, from 1908 to 1930, he played a mere 115 times for Somerset. He was just under forty, making one of his sporadic appearances, when he took 9-62 against Hampshire at Weston-super-Mare in 1928. Those who were there tell us, with graphic detail, what a marvellous achievement it was.

In Ceylon, he punctuated his working life with cricket, soccer and hockey, being naturally talented at all three. Ultimately back in this country, he would go to the county ground and say in eventide reverie: 'Perhaps I should have played more for Somerset.'

'*Now* you tell us!' John Daniell would boom back, smiling affectionately at his too occasional team-mate.

If Greswell only played when home from Ceylon, Robson and Lewis made up for it. They were the definitive toiling pre-First World War pros. They took orders, mumbled under their breath and got on with it. Robson and Lewis: the two always went together in the imagination of my childhood. Just as Wellard and Andrews did later.

McDonald and Gregory, Larwood and Voce, Hall and Griffith, Trueman and Statham; we think of fast bowlers in pairs, one complementing the other, going off the field with muscled arms round the weary partner's shoulders.

We think of Robson and Lewis in tandem. They were also my heroes, not least for the way they were underpraised. They both perhaps had cussed streaks but they gave meat and mind for Somerset. They were all-rounders who needed to bat as well as bowl. Off the field, they played billiards together at the George, where Lewis usually won. He was, after all, almost the best cueman in Taunton and at one time ran his own billiards saloon. Their temperaments and stature were different. Robson was a family man and Lewis a bachelor. But they had much in common, too. They were defiantly professional, knowing their place in the structured cricketing hierarchy, and yet refusing ever to be cowed. They were gifted footballers. Lewis played in goal for Everton, Sunderland, Leicester Fosse and Bristol City, and was tipped for an England cap. Robson was a full back for Derby County and Stockport County.

They bowled medium, inclined to fast. Lewis had the greater pace; he was also the better batsman. Yet no one should devalue either their separate or joint talents, with bat and ball. They were craftsmen-cricketers, doing their job efficiently according to their lengthy, underpaid apprenticeship. As bowlers, their shoulders sagged from an excessive workload in the lean years. Their eyes cried out silently for more support.

'Bloody hell, Ern. Just you and me,' Lewis would say as he wiped the sweat off his face.

Ernie Robson was a Yorkshireman from near Leeds. He wore a rather melancholy expression, heightened by a quite severe moustache. He wasn't much of a conversationalist and Robertson-Glasgow, who admired him, was struck by his 'silence'. Robbie was a shy man and, like so many of them, enjoyed performing on stage. He had a pleasant tenor voice; he could be persuaded to sing after an evening meal during an away tour. Earlier pro, George Nichols, who ran his own concert party and wrote the sketches himself, liked to recruit Robson for renderings of one or two popular ballads.

As a bowler he dipped late and got real pace off the wicket. Robertson-Glasgow was to write in one of his Cricket Prints for the *Observer*: 'He was the most accurate right-hand bowler of medium pace that I ever saw, a man of unequalled tranquillity in good times and bad.' Glasgie, a perceptive judge when it came to bowlers, didn't hand out accolades at that level lightly.

Robson reached Taunton by way of Cheshire in 1895. He remained with Somerset till 1923 and in that time took 1,122 wickets for them. Only White, Wellard and Langford, so far, have taken more. He also scored more than 12,000 runs, including five centuries. He never played for England, though the Australians suffered and had genuine respect for him. So they should have; he took 8-35 against them at Bath in 1909. Trumper, Gregory and Armstrong were just three who fell to him. He brushed his moustache self-consciously and fidgeted whenever someone congratulated him.

Jack Hobbs rated Robbie higher than some of the more accepted medium-paced bowlers around. He was once bowled third ball by the Somerset man. Ernie's son Victor was at the ground to see it. 'I can still remember the roar that went up. Some people still talk about it. Dad beat Jack with the first two deliveries – and then bowled him.' I've no doubt that some people were disappointed that Hobbs was out.

Vic became a good club cricketer but never quite the county player that Ernie probably hoped he would be. 'Dad was proud of me and used to take me to the county nets regularly, almost as if it was my piano lessons. I daresay he wanted me to catch John Daniell's eye.' Paternal pride was touching. And one day Ernie adeptly manoeuvred Daniell to take a stroll in the direction of the nets. 'Go on, son, get your pads on – this is your chance.'

'I can't, Dad. I've already had my turn.' Vic, looking back more than sixty years, reflected: 'Oh dear, the innocence of youth. I'd blown it! Mr Daniell walked away. My father was terribly disappointed I expect, but he tried not to show it.'

Ernie's son grew up in a household where cricket was an obsession. When the county players reported for pre-season nets, young Vic would position himself in the middle of the ground and take some spectacular catches as the amateurs opened up. He remembers hearing his father saying confidentially to Frank Woolley: 'This boy of mine is going to be a good 'un.' At the same time, he'd have been embarrassed if anyone felt he was deliberately pushing his son's claims.

There was the day when Essex came to Taunton. They were knocking up in front of the pavilion before the start of play. A boy was retrieving everything. He was darting to his left and right, snatching the ball one-handed and bringing off some extraordinary catches from beefy practice shots. Jack O'Connor, Essex's 12th man for that match, nudged Ernie Robson as he strolled past. 'See that lad out there in short pants, Ernie? He's fantastic. He hasn't put anything down. Don't know who he belongs to – but I reckon he'll be a county cricketer one day.' Robson looked to where O'Connor was pointing. He saw the agile and ostentatious fielding, and he was mortified. It was Victor. 'Dad had a few quiet words with me after that. He didn't approve of an eleven-year-old showing off like that.'

The county ground was Vic's emotional home. He ran bets for Mervyn Hill and a few of the others, amateur and professional. He was allowed to sit in the 'players' pen' with the Somerset pros; he called them all 'uncle'. He remembers Sammy Woods, in his loftier amateurs' perch, making the other occupants roar with laughter as he rattled off sporting and country-house stories in his loud, monopolistic voice. He also remembers Sammy going to the gentlemen's county club in Fore Street every day without fail.

Someone once asked me why I enthused so much over an introvert Yorkshireman I'd never seen. 'Because he took a hat-trick against his native county . . . because he was the first Somerset pro to score 1,000 runs in a season . . . because he was the first to hit a championship hundred . . . because . . .' My point had been made and I didn't need to go on.

His bowling was probably better than his batting but the latter could be tenacious and unselfishly moulded to the needs of the innings. He wasn't averse to a slog and once put on 150 with Lewis in fifty minutes. They enjoyed that; the flicker of a smile could be detected under the extravagant moustache.

Robbie conserved his energy. He was still bowling unchanged with White at the age of forty-nine, still hitting a hundred a year later. The finest catch of his career also came when he was fifty. He was fielding at mid-off to

White, when Herbert Sutcliffe smote hard and almost straight. Robson clung on to the catch high above his head.

His most relished moment was neither against Yorkshire nor the Aussies. It was against Middlesex at Weston-super-Mare in 1922. He won the match with a six in the last over. The intrepid blow over the conifers so thrilled 'Dar' Lyon's father that he made out a cheque for £50 and gave it to Robson after the players came in. It was a six that lived in history – and will outdistance in memory any of the ferocious sixes from Botham and Richards. Who'll ever interpret fully the romance of cricket?

There was another valued role of his that shouldn't be forgotten. He was appointed, in an emergency, as the temporary groundsman before Harry Fernie took over. Ernie used to play *and* look after the ground. He'd stay out on the field at the tea break, often after a long, wearying spell as a bowler, to touch up the crease and sweep the wicket. One of his duties, of course, was to prepare the wicket for the next fixture. 'Ernie's too honest – he'd never do it with his own bowling in mind!' they would say.

During the First World War the county ground became overrun with rabbits. The old scoreboard wouldn't have been able to cope with the soaring statistics of their breeding habits. Burrowing was becoming an acute problem. One day, Woods knocked at Robson's door in Taunton. 'It's these bloody rabbits, Robbie. You're a good shot. Get rid of 'em, me dear.' Robson set off for the county ground, with his faithful spaniel and his 12 bore. The dog flushed the rabbits out from under the stands – and Ernie popped them off by the dozen for dinner.

The end of his long and loyal career with Somerset has a certain poignancy. He was fifty-three years and two months when he played his last game for the county, against Warwickshire in 1923. The legs were giving out on him, the health was less robust. He no longer had the inclination to run up and down the few steps of the Ridley Stand, his preferred form of restrained pre-season training. I go back to son Vic.

> Dad was taken ill during the game with Warwickshire. He came home to rest. To his great regret he missed the Weston Festival. By now he'd put his name down for the umpires' list and actually made his debut for the visit of the West Indians. He couldn't let go completely as a player and decided on just one last match, the normal end-of-season fixture at Bridport arranged by a local benefactor.

Jack Hobbs, Phil Mead and other good friends were playing. Robson looked 'ghastly'. By now he was a very sick man. He died the following May, from cancer.

The Somerset County Club, in its Year Book, recorded: 'He was deservedly popular on any ground at which he appeared, and especially at Taunton where his seraphic walk to the wickets was always sure to evoke a rousing cheer.'

Albert Edward Lewis was always known as Talbot. He was an imposing, self-contained individual. There was a bearing about him which demanded respect. He was a tall, erect man, rarely seen without his prominently displayed watch chain or a rose in his buttonhole. Everyone said the same thing: 'Talbot was his own man.'

He was born in working-class Bedminster and returned to Bristol to die in 1956. But much of his life revolved around Taunton, where he played his cricket, ran his businesses and clocked up his regular century breaks at billiards. His private life was his own affair, though many looked on him as a ladies' man. For some time his home was a minute bungalow in Taunton's Stoke Road. 'It only seemed to have one room but that reflected the private lifestyle of Talbot', said a near neighbour.

Lewis joined Somerset just before the turn of the century and stayed till 1914. For several years he was the county's leading all-rounder. He wasn't troubled by false modesty. As early as 1901 he was opening up with Palairet and figuring in a stand of 258 against Sussex. He liked to bat high in the order, though succeeding captains tried to protect him if they needed him even more for a marathon bowling stint. His benefit year was 1909; he strode out at Taunton and caned the Kent bowlers for 201 not out.

He used his height and got some bounce as a bowler. He was more fast than medium, more a good length and line man than a manipulator of movement. He took 522 wickets for the county, mostly from balls well up to the bat. But on a humid morning he'd surprise his colleagues – and himself – by the extent he could swing the ball.

With Robson he went on tour to India under John Daniell in 1910; he went back there briefly after the war to do some coaching. Injury had really put an end to his own playing career. Later he did his best to encourage young local cricketers and ran a team of 'likely lads'.

In the early 1930s he took a side, including Victor Robson, to play a match at Yeovil, where the club side was captained by Sydney Rippon, himself well known as an idiosyncratic Somerset batsman.

> I'll never forget it. Mr Rippon was on 99 and going very well indeed. Suddenly our wicket keeper, Les Davey, asked if he could bowl. He took off his pads and his first delivery was a bad one. It bounced several times on its way down the wicket. Mr Rippon, to his dismay, got an inside edge and was caught.

Back to 1909, when fixtures were down to sixteen to save money and Somerset actually emerged £300 in credit. It was also the year that John Cornish White, from Taunton School, who had a stern adult's face and a bowling action like his coach Ted Tyler, had his first game for Somerset.

Daniell had reason to be pleased with the modest improvement, if not with the penetrative qualities of Harry Dean. Lancashire's left-arm pace bowler took 9-31 against Somerset at Old Trafford; in an unrelenting encore a year later, he took 9-77 at Bath.

There is, at best, virtually nothing to be said about 1910. Silence is the most discreet commentary. Not a game was won. Fifteen fixtures were lost. Just under forty players were used. One or two we suspect, would have done well to make the 3rd XI at school. Daniell was injured and didn't often play. The captaincy seemed to be permutated by frantic processes of elimination.

The professional Fred Hardy, never more than a journeyman cricketer, hit 700 runs – and that was better than any of his team-mates. He opened the innings in sixteen matches, and had nine different partners.

We remember Hardy less for his cricket than the tragic ending of his life. In March 1916 his body was found on the floor of a lavatory at King's Cross station. He had cut his throat. He was a private in the County of London Yeomanry and his mind was unbalanced by thoughts of having to return to the front. There were many victims of the war who didn't die in the trenches. Private Hardy knew what the carnage was like and he couldn't bear the prospect of going back to it. He anaesthetised the mental pain with alcohol and killed himself with his pocket knife.

All he ever wanted from life was the chance to play cricket. He had left his home in Dorset to join the Surrey staff. Soon he was scoring hundreds for the colts. But he was a countryman at heart and preferred the West Country to London. Fred Hardy, a friendly, sensitive soul, joined Somerset in 1902. He stayed till the outbreak of war, batting left-handed and bowling medium pace.

There were two notable innings by him in 1910: 91 against Kent and 79 against Surrey. It wasn't so much the runs he made in these two games at Taunton as the way he made them. Nor in a weak side was he to be disparaged as a change bowler. He got the wicket of Wilfred Rhodes in successive seasons – once, it's true, when the Yorkshireman had scored 201 – and dismissed Frank Woolley when he was uncharacteristically stuck on 99.

Hardy's last match for the county was against Kent in 1914. He opened the innings with Dudley Rippon. 'See you again after the war', his Taunton friends said. They never did. In his home town of Blandford and back at the county ground in 1919, when cricket re-emerged, people were saying: 'Did you hear about poor old Freddie Hardy? Sad the way he went.'

He wasn't the only Somerset player to take his life. All of them, whatever the veneer of affability, were profoundly private individuals. There was only so much they could take.

In those last few years up to the war, the county's cricket had been singularly undistinguished. Greswell came back, bronzed, from Ceylon for a full season in 1912, but it was far too temporary. Daniell sighed and only wished there was scope for tea-planting along the Vale of Avalon. The captain also viewed the championship table in glum helplessness, wondering what he'd let himself in for.

Still, at least the newcomers turned up with nominal expansiveness. You couldn't do much better than Humphrey Seymour Ramsay Critchley-Salmonson. He came from Dorset and went to school at Winchester. His form as a public-schoolboy fast bowler was said to be quite sensational. Coaches and sports masters added credence to the exciting rumours. He came in off a lengthy run and delivered the ball with a windmill action that brought added fear to callow and timorous fifth-form batsmen. Somerset didn't know their luck. They sounded out the family and arranged for this well-built boy wonder to play for Somerset Boys against Wiltshire. All the committee turned up to watch. They liked everything they'd heard. And, socially conscious as ever, they liked very much the sound of the name.

Critchley-Salmonson had the presence of an adult. He pinged the ball down; he produced some movement through the air. He impressed the whiskered committee members, even though he failed utterly to get past the stylish defence of a slight and unsmiling fifteen-year-old from Box, whose name turned out to be J. C. W. MacBryan. In fact, the pair of them ended up playing for Somerset.

Critchley-Salmonson promised so much. Yet he made only fourteen appearances for the county and took a negligible 24 wickets. He went off to the Argentine, and when he came back, both the pace and the enthusiasm had waned. He remained, like the more refined Greswell, the match winner who might have been.

MacBryan was a different proposition. He never forgave his rather pushy father for sitting next to Murray-Anderdon at that boys' match and engineering young Mac's county debut.

I was given an amusing and detailed account of what happened. The dialogue went like this:

'Now then, Doctor, you say you live in Wiltshire. Such a pity about that.'

'Well yes, but only just over the border.'

There followed a long, contemplative pause. Murray-Anderdon, the county president, was a practised hand at a little bending of the rules. He looked Doctor MacBryan up and down.

'I – em – don't suppose you have any property in Bath, now?'

'Indeed I have, Mr President.'

And so the immensely neat and correct J.C.W. joined Somerset. He'd have preferred it to be Middlesex or Surrey. More of the talented Jack and his complexes later.

Tom Young made his debut at about the same time. He stayed for 310 matches, ending up as the senior pro. There is time ahead to evaluate his contribution to the county and to ponder the question of why a succession of skippers didn't use him more as an off-spinner.

Jim Bridges (first game 1911, last 1929) was used liberally as a bowler. The war cut across his career but he still took 684 wickets. His action was high, his in-swing calculated, though too many catches went down off him. He was a Weston-super-Mare man and his honest, in-swinging skills were much admired by Bill Andrews, who followed him to the resort and demonstrated that kind of bowling with even greater verve and success.

Bridges started as a professional and ended up an amateur. For some years he kept a pub at Weston; it was well patronised by the players who liked the ale as well as Jim's pretty daughters, according to one good-natured gossip.

His batting was unconventional. He joked that there was a case for him to go in higher in the order; maybe he wasn't always joking. His stand of 143 with Holland Gibbs in 1919 is still a county record for the tenth wicket. They were two Weston lads, Gibbs having one of his only three matches for the county side, and they did it with some pride at Clarence Park.

The two batted with tremendous resolve and some luck. Gibbs, being played as a wicket keeper, strove to give Bridges his only hundred. But he was run out as they pounded their aching limbs down the track for another boyish single. They came in, side by side, to much applause. They did their best to hide their disappointment. Jimmy Bridges was 99 not out.

Robertson-Glasgow had a lot of time for Bridges. There may have been lack of recognition but never lack of dignity when they assumed omnipotence at 10 and 11. They exchanged banter and dubious compliments. One of R.C.'s favourite stories was of the evening when Bridges heard a rattle behind him and set off for the pavilion, convinced that he'd been bowled. This astonished the Worcestershire wicket keeper who had the ball in his hand, and the stumps were intact. He was an old-fashioned pro who played the game instinctively and pondered the etiquette afterwards. He knocked off the bails and appealed for a stumping.

As Robertson-Glasgow recalled: 'Bridges was stumped in his absence. But, as he was walking at right angles with the crease, the umpire gave him the benefit of the topographical doubt. He resumed, and we troubled them for some 50 runs. As we finally walked away, he said, "He won't bowl another one like that this year. Just a fluke . . . just a fluke."' We assume he was talking of the ball that finally got him, not the one he wrongly thought had done so.

My penchant for pausing to savour the ring of an aristocratic name must be plainly evident by now. Bruce de la Coeur Hylton-Stewart, educated at Bath and Cambridge, came down in 1912 and immediately created a stir by appearing as a change bowler to take 5-3 at Stourbridge. He sent down 2.2 overs and one was a maiden. Hylton-Stewart had every right to cherish it, like his one first-class century.

While haphazard, optimistic recruitment went on, familiar faces disappeared. Major Vernon Hill's was one. Now he had more time to devote to Woodspring Priory, near Weston-super-Mare, which he ran as a farm, from where the cows supplied much of the milk for the old Great Western Railway buffets. There was a Welsh inflection to his voice, an autocratic brittleness in his manner.

Local historian John Bailey, a former editor of the *Weston Mercury*, stumbled across a delicious story during some research. It seems as though there was some pilfering going on among his staff. Major Hill's individualistic remedy was both theatrical and effective.

As the farmhands lined up to be paid one Friday, he led them out to a five-bar gate and pointed to where he'd lined up five bottles. He was carrying his gun and, pulling the cartridges from his pocket, he fired five times. Each bottle was smashed. 'I'm making no accusations but that's what will happen to anyone I catch stealing my stock.' There were no more losses.

The Hills, who came originally from Glamorgan, had strong cricketing links with Somerset. Vernon's brother Eustace had a few matches. His sons Evelyn and Mervyn, who both went to Eton, played for the county. 'When I started, I used to think Evelyn, all 6 foot 4 inches of him, was for a few overs the quickest bowler in the country', Bill Andrews used to say.

Massey Poyntz was the captain in the two years up to the war; he'd taken over from Daniell. He was a tall man who slammed his hair back with a distinctive parting in the middle. His brother Hugh also played, but less frequently because he was an officer in the regular army. No one had an excessive regard for Massey as a cricketer. He would strike bellicose blows from the middle order, though he lacked technique and consistency. Alongside Braund, he proved himself a very passable slip fielder. His captaincy of a thoroughly poor team brought him more praise than criticism.

John Daniell's son Nigel had a privileged upbringing in the spiritual sense. Woods was one godfather, Poyntz the other. 'When father brought the family up to Bristol for the pantomime, we all called on Massey who lived in some style. It's funny what you remember. The housekeeper brought out the marrow and ginger jam. I was so nearly sick!'

MacBryan once stayed with Poyntz at his Bristol flat. 'I was confronted by this massive coat of arms. Massey told me that he could trace his family back to William the Conqueror.'

Braund had by now forgotten all about leg-spin. The fingers had lost their wizardry. He'd wretchedly lost his length and taken too much punishment for a wise old pro to stomach. But the runs were still coming. He was like an impish, resolute young Surrey exile again as he clobbered Worcestershire for an undefeated 257 in 1913.

There wasn't too much to smile about in 1914, certainly not for those with a prophetic nature. At least the Rippons arrived – to generate confusion and good humour. They were twins, Albert Dudley Eric Rippon (Dudley) and Arthur Ernest Sydney Rippon (Sydney). They looked uncannily alike. They batted alike. They drove a succession of scorers and cricket writers to distraction.

The family came down from London to live at Radstock. The twins were sent to King's College, Taunton for their education and quickly showed their aptitude for cricket. In 1908 they opened the innings together in a house match. The stand, with shots of exceptional quality for that standard, was worth 397. Sydney scored 218 of those runs.

Dudley took a job on a Bath newspaper and began scoring his 1,000 runs in a season of local club cricket. Sydney joined Knowle, the leading Bristol side. Their feats earned many column inches. After one of his increasingly mature and polished innings for Knowle, the Bristol press reported:

His batting this season has been brilliant. This was his third century, a phenomenal feat in afternoon cricket. Under the watchful eye of that fine exponent, Walter Hale, the former Somerset and Gloucestershire professional, Rippon should achieve very high honours in the cricket world, and when the Somerset executive tire of the many fruitless experiments with players of doubtful ability, they will awake to the fact that in the Knowle batsman they have one of the very best brand.

And, in fact, they both were selected. Dudley had an excellent first season. He twice carried his bat in the early matches. At Bath he hit a chanceless hundred 'and was cheered all the way back to the pavilion'. As a member of the family said: 'Just think what might have been achieved if he hadn't been severely injured in the war.'

There are many stories told about Sydney, all with affection, which will be recounted in good time. For the moment we can spice the expectancy with what happened in his first county season, when Gloucestershire came to Taunton.

Tommy Gange, the South African-born professional, got a ball to rise awkwardly at the young, ingenuous amateur. It struck him on the head and he collapsed in a spectacular, spreadeagled heap across his stumps. Rippon lost his bat; the three stumps went in different directions. Like all the best comedy, it carried a hint of panic and pain. Gilbert Jessop rushed up to the distressed batsman and asked him how he was. Sydney picked himself up unsteadily, retrieved his bat and brushed down his flannels.

'I think, em, yes – I'm all right.'

Jessop wasted not a second. He looked to the umpire and appealed for the wicket. I turn to Rippon himself for an account of the outcome. 'I was given not out as my stroke was finished at the time.' He's unlikely to have approved of Jessop's opportunism.

Everyone was on edge in the final month of the 1914 season. Northampton asked for their Taunton fixture 'to be abandoned because of the war'. Worcestershire did come, and won in two days. Few had their heart in the game.

What a doom-ridden time for an inaugural cricket festival at Weston-super-Mare. War had already been declared. The recruitment posters were going up. Decent, unworldly young men, just out of their universities and public schools, were fingering their virgin subalterns' uniforms, heady with the romance of belligerent patriotism. The uneducated, soon also to be scythed down, were asking each other what the pay would be like in the infantry.

The county were meanwhile committed to experiment with Weston as a county venue. Yorkshire won by 140 runs, Essex by 10 wickets. Both matches were over in two days.

Alonzo Drake and Major William Booth bowled unchanged through each innings in the Yorkshire match. They'd done the same in the previous fixture at Bristol. At Weston, Drake, the frail Sheffield United footballer, returned figures of 8.5-0-35-10.

Booth, the pro with the equally unusual Christian name, was an all-rounder who was attracting growing attention. He had just done the double for the first time; he played twice for England in 1913–14. Drake's magnificence on a capricious Weston wicket didn't overshadow the belatedly recognised promise of Booth. There should have been more Tests for him. Instead, only two years after his Weston match, he was killed in action. He was one of many gifted cricketers to die in the trenches.

At the county ground in Taunton the Artillery arrived for their training, and the rabbits continued to breed in vast numbers under the stands – until Ernie Robson's spaniel hunted them out.

CHAPTER NINE
Under an Assumed Name

Where else could it have happened? The thread of surrealism was sustained at Taunton immediately after the war. One man walked out to bat in a blue serge suit; another dared to play under an assumed name.

The sartorial outrage was the last of Harold Heygate's six matches for Sussex. There were, as the lawyers might say, extenuating circumstances. For some weeks he became a reluctant celebrity. He had, after all, been a relatively innocent participant in an incident which brought a torrent of criticism – and vintage polemics – to correspondence columns and Lord's committee rooms. Now this brave and misjudged batsman had had enough; he chose to say goodbye for good to the first-class game. He was left only with arthritic joints and painful memories.

Harold, like his brother Dr Reginald, was an amateur with a passionate regard for cricket. He wished he had been chosen more often to play for Sussex. His late inclusion in the side that came to Somerset in 1919 indicated that Sussex also had problems in finding eleven players. He was thirty-five at the time and his previous county appearance had been in 1905. Worse, he was patently unfit. He had been wounded in the leg during the war; arthritis had followed and he walked with a limp.

Sussex did their best to hide him in the field. When it was his turn to bat, Harold Heygate, once an assertive No 1, went in last. The prospect of any embarrassing short singles was no more than an academic point; White bowled him before he had scored. Heygate stayed in the pavilion the next day. He sat morosely in his blue suit, rubbing his throbbing knee and hoping that his county would not need him; nor should they have. They bowled out Somerset for 103 in the second innings; that left Sussex to score 105.

The batting that followed was calamitous. Tauntonians sensed that high drama was looming and returned to the county ground. Soon Sussex were 48-6. Their captain, H. L. Wilson, still there from the start, remained shaking his head as his succession of partners left him in a silent, sheepish trail. By now the Somerset players had been given the firm impression that Heygate wouldn't be taking any further part in the match.

Wilson looked anxiously at the scoreboard and then at the incoming professional, Roberts. 'Just stay there', he implored. Roberts did more than that; he scored a courageous 28 and with his captain saw Sussex to 103. Somerset's captain Jack White, at mid-off, ruminated as only a Stogumber farmer could. His thought processes were ponderously astute rather than imaginative. But to the surprise of his team-mates he suddenly chose to gamble on Dudley Rippon, an inexperienced county bowler. Rippon, saturnine of features and inclined to be self-deprecating when it came to his military medium, dismissed Roberts and George Stannard with successive balls. Another run was scrambled; Miller was caught and the scores were level. Nine wickets down – and all eyes turned in the direction of the pavilion. Jack MacBryan, who played in that match, told me: 'We assumed that was it, a tie. If there was any uncertainty at all, it ended when the umpire A. E. Street took the bails off and began to pull up the stumps.'

But wait. Here comes a bizarre moment of sporting history to savour. 'Hang on, Alf, put the stumps back', someone said.

Through the amateurs' gate on to the field came the unmistakable limping figure of Harold Heygate. His pads had been hurriedly strapped over his serge trousers. He had thrown off his coat but was still wearing his tie – and his black shoes. He dragged one foot after the other; the progress was lamentably slow. Some of the spectators wanted to applaud. They hesitated, not too sure of the etiquette.

Out on the square there was some confusion. Some of the Somerset fielders, already on their way back to the dressing room, stopped in their tracks. Wilson went into conclave with White, the one plainly embarrassed and the other seemingly acquiescent. One or two of the pros were muttering in disapproval. Had the sweaty accuracy of Jim Bridges and Ernie Robson over the two innings been in vain because of what now looked suspiciously like a devious change of heart? Not everyone could agree afterwards about the extent of the agreement between the two captains. What was not in dispute was the time it took the war-wounded Heygate to reach the crease: it was almost four minutes.

Umpire Street had no qualms about the necessary action. For a second time he pulled up the stumps. Heygate was 'timed out' and the match was ruled a tie. The other umpire, Fred Roberts, the popular Bristol landlord, was perhaps swayed by regional allegiance on this occasion. He doggedly refused to contribute a point of view and stayed out of the controversy.

The match became known as 'The Heygate Incident'. It monopolised newspaper editorials. *The Times* subsequently thundered away for a few paragraphs. Sussex officials were less than enamoured by the way the match was arbitrarily determined as a tie. Mental images of the disabled Heygate were sustained; adjectives like 'unsympathetic' and even 'callous' were bandied about. For some time it remained a highly emotive issue. Street, a competent umpire of Test-match stature, was branded as over-officious.

'And the umpire didn't at any time call "Play" as he should have.'

Not everyone blamed Street; some were critical of White, the Somerset

Clarence Park in 1919. The county team (*left to right*) S. Rippon, J. Bridges, D. Rippon, Chidgey, Poyntz (holding dog!), Robson, Daniell, White, N. Hardy, MacBryan, Braund, Scott McAuley (scorer)

captain, who it was suggested compounded the confusion by changing his mind and giving way to the clamour of dissatisfaction from the professionals in particular. Who appealed? 'We don't know', said the Taunton committee in a maladroit attempt at diplomacy. In fact, it was Braund, never a shrinking violet when points were at stake. He was the spokesman with a valid point of view.

Another strand to the drama emerged when it was admitted that several prominent members of the Somerset club, including Sammy Woods, had encouraged Heygate to put his pads on after all.

Nothing like this had happened before and the MCC agreed it called for an investigation. The umpires and the two captains were asked to submit evidence. A formal statement announcing the findings ended: 'The committee agree with the decision of the umpires.'

That was in the May. By the June, Sydney Rippon had some sort of identity crisis, though he spurned any form of disguise as melodramatic as a blue serge suit for the match. His problem was that he was a civil servant employed by the Inland Revenue and there was an obvious clash of interests when it came to the match against Gloucestershire at Taunton. There have over the years been various theories about why he chose to play under an assumed name. It seemed sensible to go to his son, the Rt Hon Geoffrey Rippon, QC, MP, for an authentic version.

The fact is that my father was on sick leave from the Civil Service at the time and shouldn't have been playing. He was needed by the county, so he appeared on the scorecard and in the press under his grandmother's name. Everyone treated it as a huge joke when it emerged what had happened. I suppose today there'd be an absolute furore.

The county certainly needed him. He played with much aplomb to score 92 and 58 not out. Those who only read about it in the newspapers were quickly questioning the pedigree of this suddenly produced newcomer. Who was this 'S. Trimnell'? Where had that ubiquitous scout John Daniell found this one? And why hadn't the public been forewarned of such emerging talent?

The *Western Daily Press*, an august regional newspaper in those days none too approving of some of Somerset's more unconventional excesses, observed neatly: 'S. Trimnell who is far better known facially to Somerset cricketers and supporters than he is to the general public . . . played in capital style. Although his name is new, he is by no means a stranger to county cricket. But in this match he has done better than ever before.'

All of which, we can only imagine, left many readers confused and intrigued. The Civil Service found out inevitably before very long. Their reaction was benevolent and Rippon's promotion prospects were not put in jeopardy. By the time the county Year Book and *Wisden* were printed, 'A. E. S. Rippon' was back in the records. A few conscientious statisticians and the more unimaginative occupants of MCC committee rooms could no doubt have done without the little jape.

The match itself was a pleasing one for Somerset. It was watched by nearly nine thousand spectators and was won by Somerset by 7 wickets. Laurie Key, who was asked to stand down to make room for 'this Trimnell fella', took it all in good part.

Rippon may have been on sick leave but he was nimble enough with his driving as he assembled his perky 92 before skying a catch off Charlie Parker. That magnificent bowler, with all his complexes about the class structure and upstart amateurs as he saw them, no doubt allowed himself the rare luxury of the flicker of a smile as Philip Williams held on grimly to the catch. 'They all bloody well count – even if it takes some Old Etonian to get rid of a bloke who only plays under his grandmother's name', we can imagine Parker saying.

That was in Somerset's first innings. Then came Robson, pitching unwaveringly on the same minute blade of grass – which he had possibly left just visible during his rigours as temporary groundsman – to take 5 wickets for 9 runs. And eventually it was Sydney Rippon and his twin Dudley 'who made victory certain when they took the score from 16 to 113 . . . there were a large number of bowling changes, including the introduction of P. F. C. Williams, whose lobs created a mild diversion', said the Bristol morning paper.

For most of the county cricketers it was an odd sensation coming back to play again after the war. Too many friends were missing; too many lungs were still full of mustard gas; too many boyish smiles had been replaced by weary and saddened eyes. The matches were down to two-day duration in 1919. Somerset did well to fulfil twelve fixtures; White and Robson did well to bowl unchanged whenever they were asked. White had already grown into a man and a bowler of great promise. He betrayed few emotions but there was usually a trace of petulance on those leathery features when he was asked to take a rest.

New players continued to appear and, blissfully, were soon forgotten. Others of more merit arrived in that artificial post-war year. They included S. G. U. Considine and Philip Foy. Considine, known either as 'Consy' or by his third Christian name, Ulick, was a Bath solicitor who played almost ninety games for Somerset spread over sixteen seasons. People remember him for his fielding; for the brilliant way he patrolled the wide arc of the off-side. 'Best cover point I ever saw', claimed Robertson-Glasgow. An elderly supporter told me with undisguised nostalgic affection: 'He went like lightning for the ball – nothing ever seemed to get past him.'

Nor was he a bad middle-order batsman. Once, at Bournemouth, he was said to be going 'like a runaway horse'. The cover drives were racing away, almost indecently, to the boundary. Consy's partner MacBryan thought it would be the ebullient young batsman's undoing and with a paternal gesture he began to farm the bowling himself. 'John Daniell was furious with me. He thought I was being selfish as Considine was going so well. He rebuked me publicly and completely misunderstood what I was trying to do. It hurt me very much. Consy didn't complain.'

Considine was a fine rugby player, at stand off half for Bath and Somerset, and on the wing in his one game for England. He was badly injured in that solitary international and never again showed the same zest at sport. There were unhappy and tragic aspects to his private life after that, and by the age of forty-nine he was dead.

Foy played most of his cricket in the Argentine. He did well as a fast bowler when Lord Hawke took an MCC party out in 1912. Foy was born at Axbridge and he eagerly played for Somerset when home on leave. His best season was 1920; the county wished he could have played more often.

Somerset opened 1920 with a defeat against Sussex at Bath. Even more sadly, they lost Dudley Rippon for good, his nerve failing him in the middle of the match, and he never played for the county again. The Rippon twins were both seriously wounded in the war; it was a vain hope that they would ever be quite the same again. Separated in the war, one posted to France and the other Egypt, they corresponded regularly and looked forward with romantic, unrealistic optimism to a renewed playing career with Somerset.

Dudley had done so well in his first season. He had walked to the Recreation Ground in Bath, from the *Chronicle* offices where he worked, and shaped immediately like a genuine prospect. 'Come on back with us when the war is over', the county had said to him. When he reported for the fixture with Sussex in the May of 1920 he looked strained and withdrawn. He was out without scoring in the first innings, after a moment of wretched confusion in mid-wicket with his partner, twin Sydney. It was painful for both of them; they were always encouraging each other and from schooldays had an intuitive understanding when it came to running between the wickets.

Against Sussex, Somerset had batted two men short in the second innings. Dudley couldn't face it; Braund was sent home with influenza. The only discernible consolation was Sydney Rippon's hundred. 'He scored his century in two hours and a half without making a mistake of any kind', reported *Wisden*. His joy was lessened by the way Dudley was run out.

Sydney was wounded at the first battle of the Somme. Meningitis followed and he had a thoroughly bad time, the experiences leaving him often highly strung. His expression was always inclined to be rather lugubrious and the big, distinctive glasses that he latterly wore added a quaint professional veneer to his face. The pros liked him; they also said he was strong on eccentricity. He was full of mannerisms. At the crease he would twirl the bat with a more exaggerated flourish than Hobbs. The home supporters loved it; they waited good-naturedly for the ritual and then rose in a crescendo of delight as the bat handle rotated rakishly through what seemed like 720 degrees.

Robertson-Glasgow was always writing about Rippon's 'Swedish exercises'. They were carried out with well-defined structure between nearly every delivery: individualistic physical jerks that pre-empted by many years the bizarre body language of Alan Knott. Sydney's oddball routine, enacted with both a sense of the theatrical and an unconcern for time, would irritate opposing bowlers.

There are many stories about A. E. S. Rippon and most of them are true though told with a chuckle. At Pontypridd, when Somerset were playing Glamorgan, he was in with Reggie Ingle. The former county captain remembers it vividly:

> Sydney hit to cover and called for a run. It was a very risky one and I got in only because the wicket keeper fumbled the ball. At the end of play I was changing and had only my shirt on. I turned to Sydney and recalled how I was almost run out. I suggested that it was a damned silly run. He picked up a bat and chased me. Guy Earle followed. We ran out of the dressing room and down the steps of the pavilion. Then, I'm grateful to say, Sydney tripped and fell. Guy sat on top of him until he'd calmed down.

That night, Ingle and Rippon were staying in the same hotel. 'At three in the morning I heard my bedroom door open. Sydney was standing there. I had a moment of apprehension. But it turned out that he couldn't sleep and only wanted a chat. He could be perfectly charming and a grand fellow. . . .'

Grand guignol cricket-theatre, starring Rippon, again involved a scampered single. It was one of Horace Hazell's earlier county matches for Somerset.

I was wondering what I'd let myself in for. Mr Rippon was run out by George Hunt, one of the pros. He marched straight into the poky professionals' room, as it was then. He was talking away to himself and didn't notice me. I was more wide-eyed than usual as I saw him take up a position of some menace behind the door. He was obviously waiting for poor old George to return. I crept away to find Mr Earle, who was captain for that match. I blurted out that I thought Mr Rippon was having a bit of a queer turn. The captain went in to see him and quietly led him away.

Horace is a rich source of A. E. S. Rippon stories. One of the favourites must be of the away match where Rippon was 99 not out at the end of the first day.

He was wearing some new pads and complained that they were too stiff for taking quick singles. So back at the hotel he buckled on his pads again and spent nearly two hours running up and down the corridors. The staff and fellow guests stood around, blinking in amazement, not quite sure what was happening. At last Mr Rippon was satisfied the stiffness had gone. He went to bed — and was out first ball in the morning!

Such memories of Rippon survive: of him riding to home matches on his motor bike; of him pushing his cap further and further round during a successful innings until the peak was almost at the back; of the cricket ball he kept in his office desk 'so my fingers stay supple'.

These engaging traits should not waylay us in our judgement of him as a cricketer. He played more than a hundred times for Somerset and scored half a dozen hundreds. His contrasting styles could be as absorbing as his whims. He could be a most attractive driver, especially alert for bad balls that might be punished; he could be cussedly defensive. Something of his philosophy as a batsman came through in the course of an article that he wrote:

Don't chuck your wicket away by being chicken-hearted or thinking that instead of a bat you have a scythe in your hand. . . . I often think that when it is a race against time, the quickest rate is secured by methodical acceleration rather than by abandoned actions. Each time a wicket falls, time is lost and the new fellow has to get his eye in.

Geoffrey Rippon shared his father's love of cricket. 'It was a highlight of my life to see him play, perhaps at Taunton or Yeovil. Just occasionally we played together in club cricket and that was an especial thrill. You can imagine how proud I was to see him come back and play against the New Zealanders in 1937.'

Whatever the collective winks and the post-match jokes at his expense, Sydney was a talented cricketer, and his son had every reason to bask in that. There were laughs out loud when Cardus wrote that A.E.S. looked as though he was praying when he went down on a knee to sweep for four. There must also have been immense pride as Geoffrey, years later, read the reports of the 1922 match at Cardiff Arms Park. It was a fixture when the ball was turning and the magnificent J. C. Clay was able to come up with figures of 5.2-4-9-5 in the first innings. By the end, Somerset were left to score 162 and no one really thought they would. The crowd had magically soared from one to three thousand, most of them anticipating Glamorgan's first win of the season.

Rippon had already gone once for a duck, intriguingly stumped first ball off John Johns, an amateur from Briton Ferry, whose dramatic entry to first-class cricket was not even rewarded with a second appearance.

Somerset won by 9 wickets. In perhaps his finest innings, Rippon scored 102 not out on the last day. All the headlines referred to 'Hurricane Hitting' – alliterative and apposite. A report in one of the South Wales newspapers said: 'Rippon rounded off his innings by hitting Symonds for 18 runs in five balls. Altogether he was batting an hour and a half and hit seventeen fours. He scored with tremendous vigour and gave the most attractive display seen on the Arms Park this year.'

Rippon made news even when not in the team. Once, when the train was just about to pull out of the station on its devious route to Worcester, Sydney, waving the team off, noticed some smoke curling along the adjoining carriages. He tapped on John Daniell's window. 'I don't want to bother you but I think the train is on fire!' The captain, maybe not in the mood for an early-evening practical joke, went back to his book. Rippon, more shrill this time and urgent, repeated his warning. Daniell looked up, sensed the danger and with an assertive military manner that he had never quite lost, led the team to safety through the window (the doors had already been locked).

A.E.S. was once 12th man for a visit to the Oval. The steward on the gate would not accept his explanation that he was part of the Somerset party and charged him a shilling. Rippon, with understandably huffy reluctance, handed over his silver coin and went striding away in search of his captain. Daniell was equally offended and realised that the Surrey secretary was R. C. N. Palairet, once a Somerset amateur. 'Tell Dick from me that unless you get your shilling back, we won't play the match.' The manner was unequivocal. Petty officials and inflated gatemen assumed exalted rank at their peril when it came to dealing with the Somerset skipper. 'I quickly got my bob back', Rippon later wrote.

He was an intelligent man and one, despite that plaintive countenance, with occasional shafts of laughter. He was thrilled that he and Dudley should have played, in a unique piece of cricketing history, against the Denton twins of Northamptonshire. And there was plenty of evidence that he relished and extended the confusion that was often caused. The Rippons would at times part their hair differently and wear dissimilar blazers as they strolled around the boundary between innings. One would use a tie and the other a belt to keep the flannels up and assist the scorers. But they were

Blazers very much on parade. (*Above*) The Rippon twins, Dudley (2nd left) and
Sydney (3rd left) during the 1914 match with Northants when they took on the
Denton twins
(*Below left*) Ernie Robson, wholehearted all-rounder – and tenor
(*Below right*) Three Somerset lawyers – E. F. 'Bunty' Longrigg, R. A. Ingle and
S. G. U. Considine

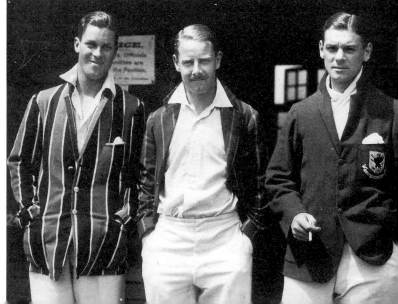

known mischievously to change the system at teatime. There was veiled, eye-winking talk, impossible to substantiate, that on one occasion Dudley had to leave temporarily during a match and Sydney batted in his place; certainly in a schoolboy match A.E.S. once got three ducks, two for himself and one for his brother. I have before me a newspaper report of a county match at Worcester in 1919. It was simply headed 'A Curious Mistake' – and it solemnly related how the wrong brother had been given out the previous day. The slip called for an agency retraction so that the records of a nation could be put right. Another example of Rippon drollery?

From 1920 to 1922 the county came tenth in the championship table; some brief improvement was deceptive and by 1925 they were back to fifteenth. In the process, Braund and Robson said their farewells. There were mutual regrets. Braund scored 17,801 first-class runs and took 1,114 wickets. He also held 547 catches, most of them in the slips and a high proportion quite superb. Robson was fifty-one when he scored his last hundred for the county in 1921; in all, there were 12,620 runs and 1,147 wickets from him. And Somerset never had a bowler of more endless accuracy.

Men of merit went; others of talent and personalised skill arrived. There were, for example, Robertson-Glasgow and M. D. Lyon, Tom Lowry and Guy Earle. Perhaps we should take them respectfully in rotation.

'Crusoe' or 'Glasgie' or 'R.C.' or, as I once heard, 'that old charmer who hides his scholarship and private pain with a classless smile' came to Somerset at the bidding of John Daniell. The county captain apparently had little regard for Robertson-Glasgow's in-swingers or straw hat or dancing pumps or conversational diversions, all of which were taken on to the field with him. Nor, as everyone is aware, had he of the game's bureaucrats who set down tiresome demarcation lines for residential qualification. Crusoe was a Scot who had a tenuous direct link with the delightful village of Hinton Charterhouse. But a cousin who lived there was the MP for Bath and that sounded a formidable argument to the captain.

Whatever the skipper's reservations about in-swing, or some of Robertson-Glasgow's wayward line in the opening seasons, the decision to bring him west from the Parks was a sound one. Daniell liked patrolling the universities' boundary in search of likely lads. Crusoe's refusal ever to take cricket too seriously and manifestations of his gently humorous and quaint persona brought sideway glances of disapproval from his captain. But at heart, Daniell liked him; everyone did. 'Just concentrate on the game a bit more, Glasgie, for heaven's sake!'

In 1923, the mildly maligned in-swinger took 108 wickets. The following summer he bowled quite magnificently for 9-38 against Middlesex. You won't find much about it in his published work; not once was he a man to linger on his own talents. 'I did get into the Gentlemen's side against the Players at Lord's', he mentioned almost as a throwaway. He was more overjoyed by the fact that three more Somerset men, White, Lyon and MacBryan, were there with him.

He fielded with the slightly distant air of the poet he was; he could be a trifle exasperating to a battalion commander intent on sharpening the reflexes. But Robertson-Glasgow wasn't a man of war. When he put a catch down, he fluttered the white flag of peace and stifled any intended criticism with an angelic apology. He was a good team-man because he loved the team rather than the individual. He loved the human race, and it showed – perceptive, joyful and comic – in the way he wrote. Our eternal regret is that he *under*-wrote: if only he had given us more of that lovely, romantic, refreshingly unaffected prose. His imagination warmed to the absurd as well as the wondrous. Never once was there malice in his cricket or his writing. It was the world which perhaps became too malicious for him in the end. He took his life in 1965.

As a junior cricket writer I once shared a press tent with him, at Glastonbury I believe. He was working for the *Observer* and I was very much in awe of him. He was, I remember, pleasant, unobtrusive company. If I hoped for a gregarious manner and anecdotal jollity I was disappointed. He was a quiet, courteous man who shared the only phone and took occasional liberties with the day's more prosaic facts. Oddly, I made a note at the time that he seemed sad to be coming back to Somerset. Perhaps by then he knew that his happiest days had gone for ever.

He had come to the county in 1920; so had 'Dar' Lyon. Dar went on to play 123 times for Somerset. Occasionally he was captain; at times he kept wicket, and did it very well. His appearances tailed away as he had to think more and more about his legal career. He was a most attractive batsman, straight and clean in his hitting. In 1924 he must have been very near to a Test place. He had scored 219 against Derby at Burton-on-Trent and was summoned to Trent Bridge for an England trial. Many felt he was very unlucky.

Malcolm Douglas Lyon came to Somerset by way of Rugby and Cambridge. He didn't lack forthrightness and a competitive edge. These qualities were usually evident when he found himself playing against Gloucestershire, captained by brother Bev. The brothers would bare their teeth while the match was going on.

Bev, arguably the most creative and best captain of his day – he was advocating or predicting as long ago as the twenties trends, then considered risible, that were accepted in the sixties and seventies – revealed few sentimental feelings when Dar walked to the wicket. At Taunton in 1930, Bev's normally laughing eyes flashed in annoyance as Tom Goddard at mid-off put Dar down when he had scratched his first two singles. The batsman carried on to make a double century.

Contemporaries used to talk of the rivalry, a single-minded Jewish passion, when the brothers were locked in conflict. 'Forget the holiday crowd – just stay there', Bev told Reg Sinfield who went out and informed the umpire: 'Sorry about this but I'm here till half-past six.' It was dreary stuff but a magnificent, cussed recovery. Somerset's elation drained away; Gloucestershire won by 8 wickets. One assumes that the Lyon brothers, both sociable and engaging characters were soon on talking terms again.

Dar, who could be a beautiful driver, scored twelve centuries for Somerset and another for the Gentlemen at Lord's. His sweetest moment was probably the hundred that came on his championship debut against Worcestershire.

He was appointed a magistrate in Gambia in 1932, although he made sporadic county appearances after that; from 1948 to 1957 he was Chief Justice in the Seychelles and held an important judicial post in Uganda.

A book like this should surely range over all shades of human behaviour, even where there is a whiff of scandal. Lyon and Earle were fellow amateurs in the years between the wars. Many devotees of Somerset cricket were shocked – and the large number of captive gossips inside and outside the team were titillated and found ample conversational mileage in a marital switch which resulted in Lyon taking Mrs Earle as his new wife. Everyone knew about it; at committee level there were polite coughs. One intimate of the times told me: 'I don't think the two cricketers much spoke to each other again.' Nigel Daniell recalls: 'M. D. Lyon's father, who was quite upset about the whole thing, came to see my father. They were closeted together in the sitting room for ages. My sister, who was only eight at the time, whispered to me that they were discussing how naughty Mr Lyon had been!'

In another, happier context, Dar could be 'very naughty' in his batting and show a complete disregard for famous reputations. He played wonderful little Clarrie Grimmett as though he had never heard of that dextrous wrist-spin and battered the Australians for 136 at Taunton in 1926. He had already steered his way to an aggressive hundred on his first appearance for the Gentlemen at Lord's. Maurice Tate, Cec Parkin, Roy Kilner, J. W. Hearne and Frank Woolley all offered him genuine, if grudging, praise.

Lowry and Earle both joined Somerset in the early twenties. They were strong, capable players, not over-obsessed with ideas of batting refinement above all else. The New Zealander Lowry captained Cambridge and later his country. He was a gregarious individual, proud of his prodigious strength, his wicket-keeping prowess and his knowledge of horses. Indeed everyone knew of the power of his biceps, especially hotel managers. His party piece, in the early hours on an away match, was single-handedly to lift and transport solid pieces of hotel furniture from the foyer to the first-floor landing. They were never damaged and the feat of strength was always carried out in boozy good humour. It could take up to half a dozen members of the hotel staff to return the furniture next morning.

Lowry's wicket keeping, on occasions needed by Somerset, was both casual and brilliant – but not often at the same time. After a bad night, his reflexes could be embarrassingly sluggish. Then he took countless blows about the body without flinching; he didn't always bother to use his gloves. As for the horses, Tom's father was a racing man and he ended up himself a highly successful horsebreeder.

He batted with a pugnacious style and amused his team-mates as much by his choice of vocabulary as his headwear. Though he didn't manage to make any of his eighteen centuries for Somerset, he was usually a good influence on morale. He had the personality to be a leader; apart from captaining New Zealand seven times, he managed them on their 1937 tour, and became president of the New Zealand Cricket Council.

Guy Fife Earle put his broad shoulders to good use. He was one of the county's great hitters. Sometimes he cross-batted; mostly he hit straight, true and high. He cleared the river at Taunton, the evergreens at Weston. Schoolboys made him their hero and fought for the battered ball as it bounded off the crumbling tombstones in St James's churchyard. He lacked Botham's technical skills but would have tried to match him blow for blow. Against Gloucestershire at Taunton in 1929, his 59 took him a quarter of an hour. There were other ferocious cameos in that calibre.

Lancashire's bag o' tricks bowler Cec Parkin (six different deliveries an over) claimed that Earle hit him a greater distance out of the Old Trafford than anyone else. I got the authentic version from Cec's son, Reg, himself a county player. 'Dad went up to this Guy Earle next morning and told him he owed 4s 6d. He wanted to know what for – and Dad said "Because I needed bloody taxi t' get ball back!" He'd never seen a hit like it.'

Earle, who stayed ten seasons with Somerset after a few games for Surrey, batted with a ferocity which suggested he was everlastingly trying to exorcise the memory of the Eton and Harrow match (Fowler's match) in 1910. He led Harrow and they should have walked it; instead they lost by 9 runs. Young Fowler was magnificent with bat and ball; and everyone with Harrovian allegiance at least blamed Earle. He had kept himself on to bowl too long; he had then unwisely opted for the heavy roller. This good-looking schoolboy skipper protested in vain; he rather resented the unkinder things that were written about his supposedly suspect leadership.

He occasionally captained Somerset and did it very well. During the 1926–7 tour of India with the MCC he blasted 130 one sleepy day at Bombay, and with Maurice Tate startled the assembled company of tropically suited expatriates by scoring 154 runs in just over an hour. In 1932, Earle went with H. M. Martineau's party to Egypt. He was badly hurt in a motor cycling accident and forced to leave cricket for good, earlier than he had intended.

The batting was stronger than the bowling, overall, during Somerset's undistinguished twenties. But Jack White, taciturn as ever, was wonderfully constant. He didn't spin the ball; he flighted it. Maturity and cunning had superseded the gawky, tentative beginnings of the boy from Taunton School who had set out to model himself on Ted Tyler.

'Farmer' White grew visibly by the year. His looks were rather severe and old-fashioned. The emotions were always kept well out of sight, unless it was to admonish a fielder inclining to somnolence in late afternoon. He believed resolutely in the puritan work ethic; he got up early to till the red earth where his family farmed, hoping for a rewarding harvest in the late summer. So he toiled as a slow bowler, sleeves rolled up and face burnished permanently by the sun, equating his haul of wickets with the sum total of his labour in the fields around Stogumber.

From 1921 he was an England player. But nothing is more revealing than his bowling record for Somerset in those years. In 1920 he took 130 wickets (average 14.45); 1921 – 137 wickets (15.56); 1922 – 146 wickets (15.11); 1923 – 141 wickets (15.43); 1924 – 135 wickets (14.34); 1925 – 121 wickets (16.53); 1926 – 127 wickets (19.08); 1927 – 104 wickets (19.50); 1928 – 128 wickets (19.15); 1929 – 149 wickets (14.63); 1930 – 111 wickets (17.66); 1931 – 128 wickets (20.36) . . .

During the Bank Holiday game at Bristol, back in 1920, his extraordinary figures were 9-4-10-7. Gloucestershire were all out for 22 in reply to Somerset's 169. How did Somerset still contrive to lose? A dozen theories could probably be offered, and the most valid would be the exquisite batting of Charles Townsend, coming up towards the end of his eventful and talented career in county cricket. Yet the truest explanation of all for such self-destructive, almost comic, tendencies must be, simply, the nature of the beast.

Somerset have, more than most, taken on at some point and plundered the champions of the day. They have, far more frequently, walked away from a captive prey. It would need more than a groundful of psychologists at Taunton to fathom out the reason for such a historic quirk.

At Worcester in 1921, White took all 10 wickets in an innings for 76 runs. In the same season Gloucestershire's Charlie Parker did the same against Somerset. Cricket was always a levelling process down in the West.

While White was taking most of the wickets for the county, Jack MacBryan was heading the batting averages six seasons out of eight. He did it with a straight, cultured bat. According to Sammy Woods, J.C.W. was both the most correct and best opening batsman in the country, a view maybe tinged with late-night amiability. He had no bottomless inheritance, like one or two of the others around at the time, and saw that at some stage he had to think of employment outside the game. There should have been more than 156 matches for Somerset; these and a few other first-class fixtures brought him 10,322 runs and eighteen centuries. The surprise is that he did so well when, because of a rugby injury playing at stand off for Bath against Pontypridd, he was unable to off-drive with any real freedom. He was also wounded in the buttocks and taken prisoner in the retreat from Mons; he spent three and a half years as a PoW.

Jack was a sophisticated, intelligent man, with a waspish tongue and a low opinion of many of the amateurs who played regularly or spasmodically for the county. He was acerbic in his open assessments of their skills and attitudes.

'You're a bad-tempered old devil, Jack', people would say to him.

He'd sniff in dismissive comment. 'I speak as I find. Some I like and some I don't.'

He didn't like Peter Johnson, a fellow stockbroker, and he didn't mind who knew it. Nor was he over-enamoured with John Daniell, though he softened his criticism here with genuine regard for the way the county captain had, with no real funds, worked almost on his own to re-establish the club after the war. Dar Lyon was his kind of amateur, second only to Woods. 'Dar is a grand chap and a very fine cricketer. Don't know what the Test selectors were thinking about.'

MacBryan played just once for England himself. He was selected to play against the South Africans at Old Trafford in 1924. On the scorecard his name came after Sutcliffe and Sandham, ahead of Woolley and Hendren. But it rained and there was less than three hours of play. Jack stood forlornly in the slips; he never batted for his country. He was strongly tipped for a place in the tour team to Australia after that. 'The chairman of selectors told me later that Peter Johnson had said I hadn't the right temperament.' Such experiences – in sport and in his private life – tended to make him bitter. He could also be a man of considerable charm and kindness. In the late years of his life, when I got to know him well, he seemed quite happy to compound the paradoxes. His critics claimed he was inclined to be a snob. Yet he repeatedly said he preferred the professionals to the amateurs for much of the time. 'It was the biggest compliment of my life when I heard Wilfred Rhodes tell the umpire George Hirst after one good innings of mine that I played more like a Yorkshire pro than a Somerset amateur.'

What one came to admire about MacBryan was his searing self-honesty and lack of hypocrisy. He didn't go in for irritating and affected modesty. Before I met him for the first time I wrote a vignette suggesting that he was 'on the fringe of the Somerset elite'. He came back at me, barrels blazing. 'What do you mean . . . on the *fringe?*' It was the unlikely start of what proved for me a treasured friendship. When he died in 1983, he was our oldest surviving Test cricketer.

His forte, apart from some delicious square cuts, was his impeccable footwork. He learned it from the headmaster of his prep school at Bath, in the dining room. The feet never once let him down when he compiled 290 with his good friend M. D. Lyon against Derbyshire in 1924; it still stands as a county record for the second wicket. The year before, he'd built a partnership of 251 with Tom Young against Glamorgan. Young had more than three hundred games for Somerset, spread over twenty-two years, though the war took him away and service in France ruined his lungs. He was a laconic, frail man who ended up as the senior pro. Cocky newcomers found him slightly moody and intimidating. It was only his ill health that made him moody. He was quite a disciplinarian as he kept an eagle eye on the noisier young professionals. Horace Hazell, the left-arm spinner who eventually emerged from the shadow of White to get his chance, says of Young: 'I admired him – he was good for us. Tom was very strict and didn't approve of us signing autographs outside the Oval. He didn't want us getting big ideas too quickly.'

Bill Andrews was intrigued when he noticed that Young was keeping his pads on after going in first and making 32 against the Nottinghamshire of Voce and Larwood.

'What, what's the idea, Tom?'

'Waste of time taking 'em off, son. We'll be soon bloody well in again.'

He had a pallid, pragmatic sense of humour. He had, too, a sturdy range of attacking shots; one or two he was apt to use imprudently. Tom could be a small man with a streak of adventure. There were more than 13,000 runs from him and eleven hundreds. His best was 198 against Hampshire at Bath, when all his local relatives and friends were in the crowd. As an off-spinner he took 388 wickets. By an astonishing oversight, Daniell and more so White failed to acknowledge his virtues as a bowler. Until well into his career, he barely bowled; Don Bradman was a good deal more forthcoming. Against the Australians, Young took 5-70 and dismissed Bradman after he'd reached his century. 'What a good off-spinner he is', said The Don afterwards. Why ever did Somerset take so long to reach a similar conclusion?

It is possible that Tom's introverted nature worked against him. He was certainly a brave cricketer – in the way he held on to a close-range catch from F. T. Mann at Lord's in 1927 ('The best I ever saw', said the batsman), and even more so in the way he tried to pretend that his wheezing lungs weren't getting worse. He was dead by the age of forty-five.

CHAPTER TEN
History for Hobbs

If the great Bradman tip-toes into these pages, then so surely should Jack Hobbs. In early May 1923 he came to Bath in search of his hundredth hundred. Because of the rain, only 3 overs were possible on the first day – and Hobbs was out first ball to Robson on the second. But he was in again by the evening and had reached 19 before the close of play. The Master was in something of a state and paid for a front seat in the upper circle of the Bath Theatre Royal to calm his nerves.

The self-induced therapy didn't entirely work. Next morning he began by running out Andy Ducat and Shepherd. Percy Fender came in with as reprimanding a look as you could in truth summon up for the Master. He'd have been the third partner to depart if he had been as co-operative over a madcap call for frenetic athletics as Ducat and Shepherd had been. Fender glared and sent Hobbs a long way back. The illustrious opening batsman made his crease again, cap askew and dignity disturbed. With an odd reversal of loyalties, more sentimental than geographical, the crowd extended a collective sympathy for Hobbs and willed him to succeed. Some violent blows by Bill Hitch, to give the initiative back to Surrey, also helped.

Hobbs describes the final moments of elation in *My Life Story*:

At lunchtime on Tuesday I had reached 50; and thereafter I plodded on, without knowing much about my total because the scoreboard at Bath did not give any individual scores. After I had hit 6 and 4 in one over, however, I noticed Strudwick, near the scoring tent, holding up six fingers, and I tumbled to the fact that I was only six short of my hundred . . . Now I was 97. I hit a single to cover point; it was my fourth consecutive single but this time the return went for two overthrows. There was a tremendous burst of cheering all over the ground. A hundred hundreds. It was not the best of my centuries but I had never had to work so hard for one. Robson was a wonderful bowler . . .

Two seasons later, in mid-August, Hobbs returned to Somerset: Taunton this time. He had never before scored a hundred on the ground. But here he made history, to the unmitigated joy of unbiased West Countrymen, press photographers and impatient romantics. This was where, in one match, he equalled and then passed W.G.'s existing record of 126 first-class centuries.

Hobbs had stroked his fourteenth hundred of the season a month earlier; since then there had been for everyone what seemed, unreasonably, like an indecent wait. Each successive match brought fresh speculation in the sports columns. It was making Jack nervous; when it was Surrey's turn to bat – Somerset had been bowled out for 167 – he was again in trouble with his judgement of a run. He played to mid-on and with the rashness of an unco-ordinated novice asked D. J. Knight to go for a single. After a few hesitant paces he saw the folly of a non-existent run and tried to send Knight back. That stylish and good-hearted amateur weighed the consequences, saw to which end the ball was being thrown and kept going. He very consciously gave his wicket away. Again, far from vintage Hobbs; already caught in the covers off a no-ball from Jim Bridges and running out his partners again. But he was still 91 at the close of play. That must have pleased the Somerset treasurer as he anticipated another big gate on the Monday. Another weekend of waiting was the last thing Hobbs wanted.

The press photographers and newsreel cameramen hovered around the team hotel. He went to church for matins but mostly stayed in his room. Ever superstitious, he managed to swap with Andrew Sandham – from room No 9 to 37. He hated nines and always said thirty-seven was his lucky number.

From the dining room window I was greatly amused to see a shoal of reporters and photographers who had come off the train from London . . .

I slept well that night and awoke fresh and fit. When I arrived at the ground, there was a huge crowd waiting at the gates. But evidently the authorities had not sufficient entrances or gatemen, for the crowd was not all inside when the time came for me to continue my innings. John Daniell, the Somerset captain, asked me if I would mind waiting until those outside had been admitted.

As soon as I reached the wicket I was all right. A few minutes later I had hit up the nine. It would be a great mistake to think that Somerset were kind enough to make me a present of those runs. Robertson-Glasgow was bowling for all he was worth, and J. J. Bridges was

working on leg-theory with such effectiveness that he beat me with it
for 101.

Jack Hobbs' own words. And leg theory, indeed, from Jim Bridges, the
affable licensee from Weston. So he pre-empted Larwood after all!

It was a push to leg off Bridges that gave Hobbs his 126th hundred.
Players started shaking him by the hand. The crowd roared 'Good old Jack'
in rural unison. Fender came on to the field with a tray of glasses and what
looked suspiciously liked good quality bubbly. 'Oh good gracious me, no!'
John Berry Hobbs used to say with an expression of feigned pain at any
suggestion that a predominantly abstemious nature should be discredited,
however lightheartedly.

The photographers went away, satisfied, to develop their pictures; the
newsreel cameramen returned to London. That small, lofty press box, which
had threatened to collapse under the weight of alien sports writers, was
suddenly depopulated. Even the spectators, elated at what they had seen,
didn't bother to come back on the third day.

There was, of course, more to come. First, MacBryan fashioned a quite
exquisite 109, with sixteen boundaries as if to underscore the historic
majesty of the occasion. Everyone agreed it was his finest innings. And then
it was time for Hobbs again; a Hobbs without cares or nervous twitches or
wayward calls for runs that should never be. Sandham, knowing that only
183 runs were needed, unselfishly left it to his partner. It was a win for
Surrey by 10 wickets; Hobbs had just got there . . . 101 not out.

Most of the journalists may have gone by then. One still on the ground
was young Morley Richards, who worked for a weekly paper in Taunton. It
was his first big scoop. Years later, after he had become news editor of the
Daily Express and was attending a luncheon of The Master's Club to
commemorate the feats of Hobbs, Richards was able to tell him how it had
helped to pay for a delayed honeymoon. John Arlott related the story in his
book *Jack Hobbs, Profile of The Master.*

In the six years up to 1930, Somerset cobbled their way to a sum total of
twenty wins. They still managed to give the Australians a fright and in that
same summer of 1926 involve themselves in a few more columns of
contentious printers' ink.

The Australians came in late August and Robertson-Glasgow (5-78)
bowled even better than White. By the end Somerset were set to score 302 to
win in three hours forty minutes; they lost by 49 runs but for a long time the
scoring rate was exhilarating and the Tourists were pulling the big green
caps down even more to obscure anxious eyes. It was the match when Lyon
sped rhythmically along to his 136, just to show what he might have done if
the Test selectors had invited him. The Taunton ground was packed, buzz-
ing with sustained excitement. The Australians had just come from the Oval
where they had lost the fifth and final Test. It was to prove their only defeat
of the tour, out of forty matches played. Somerset came nearer to beating
them than any other county.

'If only we'd run out Everett on the first day', they reflected. It was a fair point. Everett went in at No 11 and put on 98 with Ellis in fifty minutes for the last wicket. He should have been run out when he had scored 2.

It is understood that 'Horseshoe' Collins, the Australian captain, enjoyed his stay in the West Country. He complemented a typically dogged 60 in the second innings with a couple of profitable poker schools. He was, as everyone seemed to agree, very much a betting man.

And the controversy? It happened at Chelmsford, a new county ground, and Somerset were innocent participants. Essex had levelled the scores in the second innings with 8 wickets down and time running out. Eastman braced himself for 'a winning whack' as Bridges bowled the last ball of his over. He mishit and Earle took the catch. Umpire Frank Chester glanced at the pavilion clock and saw there was less than a minute left. He pocketed the bails and ruled that Somerset were entitled to the points for their lead on first innings. He argued that there was no time for another batsman to come in and face any more balls. There was an uneasy silence – but no bad grace on either side. The human character glowed with goodness. 'Come on, Percy, carry on', said Daniell. 'Nice of you, old chap, but we must accept the umpire's decision', said Perrin, the Essex captain. It was left, with civilised detachment, to the MCC. The official ruling was that the match should be declared a tie. No such confusion over a final over would be caused nowadays, of course.

Team selection and reliability among a few of the amateurs got no easier and John Daniell decided by 1926 that he'd had enough of captaincy. There was no bad feeling; he just needed a rest from his onerous office. He had operated the county on a pittance and gone to the universities for his recruitment. In the sense that he determined his own sorties and made his own judgements, he was an autocrat. He didn't always confide to the committee in advance. The impression has survived that he was something of a tartar, a man who could bark out an order or cause the more timorous pros to quake. In his days as secretary and then president, gatemen were rather afraid of him. There could be a bluster and, on a bad day, a chilly blast, in his manner. He was inclined to be a martinet, although interestingly not at home where he was a kind father.

After Clifton and Cambridge he played club cricket in India. But the family livelihood from tea-planting held little appeal for him. He put in a manager and left the subcontinent with no obvious regrets. He wasn't a man of noticeable wealth; he and his family lived in lodgings for a long time at Weston-super-Mare and in a vicarage at Trull. Then at last he was advised to buy his own house and moved to Holway Green, Taunton in 1928.

He scored just under 10,000 runs for Somerset. He could be a bonny fighter when the wicket was bad and the ball was turning. Then he would stretch forward to smother the spin and frustrate the bowler. He could also be very cruel to those who over-pitched to him. When he was forty-six, in 1925, he hit a century in each innings against Essex; he was already thinking of looming retirement and it was a pleasing statistic to go out on, give or take a few more games. The two hundreds came when he was hobbling from a knee injury.

Physical pain seldom troubled him. As a fielder he mostly stood, alert and slightly crouched, at silly point. He relied on White's accuracy but still took some painful blows. He acquired many bruises on the legs and even face; in a match away to Hampshire, he cracked several ribs. 'Bravest fielder I ever saw', insisted Woods. Perhaps he was also swayed by Daniell's intrepid approach to rugby. 'J.D.' hooked for Richmond and England; he captained his country. He led by example, exhorting his team in a voice spiced with manly enthusiasm and expletives.

Daniell was well proportioned but not a tall man. In the front row, the bigger props lifted him off the ground. At cricket, opposing pros used to moan about his proximity at silly point. 'It's his staring eyes when we look in his direction – he hypnotises us into popping catches to him.' He took more than two hundred catches and not many of them were that easy.

'He wasn't really a dogmatic or dominant man', said his son Nigel. 'Dad wasn't even terribly good at committee work. He didn't speak very well and made his points bluntly.' Nor was he, according to Nigel, ever of the opinion that Harold Gimblett wouldn't make a professional cricketer. Gimblett had claimed that he was. 'When I first came on trial he used to say I was no good but I must say I got to like him much better and found he was a good man', said this introspective farmer's son as he mused back on his ironic entry into first-class cricket.

Returning again to Daniell's son: 'Harold got it all wrong. My father admired him tremendously, right from the days when he played as a Somerset colt.'

There were always a few apocryphal stories with a sting in them about John Daniell. Some were probably put about by old, world-wise pros. 'You antagonised him at your peril. As a professional, it could be pretty tough going if you got on the wrong side of him', I was told at first hand. Bill Andrews vouches for the veracity of the occasion when he was nominated to be the shop steward and, on behalf of the other paid players, to ask for a better contract. 'He bit through his pipe in a rage, he really did.'

Pros, piques and pipes all have their place in this history. So, indubitably, has Daniell. His influence on Somerset was immeasurable. There was his administrative skill, his single-minded tenacity, his interminable knack of plucking new players from university quadrangles, his bluff assertiveness and unfussy skills as a leader. Without him, the county might have gone under.

At the end of 1926 he put away his famous Homburg hat – he liked to play in it – and handed over the captaincy to his pal Jack White. 'What have you let me in for?' asked the farmer with, we can only imagine, much apprehension in his voice.

In the next few years a settled team was as elusive as ever. The finances were again dipping alarmingly and crowds were down. The pre-Depression mood was having its effect. Gradually, sparingly, during the 1920s new professionals had arrived to give the team some solidity. George Hunt, from

John Daniell

Pill, whose countryman's hands used to hold the catches at short leg, came first; then Wally Luckes, Jack and Frank Lee, Arthur Wellard, Horace Hazell and Bill Andrews.

Occasional amateurs included Charlie Mayo and Louis St Vincent Powell. Charlie, born in British Columbia, lived opposite me in my village of East Coker and was the first county cricketer I ever met. He kept a pet raven which was apt to terrorise the neighbours; but he was a gentle man who was killed in the Second World War. Powell, born at St Vincent in the West Indies, ended up in Taunton. He was articled to a firm of auctioneers and was making plenty of runs in local club cricket. To his surprise he was chosen to make his county debut against Lancashire.

I was waiting to go in to bat, I remember. Tom Young took one look at me, gazed in pained disbelief at my pads and told me I couldn't go in

117

like that. 'If Ted McDonald hits you there, he'll break your so-and-so leg.' And he lent me his pads. I still went to the wicket without a box. And to face McDonald!

Powell went with Somerset to play at Trent Bridge. Nottinghamshire batted first and in the bar that evening Wellard was talking to Larwood. 'See you've got one or two new players this year, Arthur.'

'That's right, Lol. Even got a bloke called St Vincent. What about that?'

Next morning, when it was Powell's turn to walk to the wicket, Larwood let go a few highly inhospitable overs. He was reputed to have said: 'Just wanted to see if he were really a saint!'

If you looked for it there was always humour near at hand. There were chuckles when Mervyn Hill, having taken a painful knock when keeping wicket, used two walking sticks (as well as his bat) when it was his turn to walk to the crease. And, of course, there was Cecil Charles Coles Case who must have been a better batsman than he looked because he scored 1,000 runs in a season four times.

'Box' Case was virtually thirty before he had his first match for Somerset. His batting technique was limited and effective. The kindest adjective to evoke his style was probably *ugly*. He didn't go in for back lifts and expansive sweeps of the blade; he didn't really go in for attacking shots at all. There was no athleticism in his movement. So many tell of the occasion when he missed the ball, fell in a ludicrous heap and then picked up a stump instead of the bat that it must be true. Some said he was an adequate fielder, others that a return from him in the outfield normally bounced four times before it reached the keeper. Well, maybe he simply wasn't a boundary fielder. Nor, come to that, was White although what stunning catches Jack took off his own bowling.

Larwood saw the game when Case picked up the stump by mistake. He wasn't feeling well himself and had sat watching Bill Voce try out some leg theory at Taunton. 'This amateur named Case was felled by a flier . . . and the last couple of Somerset batsmen made their own form of protest. One, a right-hander, faced up with a left-hand stance and was promptly out. The last man walked away from the wicket without a ball being bowled to him.'

I make the protestors to have been George Hunt and Alec Cunningham, the latter having one of his only two games for the county and no doubt wishing he was back in suburban Knowle where he was born.

Case made nine hundreds for Somerset, one of them in a Bank Holiday match against Gloucestershire. It wouldn't have been festival stuff; but there would have been enough idiosyncratic charm to forgive him. And how his Frome and Bruton friends cheered when he suddenly unleashed one of those granite-like and ungainly pulls, first bounce to the mid-wicket boundary.

Oppositions looked forward to playing Somerset, whatever their long-standing reputation for unpredictability. They knew there was always a chance to take runs off languid occasional bowlers, or knock over the castles of fresh-cheeked amateurs sampling a transitory career as a county cricketer.

But the other teams often excelled when Somerset had nominally their best eleven players available. We can think of Woolley's 215 at Gravesend, or Jack Newman's 16-88 for Hampshire at Weston-super-Mare. The holiday-makers cheered Newman with impartiality – very different from what happened at Trent Bridge a few seasons earlier when the spectators barracked so much that he lay down on the pitch and refused to get up. That brought him a public ticking-off from Lord Tennyson and later, John Arlott says, a consoling fiver.

In 1928, when Kent scored 476-9, Luckes gave away only four byes; against Surrey, who totalled 501 in their two innings, he conceded one fewer. Here was Somerset's new wicket keeper for a long time. He was so quiet, almost insignificant, that some players likened him to a phantom. He had no time for dives and swoops; but he reached the ball just the same.

Wally had his first game in 1924 and his last for the county in 1949; only Harold Stephenson had more dismissals in his career for Somerset. The 568 catches were taken with the minimum of fuss or vocal plea. The 241 stumpings were mostly executed with a rhythmic, seemingly perfunctory movement; the bails were taken off – never hurled off – with the merest whisper of leather on wood. 'A lot of us thought he was at times the best in the country. Maybe he was *too* unspectacular', said Hazell.

His health was not always good and once it interrupted his cricket. It meant, too, that he dropped down the batting order after that. His batting should never be undervalued; his only hundred, against Kent at Bath in 1937, was a hard-earned and popular feat. I asked him about it and got a typically self-effacing response. 'I was in the 90s and Les Ames suddenly asked me if I'd ever reached a hundred. I shook my head and next over I found I was facing a new bowler. Les had arranged it – and my century immediately followed. That was the kind of thing that happened in those days.'

In the same summer as Luckes was giving nothing away as wicket keeper against Surrey and Kent (1928), Greswell was demonstrating that he could still curve the ball into the right-handed batsman as sharply as ever. At Weston he took 9-62, with Hunt picking up five catches at forward-short.

Cecil Buttle saw it and sighed to himself. He never imagined himself in the same class but he yearned for a chance. He had joined the Somerset groundstaff to help Ernie Robson and then under the authoritarian eye of Harry Fernie; after the Second World War Cecil was to apply successfully for the job of head groundsman. Back in the twenties he was a very good club bowler, fast by those standards and able to move the ball away. He was always impressive in the nets when he bowled to the amateurs. 'They gave you a tanner if you could hit the wickets . . . R. J. O. Meyer even went to half a crown once or twice.'

Buttle was the son of a sergeant major and had the shoulders and torso of a fast bowler. 'Harry was always short staffed and but for that I think I'd have got a few games on some of the northern tours. I was frequently fielding for one side or the other at Taunton – but it wasn't the same, even though the ten bob was useful.' He had just two county games. 'Gloucestershire were playing us and I'd been out all the morning working on the ground. All of a sudden Mr Fernie told me I was playing. I couldn't take it in at first.'

Cecil's other match was against Notts. 'I had Harold Larwood bowling at me. He got me caught and bowled. In those days they didn't spare the tailenders. Nor did we expect it. It was their living . . . the more wickets, the more money.' After that, for Buttle, it was back permanently to the mower, the rollers and the eternal daydreams. He was to give the county club fifty years of service.

John Cornish White dreamt only at night, and then of plentiful fields of wheat or good prices at Taunton market. In the daytime, he simply got on with bowling. The action, off a token run, looked almost mechanical; that was the first mistake for unwary batsmen. It wasn't merely that he could flight the ball so beautifully; he could make it scurry with wicked intent off the pitch; he could find the most unfriendly bounce; he could vary his deliveries with a poker face. He was indeed exceptionally proficient at poker and allowed himself the rare indulgence of a smile when he fleeced a friend after the game was over.

Jack White was not seen by some as an overtly friendly man. But he was solid, dependable, straight down the middle as they say in the country. He rather lacked personality or the ability to praise younger professionals; yet you suspected he would send a few swedes and a sack of spuds in the old waggon if you were snowed-up on the edge of Exmoor.

Laurie Hawkins, who made his debut as a Somerset amateur in 1928, was quoted in the 1985 newsletter of the Somerset Wyverns (exiles) as saying he didn't consider White a very good captain. 'He was very solemn, failed to encourage the younger players and only spoke to his contemporaries.' In his autobiography, *The Hand that Bowled Bradman*, Bill Andrews wrote:

> Jack White was probably good for me in many ways but there was absolutely no warmth or encouragement in his manner. He gave me a rough ride. Many years later, Bunty Longrigg, then the chairman of the club, asked me why I didn't go to Jack White's funeral. I didn't bother to reply.

None would contest his qualities as an all-rounder. He played in fifteen Tests and was captain of England. In all, he scored 12,202 runs – with an innings of 192 against Notts – and took 2,356 wickets. He twice achieved the double. His extraordinary stamina was that of a man nurtured in the sweat of the hayfield. At times he bowled all day; in any case, he hated taking himself off. He began with Somerset as a sixteen-year-old in 1909 and finished in 1937.

Into the 1930s: with a netful of evocative names to remember warmly; some not so familiar. How many recall Reg Northway and Seymour Clark?

Reg, like brother Edward, didn't play often for Somerset. But he was a gritty opening batsman who carried his bat against Yorkshire at Bradford in

1930. It was none the less creditable that his team were bowled out for 43; he stuck it out with splendid resolve to score 21 not out.

Clark, as already recounted, has earned an indelible place – by his sheer *lack* of activity – in the expansive, surreal record of cricketing curios. His first-class career lasted for five matches and nine innings. In that time he failed to score a single run. He took the ribbing in good part, even the slanderous suggestion that Peter Smith of Essex tried so hard to get him off the mark with a bad ball and only succeeded in bowling him second bounce. 'Ah well,' said Seymour, 'I was being played for my wicket keeping!'

There were more serious aspects of the club to worry about. The balancing of the books remained a matter of elusive ingenuity. A friend even persuaded Percy Chapman to visit the West Country during the winter months and make a fund-raising speech on behalf of Somerset. Chapman, a heroic figure with popular appeal, favoured good causes as much as (alas) good living.

Nor was Young exactly in the money. He was given the game with Sussex at Bath for his benefit. As other beneficiaries from the beautiful Georgian city discovered, it always seemed to be raining. Tom's share came to less than £100. That was no way to reward this fine, if frail, all-rounder; other efforts were quickly made to boost an embarrassingly poor total, and in the end it almost reached £750.

Another Bathonian had every reason to remember 1930. Edmund Fallowfield (Bunty) Longrigg scored 205 in the home match with Leicestershire. His father, a great supporter of the county and for a time its president, was there to see him. Bunty was a lawyer and it is not difficult to imagine his neat, imposing figure in court when he did criminal work. His dark hair was sleekly brushed and much of his life as a county player, restricted because of his work, was spent crouching alertly at short leg. But clearly he also occupied the crease with a skill not to be undervalued. He loved batting at Taunton most of all – and he seldom looked like getting out against Leicestershire. As a left-hander, he played the leg-spinners of the day better than many of his colleagues; he could run into trouble as he sparred when the ball was flying around more.

In 1930 he hit 1,351 runs for Somerset and was looking a decided asset. A few of the committee, ungenerous of spirit, were a little less sure of a tall, noisy, stammering warm-natured newcomer called William Harry Russell (yes, Bill) Andrews. By the end of 1932 they were looking at their books, wondering how they could trim a few edges, and releasing him. It was the first of the four times they sacked him.

His career was to extend over 224 matches for Somerset, ending at least as a player in 1947. He completed the double twice and took 100 wickets on four occasions. Many believe that but for the war he would have played for England; he thinks he would have done so but for Wally Hammond who he always suspected of vetoing fleeting Test inclusion just before the war. Bill had strong personal opinions and he was never remotely afraid of expressing them. They were without malice. For someone who didn't even play for his country, he became one of the best known professionals in the game – and certainly one of the best liked. An indiscretion was invariably followed by a strong, friendly arm around the shoulder. He rattled off more stories about his contemporaries than anyone else in cricket. Some of them, the least libellous, were included in his acclaimed autobiography. He permutated the others at scores of cricket dinners until the robust fast bowler's legs gave up on him and a gregarious nature ebbed away as, in the eighties, he stayed more and more at his Worlebury home, overlooking the golf course, near his beloved Weston-super-Mare.

When his family moved there to live, Bill began by selling scorecards and then operating the scoreboard at Clarence Park. He saw the beautifully rhythmic Ted McDonald bowling for the Australians at Taunton in 1921 and knew that here was the model for him to imitate. The Andrews action – '12 o'clock high' – was one in turn for schoolboys to copy.

To the despair of his father, he gave up a steady job in a solicitor's office for cricket. His debut, in the May of 1930, was against Warwickshire at Edgbaston. He got Bob Wyatt caught at short leg and also held a scorching catch at mid-off. By then he'd been moved out of the slips after putting down a sitter from Jack Parsons.

Soon Arthur Wellard was fit again and Andrews dropped out. He went back to the Somerset village of East Coker, where he had been employed as the pro and groundsman for the local cricket club at the time he received the call from the county. There follows one of his best stories. He was out cutting the outfield one June morning when a telegraph boy arrived. The cryptic message said: 'Report Bradford to play versus Yorkshire . . . White.'

The match had started that day and it was now eleven o'clock. Bill hitched a lift in a pony and trap to the station in Yeovil, where his request for a single to Bradford led to some confusion. The ticket collector assumed the traveller meant Bradford-on-Avon, near Bath. There are many marvellous twists and sidetracks in the telling of the story but we should leave them to Andrews. All we really need to know is that he arrived after the close of play on the first day and Yorkshire were already batting a second time. He went out next morning and took 0-64. His entry as a batsman in the first innings was 'absent O'; if people (or sports writers) had only known. But Somerset were Somerset – and that, not for the first time, meant a player could turn up halfway through the match.

Making his arrival more or less at the same time was Horace Hazell, a nineteen-year-old from Bristol who had already been turned down by Gloucestershire. He was short and chubby with the face of an angelic choirboy. His friends at Brislington CC and the other local clubs described him as 'very slow and very accurate'; he played up to three times a week and took 200 wickets a season. Brislington recommended him to Somerset and they in turn sent him during the winter to an indoor school in London.

The report sent back to the county was almost as demoralising as the way he was rejected by Gloucestershire. 'Hazell will never make a bowler, although he should try to push the ball through faster. His batting, though, has possibilities . . .'

He seldom aspired above the status of a No 11, though the players were inclined to dub him 'the Crisis King'. His slow left-arm bowling, however, brought him 957 wickets.

Like Andrews, he became one of the treasured characters of Somerset cricket in the thirties and again after the war. It was partly to do with his roly-poly build and affable barside manner. He could always laugh at himself.

> Just take my first game for Somerset, a Whit Bank Holiday match with Gloucestershire at Taunton. I nervously took the early-morning train from Bristol and hardly knew a soul when I got to the ground. Guy Earle, the acting captain, asked me where I fielded and with democratic willingness I said I'd go anywhere. He didn't take any chances and put me at mid-on where I immediately dropped a dolly from Alf Dipper. In the next over, I was put at leg-slip for Arthur Wellard. Never been there before in my life – and I soon put one down. Not an easy catch but a chance. What a start!

Hazell didn't know what to make of net practice. It carried an aura of respect for the amateurs, plenty of ritual and, as he discovered, an element of self-preservation.

> I remember the senior pro Tom Young, who was supervising the net practice, giving me a quiet word of advice about what to do when it was Mr Earle's turn to bat. He told me that as soon as I'd let go of the ball, I should dive out of the net. I was pretty green and didn't really know what he meant. Then in marched this Mr Earle, holding his bat as if it were a matchstick. I trotted up and pitched one on middle stump. He thumped the ball straight back, harder than I'd ever seen anyone hit it before. It was coming straight for my stomach. I was still in effect on trial and everyone was watching. I shut my eyes and protected my body with my hands. The ball nearly took my thumb off!

The demarcation line between amateur and professional was as pronounced at Somerset as at other counties. It was part of the social tapestry and most of the players accepted it. The system could be brutally unfair. Amateurs came in during the vacations and it was the pros who made way. There were many times when efficient Somerset batsmen, who happened to be professionals, found themselves on occasions at 8, 9 and 10 in the batting order so that amateurs of unproven ability could be squeezed in above them. There were still some signs of feudal attitudes right up to the Second World War and pros would claim they were sent to do the chasing in the outfield at the end of a tiring day.

When it came to net practice before the match, the pros were expected to do their stuff and provide rather more than their share of the bowling. They didn't protest; it was part of the ritual. The two layers of society, measured by the accident of birth alone, changed for play separately and viewed the game separately. When the amateurs used to take the field at Taunton, and at other county grounds, a bell would ring – authentic 'Upstairs Downstairs' routine – and the pros knew it was time to emerge from their poky quarters, and bring up the rear. The amateurs usually, not always, travelled first class and the pros third class.

I have over the years talked to a succession of Somerset's captains about a separatism that, because of the social order, divided a team and reminded a number of the players that they were inferior. 'It was simply the way things were done – status didn't come into it. The professionals often preferred to be on their own, in any case.' But I suspect such a statement; it seems to betray a hint of understandable guilt. Several of the Somerset captains happened to be refreshingly liberal in outlook. Two, including one who did the job part-time, claimed that at times they went out of their way to ensure that the amateurs and pros came out of the same gate. I must, in honesty, report that old pros to whom I talked were a trifle cynical of this nostalgic democracy.

Norman Stewart Mitchell-Innes made his debut for the county in 1931. He was only sixteen and probably got his chance because John Daniell knew one of the schoolboy's masters at Sedbergh. Mitchell-Innes had, at the end of term, gone off on a school cricket tour to Durham and Yorkshire, followed by the Boys' Golf championship in Scotland. Somerset heard about it when they phoned his father. 'Well then, let us know if he gets knocked out of the golf.'

The unexpected summons came.

I was knocked out of the tournament on the Thursday afternoon and on the Friday I was out on the course watching the others when a telegraph boy arrived on a bike. I was to play against Warwickshire at Taunton next day. I somehow gathered my belongings and caught the night train. I don't think I got much sleep but fortunately we weren't batting till the Monday.

Then he scored 23 and took two wickets.

'Mandy' Mitchell-Innes made his one Test appearance four years later. It was a bold selection as he was still an undergraduate, but Plum Warner had been watching when he scored a most attractive 168 for Oxford off the South Africans in the May. That kind of impeccable timing couldn't be ignored. The pundits approved. Those were the days when Varsity cricket had its own glamour and paraded its recurrent riches. Mitchell-Innes was a powerful, orthodox batsman with a mature demeanour. His great chum, Jake Seamer, who played alongside him at Oxford, Somerset and various open spaces in the Sudan, summed him up: 'He was simply a jolly good player.'

But he was out for 5 in the Trent Bridge Test. Warner had faith in him and he was chosen for the second Test, at Lord's. By now, Mandy was suffering acutely from hay fever so he phoned Warner in case he felt Mitchell-Innes might be a bad risk. 'I might be sneezing just as a catch comes in the slips . . . I, er, feel you ought to know.' Warner eventually decided it might be sensible for him to stand down.

E. R. T. Holmes came into the England side instead and made 10 and 8. Mandy went off and played for Oxford against Surrey at the Oval – and scored 132 not out, even though he had to drop down the order because he was sneezing so much when it was his turn to bat. There was much discussion about that fine innings in the sports pages but the call to play for England never came again. Ironically, every Sunday paper carried pictures of Errol Holmes shaking hands with King George V.

Like Seamer, he opted for the Sudan Political Service after leaving university. He came back on leave and played when he could. Mitchell-Innes loved the leisurely ambience of Taunton on a summer's day – and the gruff humour of his fellow players. In 1934 Somerset were batting against Notts and Mandy was sitting up in the amateurs' cubby-hole, next to John Daniell who by then had given up playing. Frank and Jack Lee were batting when suddenly there was a delay.

'What's up, Mandy – what's the trouble?'

'Em, poor Frank has been hit in the box.'

'The box? What the devil is that?'

'It's – well – the protective equipment between the legs.'

There was a snort from Daniell. A former England hooker doubtless thought the idea too namby-pamby for elaboration. Play restarted – and soon once more the fielders crowded around Lee.

'What is it this time, Mandy?'

'I think it's happened again. Exactly the same place.'

It was too much for Daniell. 'Good God, boy, in our young days we used to be able to hit 'em for four with our tools!'

There were fruitful as well as painful times for Frank Lee. Over the next few years he carried his bat three times, brother Jack twice. Frank batted at his own pedantic pace, unimpressed by bowlers' reputations or calls by sensation-seekers for coarse, alien blows from the bat. No one criticised him for the calm way he chiselled away for 59 not out in the county's fragile total of 116 against the Australians in 1934. Somerset never had a more conscientious opener.

Changes were also taking place in the early thirties. Mr A. F. Davey, who had been a capable secretary, left to take a similar post with Surrey in succession to Dick Palairet. White handed over the captaincy to R. A. Ingle, and George Hunt was the professional to be given his cards.

Hunt had been a solid, likeable, unexceptional player: a good enough bowler to take 386 wickets, a good enough batsman to score one century. He was in and out of the side; when he was out, his reliable hands a few yards from the bat were missed. He held on to nearly two hundred catches, without show or spectacular dives. Like all pros worth their salt, he was disappointed when Somerset fired him. 'It didn't help when you ran me out at Canterbury at the end of the season, Bill', he said with some feeling. Andrews was to look back on the incident with some sadness. 'I suppose it was George or myself who had to go. But he was a fine bloke and forgave me after a few days!'

Five years later, George's brother Bert had eleven games for Somerset. He was an off-spinner who made an immediate impact by taking 7-49 against Derbyshire at Ilkeston. 'Why haven't we played this Hubert Hunt before?' the committee were asking. But Bert, with a healthy cynicism about the life of an expendable professional cricketer, had preferred to stick to his weekend matches for his village team, Lodway. His pals in the parish used to say of him: 'He had the most perfect temperament we ever came across – the bowler who never complained. We could put down five catches off him, as we did more than once, and he merely smiled.' His form at Ilkeston was not sustained, and it hardly helped when Wellard inclined increasingly to part-time off-spin. Old friends, of whom he had many around the quayside at Pill just down the road from the Lodway ground, loved to quote his famous and unlikely partnership with Hazell, against Yorkshire at Bath. Hedley Verity conceded 89 runs in 9 overs. Hazell, with broad grin and ample girth, hit Verity for 28 in an over with four thumping sixes. Hunt, affected by the levity, pitched in with two sixes and two fours himself. It seems like a mean postscript to record that Yorkshire still won by an innings.

Reginald Addington Ingle, born a Cornishman, practised as a solicitor in Bath. He had a considerate father, also a lawyer, who gave him extended leave so that he could play cricket. In just over three hundred matches for the county he scored ten centuries. Here was a batsman, handsome in appearance and often in style, who liked to go for his shots. In 1928 he had taken two hundreds off Middlesex in a game at Taunton; he wasn't one to flinch against fast bowling. A modest man, he was quietly proud of the time he leaned back to hook Larwood for six, and when he cover-drove his way to the 70s off Ted McDonald and Lancashire as they dominated the championship table. 'I got hit on the elbow by Mac in the second innings and had to go off. Not too much sympathy – the bowler said he'd probably kill me next time!'

He'd been playing for the Incogs at Sidmouth one day when he was surprised to receive a telegram (a recurrent theme in the history of Somerset) asking him to come into the county side for the approaching match with Essex. 'I fancy Jim Bridges had played with me somewhere or other and had recommended me to John Daniell. I did manage to get a half-century on my debut.'

Ingle was later to lead Somerset for six seasons. The pros liked him and some said he was the best they had had. There was an immediate improvement when he took over; the county went from thirteenth to seventh in the table. He set a zestful example himself with his fielding in the covers, though he tended more to the customary mid-off with the responsibilities of captaincy.

His relationship with the professionals is well illustrated by this incident when the pros were leaving the ground after a match. There was a man waiting by the exit. Ever diplomatic, Ingle asked me not to mention the name of the amateur cricketer concerned.

The man at the exit said he was waiting for one of my amateurs and used to put money on horses for him. They were told that this particular amateur was a very good judge of a horse and next morning they asked my amateur if he had any useful tips for them. He gave them a horse, they put their money on, and the horse went down. When they were leaving the ground, they saw the same man outside and said they understood that the amateur had had a bad day. To their surprise, they were told that his horse had come up. I was very displeased when I heard from them what had happened. I assured the amateur that if he ever again gave a false tip to any one of my professionals, he'd be out of the side.

Like Mitchell-Innes, Ingle suffered badly from hay fever and had to withdraw from the team several times because of it. 'It always seemed to be worse on railway journeys – I suppose it was the dust. While the others played cards, I climbed up on the corded rack and tried to get some sleep.'

But the time came when he had to devote more of his energies to the law practice. For years he had gone into the office to work during the winter months; now it was time to put his bat away and get on with his court work. He became a highly skilled defending solicitor, and found himself much in demand among the gypsy community. 'I defended a gypsy in my very first case and got him off, seemingly to the delight of every Romany in the area.' Soon he was travelling around the country – or so it appeared – trying to get a succession of gypsies dismissed from the dock without conviction. In the ways of the successful advocate, Ingle had an impressive courtroom manner and even a sense of the theatrical. In a case of alleged poultry stealing at Chipping Sodbury, Mr R. A. Ingle, defending solicitor, was in no mood to spare the already uncomfortable police constable in the box.

'How, for heaven's sake, do you call a hen? Go on, show us, officer . . .'

And the red-faced policeman was forced to utter clucking sounds. The gypsies, liberally sprinkled around the public benches, roared with laughter. The chairman of the Bench was not amused.

A final reflection on Ingle. Whatever his success rate with the pros, during his term as skipper he could be a rigid disciplinarian. Two senior professionals stepped badly out of line on one away tour in the north. On the train journey back to Taunton, Ingle sent for them. His reprimand was scathing – but limited to the privacy of that compartment. 'I'll let you know when I want you to play for me again', he said as they made their sheepish exit.

It was a brave thing for him to do. One of the offending players was a leading batsman, the other a key bowler; Somerset could ill afford to be without either of them. 'I told John Daniell what I'd done and he approved. The pair didn't play for a match or two and the public never knew why. These two professionals didn't appeal against my action and nor, as far as I know, did they bear me any grudge. I got on well with them again afterwards.'

Ingle liked a modest flutter, a communal joke and a frame or two of snooker. The latter could be costly. 'I was playing with Lord Portman in the county club at Taunton one evening when in came Don Bradman and the rest of the Australian party.

'What would you like to drink, Don?' asked the county captain.

'Not for me – but all the other boys would like one,' said Bradman.

Two of the new arrivals in the early thirties had been J. W. Seamer and J. H. Cameron, 'Jake' and 'Monkey' to their numerous friends in sport. Seamer was the son of a Somerset parson and it was only his time in the Sudan Political Service that limited his appearances for the county to fifty-nine. The careers, sporting and professional, of himself and Mitchell-Innes ran on parallel lines. They made centuries together for Oxford; they batted one after the other for Somerset; then they used to play against each other in the Sudan.

Jake's passion for the county could be traced back to boyhood. His hero was White and now here he was in 1932 playing with him. The match was at Hove and J.C. was out for a duck in the first innings. Then, in the second innings when Seamer was dismissed, the pair crossed halfway to the wicket. 'This new chap, Jim Cornford or something . . . what does he do?' Jake wasn't too sure but, in awe of his rural hero, he felt an instant response was expected. 'Swings 'em away, Mr White.'

Seamer retired to the pavilion and began unbuckling his pads. After a few minutes in came White. The bat was hurled into a corner, the expression was sterner than usual. In icy tones, he addressed himself to the newcomer. 'What was that you told me? . . . He bowls *bloody in-swingers!*'

Seamer had an amiable, rather beaky face. Once he hit 194 for Oxford against Minor Counties but his natural game was to watch the ball and minimise the risks.

> I sort of held the fort quite a lot. I remember stands of 60 or 70 with Arthur Wellard but my share would usually be half a dozen. It could be quite disconcerting being the back-up batsman to Arthur. He didn't always hit high into the air – he was apt to belt the ball back at shoulder-height more or less in the other batsman's direction. The first priority was to get out of the way!

There is a much-relished story about him, told by Christopher Martin-Jenkins in *Bedside Cricket*, of the innings he played at Portsmouth after 'two sleepless nights out dancing.' He curled up and went to sleep when he arrived in the dressing room, but two and a half hours later – already considerably dropped down the batting order by Somerset – he had to be

Contrasting styles of Somerset batsmanship. John Daniell, comfortable as ever in his homburg, causes umpire Bestwick to duck during a match with Middlesex in 1927 . . . Maurice Tremlett heaves a delivery from Tony Lock to the Oval boundary in 1949 . . . Peter 'Dasher' Denning carries on the zestful tradition in the 1980s

John Daniell   Price   W Bestwick

woken up as the score stood at 40 for 5. He got a single off a shot he never tried to make from a ball he never saw. He survived an lbw appeal, hilariously did the splits in going through the motions of facing the next delivery which brought his dismissal.

Head down and doubtless still spinning from the night before, he ambled off. Eventually he heard the crowd laughing and he looked up to see Lofty Herman, leaning against the square-leg boundary fence. 'Er, em, excuse me. But the pavilion is over *there!*'

John Hemsley Cameron, born in Jamaica, was the son of a West Indian doctor who came over as a member of a tour party in 1906. He was sent to Taunton School where he became a popular member of the team. Short, sturdy and jolly, his features would break willingly into a broad grin when the ball spun acutely from leg. He kept tossing the ball up and bamboozling a succession of opposing batsmen by his precocious mastery of leg-spin and googly bowling. 'Monkey' went off to Lord's in 1931, selected to play for The Rest against the Public Schools and in just over 19 overs took 10-49.

Everyone got very excited, not least Somerset. They quickly recruited him and he had his first county match as an eighteen-year-old. In all he played forty-eight times for Somerset and took a nondescript 45 wickets. Seasoned professionals were no respecters of schoolboy prowess; they battered him when his length strayed. His fingers, once supple as a Magic Circle wizard, became too chubby and he was no longer able effectively to spin the ball.

Yet how can we say that? In 1939 he was vice-captain of the West Indian touring side. He played in the first Test – one of two for him – and with rather indecent treachery dismissed Gimblett, Hammond and Paynter. 'Monkey got me with only his second ball. Lost it completely and was bowled all over the place', said Gimblett in retrospective self-rebuke.

As his leg-breaks for Somerset receded, however, his batting would periodically surface with bold, good-looking strokes. Two of his three hundreds for the county were scored in 1937.

Ingle had lifted Somerset up the table but they were still prone to batting aberrations. Just as Gloucestershire had bowled them out for 31 in 1931, Derbyshire destroyed them for 35 four seasons later. In between, at Sheffield, Horace Fisher, a slow left-arm bowler who should surely have played more than fifty-two times for Yorkshire, had an lbw hat-trick. The victims were Mitchell-Innes, Andrews and Luckes. Alec Skelding, most colourful of characters, was the umpire; the occasion, no doubt embroidered a little, went into his vast repertoire of anecdotes.

CHAPTER ELEVEN
Toothless Proximity

It's time to start praising Wellard. In 1933 he wasn't simply standing a few yards from the most bludgeoning of bats, taking blazing catches with unconcern and slipping the red-hot ball into his trouser pockets while everyone looked towards the extra cover boundary. He was doing the double for the first time.

The 1,055 runs were not composed of delicate dabs and deflections; they were not classic square cuts or cover drives. There was precious little for the purist to cherish. Wellard was a pragmatist: he liked to do what he could do best. That meant the hitting of sixes, crude and crashing, insensitive to the inner torment of the bowler. He wasn't much concerned with coaching manuals and batting finesse, nor with the reputed wiles of famous bowlers. He liked to block the first few balls with a slightly exaggerated straight bat – and then aim for the clouds. The clouds could usually be relied on to convey the ball to chimney stacks, open bedroom windows, passing streams or, in one case, a passing goods wagon. In 1933, no other first-class cricketer hit so many sixes; the pattern had been set for the remainder of his muscular and felicitous career.

But his batting was only the icing. The bowling was his forte: it was fast, intelligent and denied even more success only by slippery fingers in the slips. He swung the ball away, having thrilled West Country crowds by the way he took that distinctive leap just before releasing the ball. He liked hard pitches and could make the ball zip off at a disconcerting pace.

'Just get him out for a duck and I'll give you a bottle of champagne', Wellard was told when the late Nawab of Pataudi went in to bat for Worcestershire at Weston-super-Mare. Maybe it was the wrong kind of bribe. Wellard preferred strong ale. Pataudi scored 222, one of three double centuries for his English county. Some who were at the match said that he might have been caught behind the wicket before he had scored. Why, the champers wouldn't even have been on ice by then . . .

The Weston wicket has been maligned by a succession of detractors; that diligent cricket historian Keith Ball reminds me that Robertson-Glasgow described Clarence Park as 'always sportive'. Yet in the year that Pataudi hit 222, the wicket for the festival of three matches was so docile that Somerset did not once complete a first innings. Jack Lee scored 193 not out, Young 135, Case 111 and Longrigg 101. Limited innings or not, 2,721 runs were amassed.

Bill Andrews used to tell of a good-natured running duel between Wellard and Glamorgan's skipper Maurice Turnbull during this period. Turnbull liked to use his feet and move down the wicket when facing slow bowlers like White. But it made no apparent difference to Wellard, defiantly entrenched at silly mid-off. He kept thrusting down a bronzed arm to prevent intended fours. Suddenly, in the heat of the afternoon, the big Somerset man took out both sets of false teeth and dropped them casually in the pockets of his flannels. He was apt to do this during a match, blithely unaware of the marked change in his facial features.

It was too much for Turnbull, already frustrated by this fearless human barrier to run-making. 'For goodness' sake, Arthur. I don't mind how close you stand – but just please put your teeth back in!'

At Weston, both in 1933 and 1936, the Glamorgan captain was caught by Wellard. The popular all-rounder hit the first of his two hundreds for Somerset in 1934, at the Oval. He was on his best behaviour and refrained from damaging the gasometers. His 112 came out of 157 but it took him two hours twenty-five minutes. He was rather proud of that one. 'Just shows what I *can* do, me old cocker.' There was much approval about his new found signs of self-discipline at the crease. He sniffed and said to himself: 'That's all right now and again. But there are quicker ways of working up a thirst.'

Somerset, always looking for methods of increasing the gate money, were prepared to try other venues. They had tried Knowle, on the southern side of Bristol; now in 1934 they played at Downside, the Roman Catholic school. The headmaster of the time, Father Trafford, a keen supporter of cricket, had said he was certain the fixture would be of considerable interest to all the neighbouring villages around the Mendips. Maurice Turnbull had been an Old Boy and so Glamorgan were seen as the obvious opposition. Hugh Watts, later a master at Downside and a Somerset player, was a spectator for the Glamorgan visit. 'It was a lovely ground, of course. But it was impossible to keep out people who hadn't paid – the ground was open on all sides. The cost of putting up barriers would have been prohibitive.'

The following year both Wells and Yeovil were given their first county match. Wells had neither sightscreens nor scoreboards – but plenty of clergy and cloth-conscious students from the theological college. Bowling changes and other match details were broadcast over the loudspeakers, from the scorers' box.

Somerset were bowled out for 56 in the first innings and lost to Worcestershire by an innings and 105 runs. Reg Perks (7-21) was altogether too whippy for them and out of that sorry early total, Ernie Falck was the only home player to reach double figures. He at least had local knowledge on his side. He came from Wells and was having one of his four games for the county.

At Yeovil, in mid-August, Somerset lost to Surrey by 8 wickets. It was just as well that the visitors didn't need a full batting side in the second innings: Fishlock and Parker were both hurt in a road accident after playing on the Saturday. Alf Gover took 3 wickets for 1 run and finished with 6-37; Wellard took 5 wickets for 2 runs and finished with 6-69. In the end, Freddie Brown was the match winner with 7-70.

Young had by now given up and turned to umpiring. Robertson-Glasgow was on the point of giving up and turning more to his typewriter, though I suspect most of those felicitous phrases were fashioned in longhand. And Somerset were, as ever, throwing the game's forecasters and logicians into confusion. From 1932 to 1939, their position in the championship was 7th, 11th, 15th, 14th, 7th, 13th, 7th, 14th. The only uniformity was an up-and-down swing.

Another experimental venue for county cricket, away from Taunton, was Frome. It had white railings, plenty of corrugated iron and, in the May of 1935, it had Harold Gimblett. This was where he made his debut, after being turned down by the county; and where he went in No 8 against Essex and scored a hundred in sixty-three minutes to win the Lawrence Trophy.

It ranks with the game's great romances and has been liberally documented; especially the way he missed the early-morning bus from his home at Bicknoller to Bridgwater, and had to hitch a lift to where Wally Luckes was waiting for him. He was a stranger to the Frome crowd; the printer didn't put his initials on the scorecard because they weren't known. His mother had given him some sandwiches and Wellard had lent him his spare bat. Reggie Ingle, the captain, admitted he had no idea where to put him in the batting order. 'I was surprised he didn't send me in last', Gimblett used to say.

Gimblett had got into the team by default. Daniell had tried in vain to find a replacement for the injured Laurie Hawkins. Then, as Gimblett was leaving the county ground on the Friday for what he imagined was the last time, his unimpressive trial over and his travelling expenses in his pocket, the secretary had looked out of his office window and said: 'Do you know how to get to Frome, Gimblett?'

And then there was Luckes, on the car journey from Bridgwater to Frome, saying: 'Peter Smith will try you out with a googly.' He didn't even know what a googly was. But he walked in just after lunch when Somerset had 6 wickets down, Smith was summoning up all his compounded cunning in expectation of easy pickings, and Morris Nichols was bowling like the wind, faster by far than anything the farmer's son had met before.

He had a fresh, attractive country boy's face; it carried a look of resignation, almost indifference, as he went out to bat. He'd already been told he wouldn't make a county cricketer. What was he doing now, taking on Laurie Eastman, Jack O'Connor, Tom Pearce, Tommy Wade and the Smiths? Oh, what the heck, why not treat it like one of those village games which he loved?

The innings was, of course, a sensation. He soon straight-drove Smith for four and then simply kept going. He drove red-faced farmers out of the beer tent to where they could watch, applaud and take evasive action. His half-century came in twenty-eight minutes with a six. It all ended with a casual catch, as if he had shown what he could do and was now ready to go home for the afternoon milking. His score was 123; his time at the wicket was seventy-nine minutes.

Then followed the ballyhoo which he loathed. But there was no more talk of his leaving. He went on to hit 23,007 runs and forty-nine hundreds for Somerset. Twice he scored 2,000 runs in a season and three times only he played for England. He was the greatest native batsman the county ever had. To immense natural talents of timing and handsome aggression, he acquired technical refinement. He wasn't afraid to ask. From Herbert Sutcliffe he improved his hook shot and privately gloated when it was in the presence of his hierarchical detractors at Lord's; from Jack Hobbs he learned how to play in-swing.

Others made their county debut in 1935, among them C. J. P. Barnwell. He was yet another to be surprised by the telegraph boy. 'It was the Bank Holiday game at Bristol and I was petrified. I introduced myself to the team and I don't think they were terribly impressed. The pros were understandably a bit defensive when a new amateur turned up.'

Ingle asked: 'Where do you bat?'

'Where I'm put, sir.'

'Call me Reggie. Now then, where do you bat?'

'Usually at 3.'

'Well, that's where you'll be.'

John Barnwell, who had learned his cricket at Repton, faced up to Charlie Barnett and immediately stroked a four through the covers. Soon he tried to do the same again and played on. 'That was my first lesson.'

The dividing line between amateurs and professionals could on occasions be embarrassing or inhibiting. 'I always found the pros very helpful. One day I confided to Wally Luckes that I was bothered about getting out lbw so often.'

'Glad you asked me that, sir. I didn't like to tell you . . .' And Luckes painstakingly showed the amateur where he was going wrong as he played back. 'I hardly ever got out lbw again. The professionals in the thirties really were a grand lot.'

Barnwell also knew all about their drinking capacity – and at least one case of slight over-indulgence at Colchester before the war.

Much more recently I was staying in London. I rang Arthur Wellard and asked him if he felt like a jar. We went out for the evening. After a couple of pints, Arthur turned to me and said that was his limit. Remembering his capacity from the old days, I was astonished. There was a pause and then he grinned and said that after two pints of beer he moved on to double whiskies.

Life could be less than fair for the amateurs too. Barnwell and Michael Bennett were playing at Northampton when a telegram arrived from Taunton. Its contents were laconic and to the point. 'Room for you *or* Michael against West Indians. Which?' One of them had to give way for the attractive visit of the Tourists. 'I was pretty livid and so was Michael. Why should one of us be dropped? We didn't reply to the telegram and both turned up at the ground on the morning of the match with the West Indies. Bunty, who was captain, arrived and wanted to know what was happening. We made it clear to him that we were fed up with making way for some schoolmaster or other for a tour match. It had happened on other occasions. Eventually Michael and I tossed up – and I lost.'

Barnwell, who loved his fielding in the covers as much as his batting, was a player of versatility. He once hit Bill Voce for four boundaries in an over at Trent Bridge; he also took forty minutes without getting off the mark at Lord's. Until the 1980s he and Longrigg held the county's record for an eighth wicket stand, at Bristol.

> Bunty suddenly said he was going to declare at the end of the over. I told him I was surprised because he was 189 and going well for his double century. He laughed and said I was really disappointed because I was on 45 and wanted my 50. I asked Reg Sinfield for a half-volley and he obliged. My smite landed a foot inside the boundary. Four instead of six – and I finished on 49.

The pair got on well together. Barnwell used to play in a faded Incogs cap and Longrigg could stand it no longer. During a match in 1946, he implored his fellow amateur: 'Get rid of that bloody thing. Wear your county cap.' Barnwell rather sadly told his skipper that he had never been awarded it. Later he checked and found he'd been given it in 1937. 'No one had bothered to tell me!'

He occasionally led Somerset, first when Ingle had hay fever and then when Longrigg was needed in his law office. 'I was also sounded out about whether I'd like to be considered for the job permanently. But I used to breed silver foxes and couldn't spare too much time to play cricket.'

Captaincy, in truth, brought nothing but grey hairs. Ingle, who had a gift for what today is rather glibly known as motivation, led the county to nine wins in 1936 and that was the most they had had since 1924. Administrative worries remained on the grand scale, however, and he had to call on – at times in pleading gestures close to prayer – as many as thirty-four players. After the war, he was closely involved as a solicitor in the defence of Rosina Cornock, the Bristol woman charged with the murder of her husband in the bath. It was a celebrated trial and Reggie Ingle sat through the whole of it as well as visiting Mrs Cornock regularly in Cardiff Prison. 'I always felt certain that she was innocent and I'm pleased to say she was acquitted. But the case turned my hair white.' And we had always imagined it was due to trying to raise a Somerset side in the late thirties . . .

Gimblett followed on from Frome with five hundreds in 1936. One of them was at the start of the season against the Indians at Taunton. He played in a Test trial, two Tests against the Indians – at the age of twenty-one – and for the Players. The sheer exhilaration of his stroke play offset the technical flaws and the impetuosity. But the first signs of introspection and moodiness were beginning to show.

135

In the final match of the season, against Lancashire, he confided to Eddie Phillipson that he had lost all his confidence and was thinking of giving up cricket altogether. There was nothing really at stake. 'OK, Harold, I'll give you a few half-volleys to get you started again.' And he did: another example of a delightful camaraderie that disappeared long ago.

This was the match when a tall, lean eccentric from Bedfordshire, Rollo John Oliver Meyer, scored 202. It was his first season of county cricket and he was producing an extraordinary achievement, though few would question his ability as a batsman. It is just that the versions of how he obtained his only double century all carry an appealing thread of unreality.

Most of them seem to agree that he was in sight of a highly unlikely 200 when he turned to the wicket keeper George Duckworth and offered a contribution to Jack Iddon's benefit if the batting milestone were reached. *Wisden* does indeed suggest that some levity was introduced and that even Duckworth essayed half a dozen expensive overs. Jack Meyer would, I am sure, be too good a sport and romantic to want to contest such charming authenticity.

It had been a marvellous season for Wellard. He played with or without his teeth, loose change clanging in his trouser pocket ready for the next solo school. His 134 wickets (av. 18.17) were partly achieved by off-breaks, bowled round the wicket. At Yeovil, in particular, he imparted considerable spin against Worcestershire. But then there were his sixes. He threatened to damage the distant Cathedral at Wells, where he thumped five sixes in an over off Derbyshire's Tom Armstrong. The ecclesiastical calm was desecrated two seasons later, this time at the expense of Frank Woolley. Wellard's five sixes were equally brutal and were executed with a minimum of backlift or apparent physical endeavour on the part of the batsman. Woolley withdrew (0-40) after 2 overs; when he batted he was twice lbw to Wellard, the first time for a duck.

'Have you got something against me, Arthur?' he asked with the merest flicker of a brave smile.

At Wells, where alas they no longer have county cricket, the wiseacres still talk of Wellard's sixes. They have become part of the small, tranquil city's folklore. 'Old Arthur, he got 74 wi' only 15 shots.' It's true, those 74 runs (out of his 86 in 1936) came from seven sixes and eight fours.

Somerset went to Weston-super-Mare and never enjoyed the seaside more. They won all three matches; Sussex collapsed for 47; Wellard was threatening to go over to off-spin full-time. 'Not such hard work, cock.'

As we leave 1936 there is room at the moment for only two newcomers. Peter McRae played just twenty-five times for his county, George Rowdon once only. McRae, born in Buenos Aires, was as good at cricket as he was at rugby. He scored one century for Somerset and would probably have returned after the war. But he was a ship's doctor and died at sea in 1944. Reports suggest he showed great concern for others and gave up his place on a raft when his ship was hit. Rowdon was for many years one of the finest club cricketers in Somerset, captaining Midsomer Norton with much distinction. He scored a large number of hundreds with a neat elegance that many felt deserved higher recognition. His fleeting chance came against Essex on a green Colchester wicket, where he stood up to Ken Farnes and Morris Nichols for nearly an hour. He was 12th man once after that and was told to 'come along to Weston, just in case we should need you'. The trouble was that Somerset couldn't afford to take on anyone else. Essex, much impressed with the look of him at Colchester, expressed interest. But George went back to Midsomer Norton and the family plumbing business.

Jack Lee meanwhile left to become the head coach at Mill Hill School. Some of his fellow professionals maintained, years afterwards, that it was another case of insensitive man management. The all-rounder had still been worth his place and should have been persuaded to stay. He used to say he wanted to remain with Somerset; there was talk of a benefit. But suddenly there was a vacancy at Mill Hill. He knocked on the county secretary's door. Should he take the job? Yes, he was apparently advised.

This led to some understandable criticism of the county officials. Were they too off-handed in their treatment of the pros? Did they expect unwavering loyalty and offer too little in return? Was Lee even being encouraged on his way because of his occasional outburst at the expense of the amateurs? Here was the player, after all, who took the young, unworldly Gimblett to one side and said: 'Don't bother yourself, Harold, about having to go on to the field through a different gate from the amateurs. Just remember you're good enough in your own right to be playing – and getting paid for it. All the amateurs have to do is put on a fancy hat.'

John Daniell's son Nigel is convinced that a few of the professionals got the wrong idea completely about Jack Lee's departure. 'Dad definitely told him that the county didn't want to lose him. But in fairness to him, they thought he should seriously consider the job at Mill Hill. They felt the school appointment would long outlast his career as a county cricketer.' I discussed the issue in a previous book and said the truth probably lay somewhere between the two versions.

By the summer of 1944, his thoughts forcibly deflected far from cricket, he had been killed in action, in Normandy. He'd been a reliable player who in 241 matches for the county scored nearly 8,000 runs and took, with slow, accurate, unexceptional slow spin, nearly 500 wickets. He was apt to succeed when others failed. There were notable opening stands with brother Frank at Leyton and Weston. Twice, in 1934 and 1935, he carried his bat. The innings of 135 not out against Kent at Taunton was one of his best. No one was ever going to get him out. When the Lees were in together and going well, it was a reassuring rather than dynamic sight. And Frank, small, stubborn and left-handed, was around in 1937 for his 1,670 runs, and then 2,015 the following season.

Somerset used to experiment with their openers. Lee had Dickie Burrough as his partner when they put on 215 against Kent at Bath. Burrough was an amateur always worth his place. He scored four hundreds; his father had had to be satisfied with four appearances for the county. Dickie's local club was

Bath and he deserved two centuries in that match with Kent in 1937. He was out for 90 in the first innings and reached 133 in the second.

It was really Andrews's season. He bowled beautifully, always full length, always noisily expressive, to take 131 wickets. His batting, sharply varied in quality as his fluctuations of role in the batting order reflected, could produce sturdy and good-looking blows. They helped him to the double for the first time in 1937, and he rather proudly underlined his new-found stature as an all-rounder by doing the double again in 1938.

In terms of personal triumph, Bill couldn't have hoped to better his bowling performance at the Oval, of all places, in the June of 1937. In Surrey's second innings, his figures were 6.4-2-12-8. That, as Bill with every justification would remind you, included a hat-trick and a dropped catch which went for six. 'And I wasn't ever fit enough to bowl.'

It's true: he was hobbling with an ankle injury and was hoping that Ingle would be able to hide him away somewhere in the field. 'Don't feel up to it, skipper', he said as he was thrown the new ball. Success heals all. The limp stayed – but the grin widened. 'I still didn't know I'd done the hat-trick till the umpire told me as we were walking off the field. I'd got a wicket with the last ball of one over and the first two of the next.'

Who would dare to say that the engaging Andrews is immodest? 'I promise you that Arthur bowled better than I did and he only got a couple in that second innings. I was coming in off medium pace because of my ankle.' Surrey were dismissed for 35, their lowest total for forty-four years.

Some overnight rain had freshened the pitch but it must have been Andrews at his very best. He had Knight utterly deceived to give a simple return catch; he had a succession of batsmen playing uncertainly and edging to Hazell in the slips; he had Burrough sprinting like a man inspired to take a difficult catch off Freddie Brown. The saddest thing of all was that Wellard later came along with 91 not out at No 8, ran out of partners and Somerset lost a magnificent match by 11 runs.

Sydney Rippon came back for a few games in 1937. He had given up county cricket in 1929 following a serious breakdown. Now he was back to open the innings again in place of Gimblett who was unfit. Rippon was in his mid-forties and his form at club level was unknown. But he volunteered to go in No 1 with Lee. The match was a tough one at Old Trafford and such volunteers were embraced. Somerset were badly short of players. Andrews was batting at No 4 and Wellard at 6. Edward Hack had been rushed into the side for his only match; another club cricketer, Newman Bunce, from Lodway, was needed for his bowling.

Rippon unfurled one or two vintage cover drives in that and his subsequent matches. His running between the wicket had not noticeably improved. He now wore horn-rimmed spectacles and the spectrum of mannerisms hadn't lessened. A cricket writer at Ilford observed: 'Two onlookers were so engrossed in watching the eccentric movements and postures of Rippon, who several times sank on one knee in seeming fervent relief that the ball had missed his stumps, that they upset the bench on

One group of less familiar faces in the Somerset team which played at Old Trafford in 1937. *Back row*, F. S. Lee, W. N. Bunce, E. J. Hack, W. Luckes, H. Hazell, A. W. Wellard. *Front*, W. H. R. Andrews, K. C. Kinnersley, R. A. Ingle, C. J. P. Barnwell, A. E. S. Rippon

which they were accommodated and fell flat on their backs.'

Yes, it was good to have him back. He was in every sense an individualist – as he defiantly demonstrated by passing his law finals after retiring from the Civil Service.

Goodbye finally, also in 1937, to 'Farmer' White. By whatever standard we measure it, he was in his own phlegmatic way one of Somerset's great cricketers. He knew the game as well as he knew the wondrous ways of the banks and hedgerows of Stogumber. He was a superb bowler, a far more than passable batsman and a fielder who, although he never darted around the boundaries or pounced athletically in the covers, still took 381 catches. And only Braund or Wellard have got anywhere near that figure for the county.

Longrigg took over the captaincy in 1938. According to one professional who played under him, he was 'solid and steady rather than brilliant or inspirational'. That seems a perceptive judgement. But his arrival as leader put everyone in good heart. The county spurted up again to seventh in the table; they also won ten county matches, more than ever before. Team work was good; the side seemed to have a better balance. Bunty was also lucky: the occupational hazard of last-minute selection trauma had subsided.

Gimblett scored 1,291 runs, a little down. Lee soared to 2,015. There were few innings that you would recall a decade later. He wasn't that kind of batsman. But the immense reliability was the perfect complement to the more instinctive flailing from Gimblett and Wellard. Sheet anchors had their uses, even at Taunton, Bath and Weston, where the disciplined plodders were usually outnumbered by the cavaliers.

This small, diffident man went to Worcester in the August and so nearly equalled the world record of C. J. B. Wood, who for Leicestershire against Yorkshire in 1911 scored a hundred in each innings while carrying his bat. In the game with Worcestershire, Lee, a player of infinite patience and gentle temperament, was 109 not out in the first innings. He was last out in the second for 107. His 2,000 runs that season included seven hundreds; three of them came in a placid and reassuring row. Who says slow batsmen are unloved? The collective acclaim for him from his team-mates was always particularly warm.

There was also Herbert Francis Thomas Buse. He worked as a clerk in a solicitor's office at Bath, where he was a highly competent all-rounder in club cricket. In the winter months he was a brave full back for Bath Rugby Football Club, though that quietly dignified appearance might have suggested a less physical form of weekend pursuit. He wasn't, in truth, a man who appeared to do anything in too much of an indecent hurry. His stuttering, mesmerising run-up, as a prelude to medium pace and out-swing, had its own somnolent charm. His batting was predominantly one pace, and that was a slow one. The concentration was prodigious; he anchored himself to the crease, bottom protruding and eyes throwing out an amiable challenge to the bowler.

Bertie came in for a match at the Oval in 1929, just before his nineteenth birthday. Somerset were short of bowlers and he was handed the new ball to take on Hobbs and Sandham. He wasn't too abashed by such a prospect. In fact, he came off after 6 overs (0-22); Hobbs went on to a double century. A year later, Buse was again asked to take a few days off from his law office, this time so that he could play at Chesterfield. He had every reason to be pleased with his 4-27.

It had always been an ambition of his to play permanently for Somerset. His form for Bath, paraded in his own distinctive way, led to his being offered terms as a professional – but not until 1938. The meticulous clerical work, surrounded by solicitors, hadn't been wasted on him; he'd been taught the value of calm logic. He weighed his affection for the game against the vicissitudes of an indeterminate career that had nothing to do with nine-to-five conveyancing. 'If I don't take wickets, I can still make runs', he told himself. His ability as a proven all-rounder in high-class club cricket appealed to the county.

In his first season as a professional cricketer, he scored 1,067 runs and took 61 wickets. The maiden hundred came in 1938 against Derbyshire; it bore all the endearing and cussed watchfulness that characterised so many of the innings that followed. 'You'll be all right for us, Bertie', the other pros were soon saying.

That same summer threw up an imperishable cameo at Leicester. Somerset should logically have lost by an innings. Trevor Jones, aged eighteen, and Luckes came along on the third day to compound the delicious irrationality of the game of cricket. Jones, a stylish young batsman from club cricket in Bristol, went in at No 9; Luckes went in after him. They put on 146 for the ninth wicket, a county record which lasted till 1963. Young Jones might have been playing in a school house match, so composed was he. Leicestershire's bowlers despaired; the old Somerset cynics came out of the dressing rooms to stay and applaud.

Luckes recalled it to me with great joy not long before his death.

We were still 50 runs behind with only 2 second innings' wickets left. I can still remember how, before I even went in, the Somerset players were packing their bags, convinced that the match was over. Trevor made 106 and I got 90 not out. Then came Horace with 18 not out. We were even able to declare but the game was drawn.

Wellard and Andrews, broad-shouldered buddies, took just under 300 wickets between them. One swung the ball away, the other in at the right-hander. They were always comparing notes: about Wincanton starting prices and the cellar quality of a wide range of draught beers, every bit as much as the advantages of the gentle sea breezes at Hove, Eastbourne and Bournemouth to the early-morning bowlers.

In 1938, Wellard's haul was 172 wickets. It was more than anyone else in the country and he was looking supremely fit, more bronzed than usual after his tour of India under Lord Tennyson, for whom he took 47 wickets and had almost as many catches dropped. 'So what's new, cock?' he'd say with that philosophical shrug implying he had soon forgotten (and forgiven). Wellard made his Test debut against New Zealand at Old Trafford in 1937; now, in 1938, he was brought in to play against the Australians at Lord's. That was the sum total of recognition by his country. He would have gone to India on the 1939–40 tour but the war put a cruel end to that.

Somerset slid down to fourteenth in the table again in 1939, as if their spunky improvement the previous summer had all been a little too much for them. The return to more familiar depths was hardly the fault of Gimblett. He was quite magnificent at times, ready to harness a few additional technical adornments to that innate bravado and ebullience which were so often manifested by sixes in the opening over if the bowler were accommodating enough to offer one or two half-volleys.

At the end of his first seven matches he'd scored 905 runs; five hundreds had come in consecutive fixtures. He now headed the county's averages. There'd have been uproar if he had been passed over for the West Indies Test at Lord's – or for the Players against the Gents that year. It was ironical that Cameron got him at Lord's: the little West Indian from Taunton School, who had by then largely lost the art of leg-spin, still took a wicket in his first over of Test cricket, just as another 'Somerset' man, Colin McCool did for Australia against the New Zealanders at Wellington soon after the war.

Honest pros, a stirring part of the Somerset story. Frank Lee and Harold Gimblett walk out to open the innings. (*Below*) Arthur Wellard, Bill Andrews and Horace Hazell

The West Indians came back to Taunton to play Somerset in early August and were beaten by an innings and 72 runs. It was the first time they had gone down since the Lord's Test. Their first innings total of 84 was the lowest of the tour. Jeff Stollmeyer carried his bat for 45. Wellard (4-43) and Andrews (6-40) both bowled unchanged for 16 overs on a green top.

Wellard was given the Glamorgan fixture at Weston for his benefit. A few of his friends said he walked round the boundary between innings, talking in a Welsh accent, to advocate the advantages of a generous collection for the beneficiary. He never did, of course, though he'd have enjoyed the joke. The cheque came to £1,413, a record for a Somerset player.

There was not once any lack of volunteers when it came to a benefit match for Wellard against one of the club sides. John Barnwell took a strong county XI to play Clevedon and District during that season. 'Bunty gave me strict instructions to take revenge since we'd actually been defeated in the previous benefit fixture there. We found our form – and I found a wife, the daughter of the opposing skipper.'

Wellard played in a match at Downside School, where he quickly had a promising seventeen-year-old, Hugh Watts, out lbw. 'No doubt about it but there was no appeal. Arthur just coughed and said nothing. Afterwards I asked him why', said Watts.

The reply was accompanied by an eloquent grin. 'Because I was told that on no account were we to get you out. The county wanted a look at you!' Watts made his debut that summer at Bournemouth and had four matches then.

Buse had a bowling performance of 8-41, in just under 11 overs, to cherish when Derbyshire came to Taunton. So had Doug Wright, even more impressively at Bath. The Kent man kept springing in at medium pace to take 16-80 from the match. That was one occasion at least when his miscellany of distinctive leg-break gave him results commensurate with his considerable, if uncontrollable, ability.

For a second time the history of Somerset was about to be interrupted by a world war. There would be more casualties, some fine West Country cricketers lost for ever on a European battleground or at the bottom of the ocean. So let us pluck two final tales from 1939, true and contrasting, to distract us from depressing thoughts of imminent gloom. One is thrilling, the other rather scandalous. They were part of life on the county cricket circuit in the late thirties.

At Kidderminster, Somerset tied with Worcestershire. 'I should have been the hero and ended up the villain of the piece', says Hazell. It started well enough with Wellard and Hazell spinning out the home side for 130. Somerset were just as fragile and it was left to the last pair, Sam Weaver and Hazell, to ensure a lead of 1 run. Then Worcestershire were hustled out again, this time for 142. Hazell should have been brought on earlier; when he was called up, he dismissed five of the last six batsmen. His figures were 5.7-1-6-5. Perhaps we should leave an account of the subsequent agony to Horace.

Again, in the end, it was left to Sam and myself. We needed six when I came in. I was feeling very nervous. When it came to the last over, Dick Howorth was bowling. I swung at one and it landed only a few feet inside the boundary – I had to be satisfied with a four. We arrived at the fourth ball and I couldn't believe it – the Worcester skipper had kept most of his fielders in the deep. We were actually level now and I calculated that a push for a single was all that was needed. Howorth was bowling over the wicket and I felt that he would be able to field himself on his follow-through if I hit to mid-off or short extra cover. I decided to be cleverer than that and aim for deepish cover point. Oh dear, I should have known better. I left a gap and my stumps went over.

The Worcestershire players raced in from all directions. They picked up the bowler and carried him off the field – they thought they'd won instead of tied. All I wanted was a big hole in the ground. I didn't think my colleagues would ever talk to me again. The memory still haunts me, almost half a century later.

It was one of Weaver's only two games for Somerset. He was better known for his huge throw-in as a wing half for Newcastle United and Chelsea. Sam played in the FA Cup Final and for England at soccer. But neither, he admitted, compared with Kidderminster for drama.

Now for the promised touch of scandal. It happened on an away match when one of Somerset's very occasional players took an indiscreetly ardent shine to a pretty member of the hotel staff. His overtures were nocturnal. The player's affectionate nature was unrequited. He was given first an icy and then a noisy reception. The hotel manager was far from pleased; there was much talk of a stinging report being sent to the Somerset headquarters. A breakfast-time identity parade was also contemplated.

The incident never became public knowledge. Soothing words and apologies pre-empted the feared scandal. That was as it should be. Give or take the occasional case of alcoholic excess, usually after a wearying day in the field, there were surprisingly few disciplinary problems for a lengthy line of Somerset skippers to handle.

For the time being, from the late summer of 1939, there would be nothing at all for county captains to handle.

AFTER THE WAR

Two literary cricketers –
R. C. Robertson-Glasgow and
Peter Roebuck

Two genial spinners –
Johnny Lawrence and
Vic Marks

IN TANDEM Two 'immortals' – Harold Gimblett and Arthur Wellard

Two 'superstars' and soul-mates – Viv Richards and Ian Botham

CHAPTER TWELVE
Success — and Shop Stewards

No, of course it could never be quite the same again. The social order had changed and Labour were on the way in. Professionals returned to the county ground in 1946, back from the war. They were older, wiser and in some cases less willing to be subservient; by the next season, they were becoming restive about their modest contracts. There had been intrepid knocks on the secretary's door. Andrews, who had the best handwriting, had drafted a challenging letter to the committee. It didn't make him especially popular and poor old Bill, shop steward or fall guy according to your point of view, was out at the end of 1947.

But, whatever the hints of cynicism in the dressing room, there was an infectious camaraderie, reflecting a surging relief that county cricket was back again. Evocative smells like fresh paint and freshly mown grass were hard to resist. The reunions, among players and rural supporters, sparked memories and expectancy. After the drabness of the war years, there was an unleashed excitement about spectator sports like cricket. The sycophants were lining up to buy the pros a drink.

Somerset had eight professionals and that represented a reassuring amount of experience. Longrigg was again the captain, adding to the feeling of continuity. Despite the occupational qualms about the players' dues, team spirit was perhaps as buoyant as it has ever been. Somerset invariably walked on to the field with a smile on their face.

Opponents noticed and envied it. Gloucestershire, traditionally more serious in demeanour, were affected by it. When Wellard was taking the most outrageous liberties with Sam Cook's bowling, George Lambert summoned up some of his innate cockney chirpiness to assuage the put-upon slow bowler: 'Don't worry, Sam, he's been mishitting them so far!' That was the match when Hammond, in peerless form, chipped a magnificent six off Andrews. The bowler stopped in mid-wicket to applaud and, as the Gloucestershire wicket keeper, Andy Wilson remembers, was advised by Bunty to restrict the hero-worship and get on with the bowling.

The amateurs also much enjoyed each other's company in 1946 and 1947, not always the case in the past. Yorkshire came down to play and a crowd of the amateurs went off to a pub at Wiveliscombe. 'We ended up playing darts,' recalls John Barnwell, 'Bunty and myself against Norman Yardley and Brian Sellers. Wonderful night. The landlord sent us away with a lobster apiece.'

Brigadier E. H. Lancaster, by now secretary, had done his best to keep the club ticking over during the war years. The players had done their best to organise some cricket. But some, because of overseas postings and the limitations of Service life, hardly picked up a bat. Their joints were now stiff and there was much massage on the improvised treatment table. They still fancied their chances against Essex in the opening match. Tom Pearce crushed such romantic notions with a century on the last day. It was a narrow win; the happy crowd went home, whistling almost impartially. For them it was enough that cricket was back.

The county's one new professional after the war was Johnny Lawrence, a Yorkshireman not much taller than the stumps. He'd actually qualified for Somerset at the end of 1939 and then had to wait a long time for his chance. His virtues were teasing leg-breaks, effervescent tumbling in the pursuit of catches near the wicket, and visual humour. He came from Bingley and hoped in vain for recognition in his native county, but he got no further than the Yorkshire 2nd XI. Bradford League cricketers were sorry to see him go; Somerset were glad to welcome him.

His cheerful disposition was much to the liking of the dressing-room occupants, though his non-conformist attitudes, including his much-voiced disapproval of what is quaintly called industrial language, could be a little too inhibiting for those with a bent for freewheeling linguistics at the end of an unrewarding afternoon in the sun. He had valuable, deep-rooted Yorkshire qualities: he could on occasions bat with irremovable resolve. And he had a relish for unmalicious revenge: he often did well against his old county and achieved the hat-trick against them at Taunton in a beguiling session of 6-35. In his first season for Somerset, he scored 966 runs and took 66 wickets, some of them with his veiled googly and a few more with the ball that went straight on for an lbw triumph.

Then there were the new amateurs: G. R. Langdale, M. M. Walford, G. E. S. Woodhouse and F. Castle. We might also add Bill Caesar, a capable and competitive club cricketer who to most people's surprise came into the Somerset side for three matches at the age of forty-five. Even more intriguingly, he'd had a game for Surrey twenty-four years earlier.

Langdale and Walford both scored hundreds on their home debuts. The left-hander, Langdale, a studious looking figure in his spectacles, had been born in Yorkshire and played a few matches for Derbyshire before the war. He was a totally unfamiliar name to the Taunton spectators as he made his seemingly diffident way to the wicket at an unprepossessing No 8. He began striking the ball at once, not wantonly or with the jaunty cavalier inclinations of one of Somerset's many strolling players. There was a quite riveting fluency about the way he was getting to the pitch of the ball and cracking it through the covers. He scored 146 off a Yorkshire attack which lacked Bill Bowes but was hardly in a charitable mood. It was his finest innings; 92 of the runs came in boundaries.

'George had come down here to teach and we'd asked Brian Sellers about him. He had joked that he might be good enough for us! We used often to remind him of that light-hearted remark afterwards,' said Barnwell.

Walford had met R. J. O. Meyer at Oxford where the latter, on holiday from India, was playing for the Stragglers of Asia. Now, while still serving with the Signals in Germany, Walford had written to him, asking whether he thought Somerset could do with another recruit during the summer vacations. Born in Co Durham and educated at Rugby, Walford had earlier been approached to play for Warwickshire. But following his war service he was returning to Sherborne School to teach and some part-time cricket for Somerset seemed an attractive proposition.

He was a triple Blue; he was a fine centre three-quarter who played in two final England trials when at Oxford and for England in wartime internationals and was a hockey international who played in the 1948 London Olympics. But it was as a cricketer that he excelled most of all. He was, at his best, a quite superb batsman, orthodox and astute. His repertoire of good-looking strokes included some dazzling cover boundaries off the back foot. At the end of term-time, he arrived at the county ground and immediately middled the ball as if he'd been playing county cricket all season, instead of intermittent matches for Sherborne Sunday.

If he had chosen to play more often for Somerset, he would have established himself as a Test batsman. As it was, Micky Walford batted at a slightly disparaging No 7 in his first match, against the Indians, and scored 141 not out. The quality was a revelation; frankly he never looked like being dismissed. His technique enthralled me that day, and during several subsequent innings. I missed his 264 at Weston the following summer, against Hampshire. 'I don't remember too much about it but I daresay it was a bit of a slog towards the end', he said.

Walford wasn't a naturally gregarious man and a few of the team didn't quite know what to make of him. They all, without exception, envied him his considerable batting skills which brought him nine first-class hundreds and an average of 40.90 from his fifty-two matches for Somerset. 'I always tried terribly hard and, yes, I was very competitive indeed', he said.

That brings us inevitably to the extraordinary incident when Len Hutton was given out during his innings at Taunton in 1948. It led to something approaching apoplexy back in the Yorkshire professionals' changing room. The mutterings of deep displeasure went on for a long time afterwards though not, at least on the surface, from Hutton himself.

He had played a ball from Hazell to somewhere between point and third man and it was fielded by Lawrence. There was no question of a run and the England opener helpfully moved out of his ground so that he wouldn't impede the return to Luckes. The ball struck the wicket keeper's gloves, spun on to Hutton's pads and then rebounded to the stumps. A bail teetered and then reluctantly fell. Nothing had seemed at stake and Hutton bent to replace the bail. As he did so, he was conscious of some manufactured coughs and the audible kind of silence that is apt to accompany collective embarrassment. Then to his astonishment he noticed that the square leg umpire's finger was up.

Walford, fielding on the leg side, had appealed. Hutton, outside his crease, was given out. He had to be; technically he was run out. Those who were present say he walked back to the pavilion with a brave smile on his face. If he did, it was an eternal tribute to the philosophical spirit of Pudsey.

For days, no one would even whisper the name of the culprit. The newspapers were given bland, non-committal answers when they asked. One of the older players, loyal like the others, was quoted as saying: 'All I can tell you is that it wasn't a pro.' Nearly forty years later, Walford was to tell me: 'I saw Len not so long ago and brought up what had happened. He didn't complain in the least – but I suppose in a way it has been on my conscience all this time. It was something done in the heat of the moment.'

Kent's Billy Ashdown wasn't quite as generous in his response to another untimely appeal and we stretch back to the thirties once again, to bracket the two controversies. Playing against Somerset, this fine opening batsman pushed well forward and was hit on the pad. There was one lone shout, from the direction of extra cover. Ashdown was surprised and displeased at being given out on the optimistic appeal of someone hardly in the best line of vision. The impetuous shout had come from Somerset's 12th man, Buttle.

Micky Walford liked to win – and to win with some style. His one indiscretion against Hutton wasn't really something to harbour, though one or two of the Yorkshire professionals were singularly unforgiving; better to cherish the rich texture of Walford's batsmanship. He seemed to have an especial relish for the bracing air of Weston, where he scored six of his hundreds. When he arrived from schoolteaching in 1947, his first three innings were 90,101 and 264; this produced a stirring aggregate of 455 and average of 151.6. 'He's after your glory', several of the pros told Gimblett, teasingly. 'I heard of this so-called jealousy but never noticed it. I got on well with Harold and admired him vastly as a player', said Walford.

In 1953 he started well and then tailed away. 'I was on a special registration and someone rang and asked whether I'd give it up. I'd have been prepared to go on a bit longer.' His largely unpublicised value as a talent-spotter shouldn't be forgotten. He recommended Harold Stephenson to Somerset and had already suggested another fine wicket keeper from Durham, Dickie Spooner; when he had given up county cricket and was playing for Dorset against Devon, Walford was impressed by the bowling of Len Coldwell. 'Somerset had a look at him but didn't think he was good enough.' He went on to play for Worcestershire and seven times for England, of course.

Fred Castle was another teacher to come into the county side, like Walford, soon after the war. He was the headmaster of a secondary school at Bath and it was never easy to get time off. For his debut, against Gloucestershire, he had to obtain special permission from the local education authority and went into the school in the morning before heading for the match.

Castle was a person of varied talents. Brought up in Canterbury, he was invited to become a professional with Kent who liked the look of his assertive mid-order batting. In the same way he could have become an inside forward for Crystal Palace. He represented both Kent and Somerset at hockey; he had a fine baritone voice and was an accomplished magician. Occasionally he stood in as Somerset's cricket captain and he discovered it would need more than sleight-of-hand for him to conjure up a conquest or two. 'My first effort was at Old Trafford and we lost by an innings. There was this awful thunderstorm and we were bowled out twice the next day.'

Hugh Watts played in that match. He was still in the army and it called for a persuasive interview with his commanding officer. But, well, the ritualistic telegram had come from Taunton. 'Gimblett appendicitis. Report Old Trafford.' It wouldn't be true to say that Watts got there in time; Somerset were never that generous with their notice. At least he arrived in time to bat twice in a day.

It's as good a moment as any to mention the popular Watts' only county century. By then he was a history master at Downside.

We were playing Glamorgan and I was struggling a bit in the 90s. Len Muncer was bowling his off-breaks, too flat for the liking of his captain, Wilf Wooller, who said, 'For God's sake, Len, give them some air.' Both players were pretty short tempered. Muncer's reaction was to bowl a succession of slow full tosses. I hit three fours in a row and got my century.

Team spirit within the Somerset side, at least during 1946, was at a level never really matched before or since. It must be admitted that the standard of fielding was a good deal less memorable. One contemporary summed it up with a shrug of jocular resignation.

Some of the older players couldn't stoop too well and were also a decidedly bad risk in the outfield. R.J.O. had a terrible back. Hugh Watts couldn't throw because of a shoulder wound, and dear old Frank Lee had a double rupture. The only decent fielder was Harold Gimblett and he didn't seem to be trying half of the time!

Longrigg, however, set an alert example in the leg trap – his suspect speed would no doubt have been exposed in more distant outposts. It was to be his last year in charge. He'd done the job conscientiously and with some success; he would be sustaining his close links as chairman and president.

Somerset had made a slightly tardy start to the 1946 season. But from late June they were perhaps the most attractive side in the country. They went sixteen matches without being beaten. Twelve of those games were won, half of them by an innings. They kept compiling 500 runs in an innings and finished the season in fourth place. If they had started winning earlier, they'd have walked away with the championship. 'We were so busy renewing old friendships and wallowing again in the cosiness of the county ground that we didn't want to be rushed. Those big, unfamiliar wins had to take their turn.' Does anything better illustrate the timeless quintessence of Somerset cricket?

Wellard rubbed a painful knee, played as often as he could and still took

106 wickets. Gimblett, despite his illness, still hit seven centuries including his 231 against Middlesex. The pundits detected an added strand of defensive technique to complement the bountiful blade. When he went to Bath, the locals were continuing to talk of his appearance for London Counties the previous summer, in a match played as a benefit for the widow of Jack Lee.

Some lively descriptive writing in *Wisden* tells us:

> Gimblett, in his only innings of the season for London Counties, hit 101 in 110 minutes. Once he sent the ball soaring over a line of tall trees and the road outside the ground, into the judging ring of the local dog show, scattering people and animals. Directly after reaching his century, Gimblett broke his bat. The blade flew yards, leaving him standing with only the handle. The first stroke he made with a new bat brought his dismissal.

Now he was back with Somerset in the championship, and all was well. He was looking older and more strained; but the batting, classically chiselled and founded on exhilarating aggression, could be sublime. One or two other bats of his were badly damaged, if not quite splintered: he was inclined to hurl them across the dressing room after an untimely dismissal. 'We stayed well out of the firing range', a colleague recalled.

One of Gimblett's hundreds that first season after the war was against the Indians. I feel justified in pausing to dwell on the match. As a schoolboy I travelled with my sandwich box each day by train to Taunton and didn't miss a single ball. I cheered aloud at what seemed like an optical illusion, the collapse of India for 64 before lunch. And they'd just made 533-3 at Hove.

Wellard was unfit but for once it didn't appear to matter. Andrews, playing in brother Jack's size 12 boots, swung the ball as if inspired for 5-36. Buse, delicately deceptive, was even better (5-27). India made 431 in their second innings and it was never going to be enough. They lost by an innings and 11 runs.

The 1947 season had to be anti-climactic. Oldish men were getting older; that artificial flush of post-war excitement was rather on the wane in an oppressively austere Britain. Jack Meyer was the skipper and he simply wasn't fit enough. He was frequently in excruciating pain from his troublesome back. He stood with brave resolve in the slips, one hand trying to soothe his aching lumbar region. Against Northants, Wellard was bowling well and Dennis Brookes snicked straight towards R.J.O. It was a straightforward catch but Meyer couldn't bend for the ball. He shook his head in helpless self-reproach, put his hand into his back pocket and walked up to the bowler. 'Sorry, Arthur – here's a quid.'

Meyer could be endearing and vastly amusing. The idiosyncratic administrative skills he displayed at Millfield could also be of value to a cricket team. He had the knack of rustling up substantial meals for big players with enormous appetites in strange towns late at night. Once he pulled the communication cord on the Manchester express to order some requested food. He had a hundred theories on the game and wasn't inhibited about experimenting with a few of them. He was known to turn the batting order almost upside down, impervious to exchanges of disbelief. He didn't consider that cricket had too much to do with the dull confines of logic. At Taunton, where there had been heavy showers, the Somerset team eventually came out one man short. 'Then Jack appeared,' recalls John Barnwell, 'making his protest by walking under an umbrella and having his flannels tucked inside his socks.' It seems that Bunty Longrigg, the captain that day, wasn't too amused and ordered a less bizarre entrance.

Yet behind every incident was a semblance of a smile — though Walter Robins wouldn't have shared such an implication at the time. R.J.O. was leading Somerset on the day that Hever, the Middlesex bowler, went off with a damaged hand. The 12th man was Fred Price, the wicket keeper.

According to Hugh Watts, Robins asked Meyer if Price could come on as wicket keeper; that would have allowed Leslie Compton to make one of his rare, but not unknown, appearances as a bowler. 'Not on your life', was the Somerset captain's response. 'Right, then,' said Robins with a fiery irony in the voice. 'Just watch this!'

He opened with Laurie Gray. Then Compton, who had kept wicket for the over, took off his pads to send down the next six balls. It was a laborious process, both irritating and mildly comic. And mercifully it didn't go on for too long.

Meyer could be opinionated. He was a strong advocate for a 2nd XI when Somerset didn't have one; he called himself a rebel by nature and admitted that he sometimes made mistakes. Significantly he was mostly liked by the professionals, even if they sighed at some of his unorthodox theories. But, then, his cricket was not for a moment hamstrung by orthodoxy. His best ball was the one that swung late from leg; yet his challenge to the batsman would sometimes incorporate, partly out of sheer devilment we suspect, six completely different deliveries. It could be hard on Luckes. His admiration for the small stumper was boundless and, maybe with a pang of guilt, he opened a fund to commemorate Luckes' record-breaking dismissals for the county.

The pity is that Rollo John Oliver Meyer played only sixty-five times for Somerset. In that time he scored nearly 3,000 runs for them by attractive and resourceful means; he also took more than 400 first-class wickets. If he hadn't gone off to India before the war, he could have earned Test recognition. It was the kind of status predicted for him during his Cambridge days.

His influence was usually stimulating but it is highly debatable whether his appointment in 1947 as captain was wise. The county dropped to joint eleventh. Somerset were beaten in a day at Chesterfield; at Bristol, they were spun out for 25 and the square at Nevil Road was pointedly compared to the sands at Weston-super-Mare. It seemed like an unwarranted libel on the resort where for generations small boys had amassed vast scores while the token tide stayed out of sight.

There were still almost 1,000 runs from Walford in his restricted appearances, and a good hundred from George Woodhouse, the wartime Cambridge batsman who was being lobbied as a future captain of the county. At Lord's, at the start of the season, Maurice Tremlett made a heroic entry. It was a magnificent match and Tremlett, the former office boy at Taunton, won it with a few calculated blows at the end, clean and handsome. He'd already sent back five Middlesex batsmen, including Denis Compton for 8 runs, in a 5 over spell.

As the tall, blond Tremlett came off the field at the end, accompanied by the ever-reliable tailender Hazell, the home players lined up to applaud the newcomer. The newspapers became lyrical; his pads were hardly off before premature comparisons were being made with Tate. As in the case of Gimblett, it was too heady a performance, too high a standard at the outset. Yet 1947 threw up no single individual feat to match it; and at Lord's. Soon this amiable young man, not long out of the army, would be off to the Caribbean under Gubby Allen. It will be time later to shed our tears.

In this same 1947 summer came Miles Coope, Eric Hill and Les Angell – and out went Lee and Andrews.

Coope came from Lawrence's league territory in Yorkshire. He promised much during his three seasons with Somerset. As a batsman his range of shots was ambitious and he had one of the most delicate late cuts ever paraded in the West. There were two centuries from him but he was also a luxury, never quite consistent or disciplined enough with his repertoire to make a successful county cricketer. Hill, from Taunton School, was also rather a disappointment. He was a tall, upright opening batsman of undisputed correctness and style; he had injuries and little luck, when one remembers the succession of agile catches that dismissed him. His fielding, initially in the deep and then at short leg, was always an asset. An intelligent, sensitive man, he valued what he called the chivalry in the game then.

We were playing Hampshire and their splendid little wicket keeper Neil McCorkell was playing. I pushed a ball into the covers and thought about a run. Then I moved back without grounding my bat. 'Come on, get your bat down', he whispered. That was one struggling pro (me) against an established player. It doesn't happen today.

The farewells were as ever sad. Lee got a benefit (£4,014), partly organised with one of the game's many ironies by his departing colleague, Andrews. He'd reached 1,000 runs in a season eight times and once got to 2,000. His 15,000 or so runs had been compiled with a rather dour devotion. He became a first-class umpire of constant merit and stood in twenty-nine Tests.

Andrews was given a testimonial for the following year, though he wasn't too pleased with the conditions. Nor did he enjoy his participation in team affairs during his final season. At the age of thirty-nine he reckoned the action was still reassuringly high but it wasn't of much use when you were destined to bring out the drinks for most of the time. He'd sensed from early summer that he was due to be fired. The vigour and verve had gone from his personality; his face betrayed his inner feelings as he reluctantly came to accept that the romance of cricket that had been his life was coming to an end. But, of course, he'd be back: as a coach, committee man, counsellor to the dozens of schoolboy players, and incorrigible supporter. He would go on speaking his mind, charming his adversaries, making good and bad judgements (always positive ones), persuading Brian Close to come to Somerset, and inviting anyone within earshot to 'shake the hand that bowled Bradman'.

CHAPTER THIRTEEN

All Those Captains . . .

Surrealism takes over again when we come to 1948. It was the season when the committee claimed they were forced to have three captains. Don't you believe it; there were at least five. Take into account makeshift skippers for the occasional afternoon and the total is near seven. But let us start with *three.* The trouble was that the county couldn't find anyone of suitable pedigree who could make himself available for the whole summer. So they ingeniously chopped the season into three.

Mitchell-Innes, home from the Sudan, agreed to take over first. 'I arrived in March and helped set up the pre-season work. I stayed till the end of May and then handed over to Jake Seamer. Thoroughly enjoyed it. Great fun.' It must be said, alas, that early results didn't reflect this delightful ebullience. Somerset didn't pick up a single point from the opening five fixtures.

Within the transitory conditions of the job, Mitchell-Innes was quite a popular skipper; so was Seamer who said: 'My friends were the pros. Spirit was good whatever the strains on continuity. The players were great ones for singing on the train . . . Horace and the others.' After him, officially, came Woodhouse, who was to take over on a more permanent basis for the following year.

You would have thought that Somerset could have managed with three of them, but Watts was asked to help them out of an embarrassing emergency. 'We need you, Hugh, to lead the county against Hampshire at Bath.' Whatever the circumstances it was a flattering invitation and he was grateful that a sympathetic headmaster at Downside allowed him to ditch his history lessons for three days. Sadly he was out without scoring in the first innings. It was raining when he got to the ground on the final day. Lofty Herman was standing in front of the pavilion, with a worldly smile on his face. 'It's rare weather, skipper, for bagging a pair!' You could say the psychology had a slightly harsh edge to it. Watts avoided another duck when play restarted and offered up a silent prayer. He was sometimes known as 'The Abbot' because Andrews and his mates used to notice the Benedictine monks wandering around in their black habits whenever the team visited Downside.

Castle was also captain during that desultory, oddball summer. He led some choruses from his beloved Gilbert and Sullivan on away matches and usually carried a pack of cards for a few impromptu tricks when the rain came. They say he was in the Cec Parkin and Jack Mercer class for magic.

There were only four centuries by Somerset – and Gimblett scored them all. Commentators were saying, with some validity, that he was carrying the county's batting. He said he felt the strain of it. At the inquest, following his suicide in 1978, the coroner discussed the implications of such a responsibility over the years.

Gimblett's biggest and most historic innings, though not necessarily his best, was the 310 against Sussex at Eastbourne in the August. It was the highest since cricket had resumed after the war, and was, until 1985 – when Viv Richards scored 322 against Warwickshire – the highest by a Somerset player. Harold was apt to exaggerate and dramatise incidents that involved himself. But two concerned with that massive innings are well worth recalling.

At the time I was writing his biography, he told me:

> I stayed on the field for 17 hours 50 minutes and do you know I was then allowed ten minutes off by my captain to shower and change before I was needed back on the field. . . . And this will give you some idea of what the club thought of the professionals. Arthur Wellard went to see the secretary and asked if they'd allow a collection around the ground for me back in Taunton because I'd just made 300. The answer was no – I was paid to do that.

The Australians came to the county ground right at the end of the season. They were a marvellous touring side and were in no mood for levity and the sacrificing of a superb playing record. As it was, they won by an innings and 374 runs. They did it without Don Bradman; but Lindsay Hassett led the side on his birthday and celebrated with a hundred. Somerset were bowled out twice in under four hours and it was all over by teatime on the Monday. The Australians had declared at 560-5 and everyone from Wiveliscombe to West Chinnock went home lyrically extolling the exceptional promise of a nineteen-year-old century-maker called Neil Harvey.

None of the home bowlers got anywhere at all, apart from Jim Redman, an honest, persevering, unexceptional seamer from Bath, only a little above medium pace, who took three of the five Tourists' wickets to fall.

The Aussies as usual were complimentary about the Taunton wicket. Keith Miller, whose typically relaxed visit to the West Country had lacked too much physical exertion, turned to head groundsman Buttle. 'Well done, Cec – just like one of ours back home.' They were always saying that; The Don had, on an earlier acquaintanceship with this true, at times too docile, track, offered as much praise.

Tremlett, fast-medium and with the broad-shouldered build to match, bowled well without any real luck at all. He ended the season with 80 wickets (average 24.82). The two slow bowlers, Hazell and Lawrence, had edged above him in the final averages; all three showed genuine consistency. Tremlett, by now a new hero, not least for his striking presence and penchant for effortless straight drives that thudded against the tough fabric high on the sightscreen, was to be rewarded with an invitation to go on his second successive MCC tour, this time to South Africa.

The small, squat, gentle Luckes had played much of the time. But Stephenson had now arrived from Durham and was being significantly and tactfully eased into the team as the new wicket keeper. His approach was rather different; he was more nimble, of course, and batted with an exciting, slightly reckless relish that seldom rejected the gamble of a perilously possible single. He possessed the technical knowledge and the intuition of a fine wicket keeper. He missed little and didn't show off. As a batsman, his pads always looked too big for him. The style could be suspect; the eye was sharp and the enjoyment, especially in early evening when late-order batters were meant to be strong in the arm and not statuesque, was evident for all to see.

Because this was Somerset, traditionally full of winks and nods, team selection continued to carry an element of surprise. John Barnwell had had one season with the county after the war and was now living in Liverpool. 'When Somerset were due to play in Lancashire, I contacted Jake Seamer – it was during his term as skipper. I told him I was up there and would he like to stay with us? As an afterthought, I implied I'd be available!'

That was good enough for Jake. Barnwell came in for his only match of the season and his last for Somerset. It was a soft, drying wicket at Liverpool, much to the liking of Roberts (7-47). The slow left-arm bowler twice got Barnwell; Somerset lost by an innings.

Gimblett walked away with the batting honours again in 1949; he did it at his own predetermined pace, and that was often very fast indeed. Opposing new-ball bowlers were never allowed the indulgence of range-finders. Some of Gimblett's cover drives could be as sweet as Hammond's. His hooks were as pugnacious as they were cussed; he scattered the spectators beyond long leg and the glint of satisfaction in his eyes revealed that his memory was long and that was his contemptuous answer to MCC-tied elders who once told him to forget the shot altogether. His aggregate of more than 2,000 runs that summer was a Somerset record. There were five centuries, most of them fashioned with the beauty of innate stroke play; two of them came in the match with Hampshire at Taunton. He was to score two hundreds in another match at headquarters three years later, this time against Derbyshire.

For a long time in 1949 there wasn't a great deal to remember with particular pride. The county started with five defeats; then through much of June and the whole of July they lost ten matches in a melancholy row. Loyal West Country scribes were struggling for generous things to say. It was easier when the schoolmasters turned up. They – and the rest of the team – sniffed the invigorating sea breezes and got to work. A depressing playing record was turned on its head; there were three wins for Somerset at Weston, and another at Clacton. Sussex narrowly averted the same unseemly treatment at Eastbourne.

Gimblett, for all his handsome runs, was happy to concede a generous share of the retrieved season's honours to Hazell. The two, hardly alike in temperament, remained firm friends for most of the time. 'We only had one serious row during our joint playing career,' said Hazell. 'It was all very childish and we didn't speak to each other for a few days. Then our wives sorted it out. We shook hands on the spot.'

It was Horace's benefit year in 1949 and he took more than 100 wickets for the first time. Once, during a Bank Holiday match with Gloucestershire, Hammond was heard to say: 'I wish I had that little chap in our side – he's as good as anyone in the country when it comes to slow left-arm.' Hazell also lifted morale with his jokey ways. He considered his batting deserved greater recognition, and elevation in the order to go with it. 'Don't be fooled by my comfortable build – just remember that Harold always chooses me as his runner when he's limping.' It was an argument that defied logic but couldn't be discounted. Horace was apt to be first to the bar, additional evidence of his athleticism, and liked to lead the community singing after a victory. When rain was needed – either to save Somerset from defeat on the third day or to offer encouragement to the spinners – he'd wrap a towel around his head, turn to Allah and silence the fellow occupants of the dressing room with his wailing incantations. Fellow pros swear that it worked on at least one occasion.

This was the June, in 1949, when he sent down 105 balls (17.3 overs) without giving away a run. Famous Gloucestershire batsmen like Tom Graveney treated him with inordinate respect. The concentration, by bowler and batsmen, took on an unusual intensity. A holiday crowd, at first impatient, became absorbed by the *lack* of scoring. The young Somerset player, Leslie Angell, recalled years later: 'There was a remarkable tension among the fielders as the maidens increased. We were all so anxious not to be guilty of breaking the sequence by any error on our part.'

Lawrence, even smaller and slower than Hazell – and he tossed the ball higher – also exceeded 100 wickets in all first-class matches. Apart from Gimblett, Buse and Tremlett topped 1,000 runs. The talented, over-ambitious Coope had done so the previous year; now, like Luckes and Wellard, he wasn't to be re-engaged. Somerset could profitably have held on to Wellard longer: their judgement was often at fault when it came to saying goodbye. He was less fast and less fit but the heart was as bounteous as ever. There was an ironic twist in that he was needed again in late season after playing for Kidderminster in the League. Arthur took 1,517 wickets for Somerset and almost a quarter of his 11,432 runs came from sixes. Not once did he lose his enthusiasm as a cricketer – nor his skill with a pack of cards.

Woodhouse, a promising player at Marlborough and wartime Cambridge, did his greatest service to Somerset in giving them the luxury of a single captain in 1949. He was an unassuming, unspectacular skipper, the youngest in the county's history, and he deserves some credit for gradually finding the best blend from an indeterminate team. For the next three years, S. S. Rogers was the captain. His appointment occasioned some surprise but Woodhouse was heading for the brewery business and a full-time career away from cricket. It wasn't easy to find a successor in those days. The old-style amateur of independent means was a fast disappearing species. But Stuart Rogers, the young good-looking Chindits major, was now out of the army and ready to give it a go. He was a modest player, in the technical first-class sense; he batted with a bold and optimistic front-foot philosophy.

The crowd quite liked him, though he wasn't wholly one of the boys. 'I found him a pleasant chap and during the time I was senior pro, we got on well. Once or twice he'd ask me to have dinner with him on an away match. We'd have wine on these occasions – wine was the only drink that affected me. It made me as drunk as a handcart! The skipper would come around for me in his little sports car and we'd drive off somewhere to a restaurant,' said Hazell.

Hill, working so hard to ride his bad luck and establish himself as Gimblett's opening partner at the time, feels that Rogers probably lacked rapport with the younger professionals. It was true, of course, of several of the Somerset captains who came and went in the early post-war years. 'We were playing in Hampshire and for some reason Stuart Rogers decided to drop anchor – he imposed a curfew and ordered that everyone should be in bed by ten o'clock. The skipper plotted his evening accordingly and staggered up to bed at half-past nine . . . more drunk than anyone I've ever seen in my life!'

Rogers' record wasn't a bad one. He immediately lifted the county up the table to seventh position. There were three lively – and, some would ungraciously suggest, rather lucky – hundreds from him. One was against the South Africans. Another against Northants at Glastonbury in Gimblett's benefit match of 1952, was joyfully memorable for the fact that the last 50 came in half an hour. I was there to see it – and there was celebration at the ancient George and Pilgrim afterwards. He took a farm near Taunton for a time and was only thirty when he retired from county cricket. By the age of forty-six he was sadly dead.

In 1950 he had been one of four Somerset batsmen to pass 1,000 runs and his seventh wicket stand of 182 with Stephenson at Frome was frequently a thrilling crash-bang affair which threatened the record partnership of Woods and Vernon Hill fifty-two years earlier. Tremlett hit three hundreds with a full, clean straight swing of the bat. He was always inclined to make deep long-off and long-on redundant when he was going well. Lawrence had his best season and missed the double by 19 runs.

Brig E. H. Lancaster stepped down as secretary. Much of his time was given for the club; he was a diligent administrator who occasionally irritated those who misinterpreted his precise, military manner which he had acquired in the Indian Army. The barriers between him and a few of the professionals were not of his choosing. He didn't always find it easy to mix. An old friend of his said:

> Lanky was very generous to Somerset with his time and, in effect, money. He did an invaluable job in keeping the club going at a very difficult time. Lanky was a good secretary, though for someone as cricket-crazy as himself, he probably preferred watching on a sunny afternoon to working away in the office. When he was in India, he was a very good club cricketer.

The Brigadier was a distinctive figure, strolling around the county ground. He was tall, lean and erect; later he still came but was pushed in a wheelchair. His quiet enthusiasm for the game never lessened. More than twenty years after he'd retired I asked him for a memory from those days.

> Soon after I took over, I found out that the vice-presidents and VIPs on the ground were getting a different menu from the ordinary members. I changed that – and there were some complaints. Some people stormed off to see the president. And he told them: 'If you have a bloody brigadier for a secretary, you have to put up with it!'

What is there to say of 1951? Somerset were getting edgy about long-term prospects: short term, too. Harry Parks, the former Sussex professional, was brought in as coach. Ellis Robinson was here, by way of Yorkshire, to bolster the bowler and the close catching. The crafty old off-spinner wasn't obtaining as much turn as he used to, at least not until he reached Weston where he finished with a splendid 15-78 match analysis against Sussex. As for Tremlett, there was no more realistic thought of a career as a bowler for England; but his batting was at times tantalisingly near to Test calibre. He scored more than 2,000 runs, most of them assembled in a most attractive fashion. He 'read' the bowling so well, knew when to withdraw from a contemplated assault and was frequently the best straight-driver in the country. He made exhilarating sixes look like a controlled golf chip.

Fifteen matches were lost. One was against Worcestershire at Taunton. They needed 5 runs off the last ball and Buse, with his quaint, stuttering run and a perceptive nature that didn't often let him down, was bowling. Rogers had ensured that the boundary was well populated. It didn't help – Bob Wyatt braced himself and heaved the ball straight into the pavilion for six.

We come to 1952, the first of four seasons when Somerset were bottom of the championship table. It was, even if viewed in relation to some of the inept, lackadaisical offerings of earlier years, surely the county's nadir. Crowds were small, faces were long. There were accusing fingers and interfering vice-presidents. Committee meetings were taut if not bad tempered. 'What's happened to our so-called recruitment policy? Where's our pace attack? Where's the will to win?'

Roy Smith, on an extended trial and not short of application, clearly wasn't going to end up another Hazell. Malcolm Walker, an off-spinner, was destined to make a modest impact. Local boy John Harris was brought in speculatively at the age of sixteen, the same age as another Somerset debutant and subsequent umpire, Alan Whithead, five years later. Angell, neat, stylish, thoughtfully wary against the new ball, was never able to reproduce his prolific scoring at club level for Lansdown. The hopes had been that he might take over the Lee role as Gimblett's opening partner. It was almost achieved on occasions; the unassuming Angell, a right-hander unlike Lee, had a sharp eye and played the ball well through the off-side. He even once or twice outscored Gimblett: the response from the other end was a mildly disapproving glance.

Harold turned it on for his benefit at Glastonbury and scored a hundred in the second innings. But later he went on record as saying: 'I'd wanted the Gloucestershire game at Taunton for my benefit but was told the county couldn't afford it. Morlands did their best for me at Glastonbury but I ended up with a net profit of between £7 and £8 on the three days.'

The West Country crowds, especially the schoolboys, still loved him. He completed 20,000 runs that summer; against Derby at Taunton he went like the wind in a second-wicket stand of 200 with Gerry Tordoff, a capable left-hander who played for Cambridge that year. Tordoff could probably have established himself in the Somerset side and tightened up his technical approach to batting. Instead he signed for a three-year commission in the Royal Navy. He still managed to obtained a partial release to captain the county in 1955 – more of that later.

Stephenson, positively impish, hit a maiden century against Glamorgan to lift the gloom for at least one evening. Lawrence not only scampered for his first hundred in the match with the Indians, he did it again with undisguised elation against Essex. But Robinson was now on his way from Somerset – and so was Hazell.

As in the case of Wellard, Hazell's departure wasn't the wisest of decisions. Mobility, seldom a conspicuous asset, was on more of a decline. But he was still top of the bowling averages, still pitching on the same blade of grass and saying to himself: 'If only my fingers were bigger, I'd spin the ball more.'

The county did, in fact, offer him match terms but that was really no way to see out an old pro. 'When I heard, I sought out the president, Major Longrigg, and went into a huddle with him at Weston. He looked sad and said that the committee had agreed to start from scratch again, even if it meant being on the bottom for three years.' The following season Hazell was asked to go back and look after the Dragons, a team of potential county players, some of whom were qualifying. Sometimes he played, sometimes he umpired, always he advised; he loved it. But that official talk of 'starting from scratch' must have seemed odd to him as the county went on signing older players.

It was back to musical chairs when it came to the captaincy in 1953. The new leader was another surprise, Ben Brocklehurst, later to become the managing director and proprietor of *The Cricketer* magazine. He was an assertive middle-order club batsman; as a county player he ended with an average of just under 16 from sixty-four matches. Brocklehurst was seen by some of the players as a stern disciplinarian. It could be argued that his own nondescript form worked against his authority. He had crosses to bear, not least the fluctuating temperament of Gimblett, his senior pro.

There were two wins for Somerset during the whole of 1953, one of them against Middlesex at Lord's. It called for a neat, ironic gesture from Brocklehurst.

> We actually found ourselves in the position of needing only 8 runs with all our second innings' wickets standing. As we came off the field, the Lord's head groundsman asked which roller we'd like. I pointed to the largest one and asked for it to be given the full time. Thus nine men pushed the heavy roller . . . so that we could get those 8 runs.

But mostly it was demoralising stuff. Matches finished in two days, which was good for travel arrangements and bad for livers. And as anyone in Bath – and Buse, with feeling – will tell you, Lancashire's visit to the Recreation Ground lasted only *one* day. It was all over by teatime – and it was Buse's benefit match. Roy Tattersall headed for home with a haul of 13-69 and a shirt not even sweat stained. Buse was left gazing forlornly out across the newly laid square.

Cecil Buttle, the county's head groundsman, takes up the calamitous tale.

> There were panic stations – after all, there were two more matches to go at Bath. I was sent across from Taunton on the Sunday, and Johnny Lawrence, who had a caravan at headquarters like me, also came. There were acorns and gravel on the wicket and we raked all this off. I realised I had to take drastic action, and I decided on plenty of liquid marl and cow manure. We used a watering can to spread it across the wicket. The problem was knowing how to camouflage what we'd done. Then I hit on the use of cut grass. I sprinkled it all over the top and gave it a good roll. The weather was fine, so that helped. Johnny and I worked till nearly ten at night . . . I was sweating on it but everything was fine.

Buse had been a loyal and valuable all-rounder and of course he deserved better than a one-day benefit. He was to leave at the end of the season, with a creditable 10,623 runs and 657 wickets to his name. His style, whether in that quaint, stuttering run-up to the wicket or the posterior-protruding stance as he prepared to prod, was his own. He could be an immensely important member of the side without the merest flourish of the extrovert. He was utterly unflurried as a batsman. He had a sense of dignity and for some peculiar reason didn't approve of the evocative way John Arlott likened him to a butler bringing out the tea.

Battles with Gloucestershire – and what was that about crowding the bat? The fielders close in on left-hander Andy Wilson as Malcolm Walker, the bowler, strives for a vital late catch, in 1953

This time, a few years later, Dennis Silk swoops for the catch. Brian Langford is the bowler, Arthur Milton the batsman on his way

We could write a whole book about the Bath Festival of 1953: not only of Bertie's empty pocket or the Air Vice-Marshal's secretarial instructions to Cec Buttle to 'do something about that wicket – and quickly'.

It was here that a fresh-faced seventeen-year-old lad, just about to do his National Service, made his debut as an unknown off-spinner and took 26 wickets in three matches. Brian Langford was to stay twenty-one years as a player and harvest 1,390 wickets for the county. It was here at Bath, too, that Tremlett was fielding at silly mid-off to a young Kent opening bat, Woollett, who suddenly shifted from dour introspection to off-side venom. The ball hit Tremlett on the forehead and went on to the boundary. His sinus bone was splintered and one of the eyes was partially dislodged. It was a sickening injury; it kept him in hospital for several months and he used to joke truthfully, with the murky humour beloved by professional sportsmen, that his operation was well charted in the *Lancet*. The blow would have destroyed a lesser cricketer in the psychological sense. Tremlett adjusted his batting technique a little and got on with it again in 1954. In a confidential aside, over a beer, he'd say: 'It's never been quite the same. I'm troubled by my left eye and something has gone from my natural, attacking play.'

Tom Hall arrived from Derbyshire for a couple of seasons, to give a little more pace. The diminutive Smith showed up at times as a batsman, achieving his maiden century and a county cap. He grafted for 77 against the Australians. But that brings us to a lithe, slightly built newcomer, Peter Wight. He'd come over from British Guiana to make an instant impression as a league cricketer with Burnley.

The county decided they wanted a look at him and pitched him in against the Aussies. Almost at once he was caught in the slips: absolutely no sign of the jaunty stroke play on which his recommendation had been based.

'That evening arrangements had been made for us to play the Australians at skittles in a country pub. I must have been looking a bit down in the mouth because Richie Benaud tried to console me. He told me not to worry and that I'd get a hundred in the second innings. And I did – 109 not out.'

Rural junketing and crystal gazing with the Aussies were fun, but there wasn't too much of that. Many, close to the county club, were taking an increasingly pessimistic view. By lack of foresight and vision, was Somerset really running down this time? Was this to be the crisis they wouldn't survive for long?

CHAPTER FOURTEEN
The Passion of the Press

Journalists are readily, conveniently blamed for much that is wrong in sport. They are accused of failing to write and think constructively and not having the clubs at heart. This patently wasn't true in the case of three newspapermen in the autumn of 1953. They all cared passionately about Somerset. And they all feared that short of a major shake-up, the county was heading for untold disaster and maybe oblivion.

The late Ron Roberts was the spearhead – resourceful and determined. His journalistic pals and fellow rebels – as they were inevitably called – were Eric Hill, the former opening bat, and Bob Moore. They all worked then on provincial papers in the West Country. 'The three of them are only looking for headlines and personal glory', thundered the Taunton reactionaries. That was a petty, unjustified view to take.

Hill remembers the whole experience, with mixed feelings of pain, indignation and satisfaction.

> We were desperately worried about the state of Somerset cricket – not just the financial position but the lack of results and the overall bleakness. So, with Ron as the instigator, we decided to do something about it. We called a special meeting, at the Corfield Hall in Taunton. The place was packed and there was an incredible atmosphere. In any case, feelings were so intense that Taunton itself was like two armed camps. Bob made the main speech for us, a particularly good one, calling for reorganisation and a new approach. We won the meeting over by a distance.

But the three believed any improvements might be no more than cosmetic; they were dismayed by the way the county had presented their case. Any half-hearted promises by the committee to change direction a fraction or two were seen by the newspapermen as futile. They decided another public meeting was necessary. This time they would sweepingly ask for a vote of no confidence in those who ran the club. They believed that the only way to revitalise Somerset was to get rid of the present committee altogether.

There followed frantic lobbying on both sides. At one stage the county vetoed the trio's requisition for the meeting on the ground that some of the signatories weren't paid-up members. 'We'll call the meeting instead', they insisted.

The meeting was staged, rather stage-managed, with cold, Machiavellian ingenuity. As an example of domestic duplicity, some would claim it was unsurpassed in a long history of Somerset that was never wholly distanced from the narrow-eyed craft of cunning.

Hill again:

> The choice of venue was a cheat in our opinion. It was the Town Hall, Weston-super-Mare at 5.30 on a Friday night in November. There weren't so many cars about in those days and many working people had great difficulty getting there. A large number were ruled out.
>
> The Bishop of Bath and Wells had been brought in as the chairman, to stack the status-quo balance even more against us. There the committee sat, in a long, elevated row, looking down in all their wisdom on the plebs. Ben Brocklehurst had always asked us not to attack the players and we felt he might be on our side. But the first person asked by the Bishop to make a speech was Ben – and he delivered a blast of criticism against the three of us. He suggested we were misguided and referred to us as Faith, Hope and Charity. It was absolutely shattering. A few spoke up for us but of course the whole committee voted for themselves. We still only lost by fifty votes. The whole thing depressed us. We felt we had been stuffed by the way everything was very carefully loaded against us. If only the county had exercised as much ingenuity in running the club successfully.

In retrospect, many came to admire the stand – and the ethics – of the journalists. They had, for instance, taken legal advice at one stage and could have contested the way their move for a second meeting was superseded by the club. 'We hated the idea of dragging the county through the courts.'

One amusing margin note to the whole, unedifying business came when the Somerset establishment, very much on the defensive, produced an impressive and no doubt costly printed record, glowingly listed, of the committee's achievements.

> We looked at it in horror and realised it needed answering point by point. So we got to work, far more modestly, on the duplicating machine. Numerous members gave us money to cover the cost of stationery and postage. Maurice Tremlett was getting half a crown an hour for sending out the county's statement of attainment. Then he was coming into the *Gazette* office to help Ron, Bob and myself send out our version!

A good deal less amusing was one businessman's efforts to get Roberts sacked from the *Evening World*, Moore from the *Evening Post* and Hill from the *County Gazette*.

The likeable Roberts went on to become a highly respected national cricket writer and tour manager until his untimely death. Moore also went to Fleet Street and later worked as a press officer at Scotland Yard. Hill remains a distinguished and venerable occupant of the Taunton press box.

SOME FINE SOMERSET BOWLERS

(*Clockwise from top left*) Bill Greswell – if
only he had played more often; Bryan Lobb
– a fine season in 1957; Fred Rumsey –
from Worcestershire to Somerset and
England; Hallam Moseley – good on
bowling action and PR; Ken Palmer –
deserved more than one Test

They were three Taunton boys who decided they had to show their considerable affection for Somerset County Cricket Club in their own challenging way.

They lost the second vote but their work wasn't wasted. Their intrepid assault on a complacent set-up brought gradual improvement. Roberts and Moore were elected to the committee, Hill made captain of the 2nd XI. It was apparently too much for one member, Brig E. H. C. Frith who, before a meeting at the Castle Hotel, asked if he might speak. The chairman didn't seem to be taken by surprise. Frith wondered aloud whether it might be a good thing if members of the press would consider it advisable to resign from the committee if they had critical views to express. It looked like another snub for the journalists. Roberts, with a fine sense of both timing and irony, said: 'I second that, sir.' So three newspapermen's independence wasn't imperilled.

A new vitality was hardly discernible in 1954. Somerset had a noticeably larger professional staff but still occupied the bottom position. Angell was sensibly recalled and had his best season. A sixteen-year-old from Yorkshire, Graham Atkinson, who preferred scoring through the leg side, came in for his first game and looked a batsman of distinct promise. There were other new names: Geoff Lomax, Jim Hilton, the Australian John McMahon and Yawar Saeed. Wight didn't know what to make of some of the green, seaming wickets but still made more than 1,300 runs.

Stephenson was a joy in tandem with Lawrence. The prodigious leg-break would beat the bat and 'Steve' would knock off the bails with the merest flick. The glee on Lawrence's face as an exasperated batsman pounded forward and missed . . . the sweet anticipation and co-ordination of Stephenson . . . the collective chuckles at an opponent's discomfiture. Stephenson had eighty-nine victims that summer – and the next was Dawkes with 65.

Gimblett left for good after the Yorkshire match at the start of the season. He said he couldn't take any more. There had been breakdowns, and private and public misery. Few who watched his brilliance – fast, stylish, bonny batsmanship, full of sunshine – had any inkling of his mental battles. He played only three times for England and, in fact, manifested a disinclination to appear at the highest level. Nor did a withering, tactless turn of phrase in the surrounds of Lord's help. He was a minor public schoolboy, intelligent and acutely sensitive. For reasons not always easy to explain, he retained obsessive complexes about class, money and health.

The Somerset public loved him. His forty-nine hundreds for the county – and 23,007 first-class runs – reveal how much they leaned on him. In the March of 1978, by then living with his devoted wife in a mobile home at Verwood near Ringwood (he had chosen to get away from his native county and talk of cricket), he took an overdose of drugs, just as Robertson-Glasgow had. He'd been suffering greatly from arthritis and his inner torment hadn't eased. A memorial service was held back in Taunton and the church overflowed with old players and friends, just as it had when Sammy Woods was buried in the town.

Tordoff led the county in 1955 and they stayed on the bottom for a fourth year. He was a personable rather than an astute captain. Some of the committee found him a rather too convenient scapegoat. A former player said: 'It was hard to see who was around to take over from Ben. Gerry was a goodish player but he still had a bad side around him. It was terribly unjust that he should have been blamed as much as he was.'

Captaincy had, ever since the war – some would say before the turn of the century – been a matter of recurrent concern. There were no longer amateurs with the necessary time and money to spare. Somerset had suffered more than most because of an appalling lack of continuity. So the appointment of Tremlett in 1956 was a glowing landmark of sanity and social change. He was the county's first professional skipper.

He did the job for the next four years. It wasn't without blemish or criticism. He was tentative with some of his earlier decisions over declarations and team-mates gave him long, despairing looks. His batting was never quite consistent enough. But, in retrospect, one can make out a strong case that he was the best captain Somerset ever had. Few had a sharper tactical sense; he knew and played on the technical weaknesses of opposing batsmen; he loathed futile draws and tried to keep the matches entertainingly poised till the last few minutes.

No longer did he have his bowling to worry about. The decline had started when his admirer Gubby Allen took him to the West Indies. He was told he should attempt to bowl faster out there; he added four paces to his run-up, lost his stride and for ever after his confidence. Supporters remember with genuine sadness the embarrassing loss of line and length, and the afternoons when after yet another sequence of painfully wide deliveries, he put his hands on his hips and looked unseeingly at the ground for what seemed like a minute. In the end he said to his skipper of the day, Tordoff: 'That's it, Gerry. From now on, I'm a batsman only – or I get out altogether.' The abject misery of losing all semblance of fast-bowling technique was to be experienced similarly, in the late seventies, by David Gurr, who had arrived at Somerset from Oxford University with a beautiful action and accompanied by the kind of rational testimony which suggested that he could become an England player.

As captain of Somerset, Tremlett took the county from seventeenth to third in the table. That was in 1958 and, as this history is being written, the county have never been higher. They won twelve games. More significantly, they did it with a touch of bravura. The visible enjoyment took oppositions by surprise. Tremlett was throwing out challenges as if he were leading a side which resided by rights on the upper levels of the championship. His leadership was a restorative to shattered pride. Offsetting the apparently lackadaisical manner and batting that never quite fulfilled the stunning promise paraded at Lord's was a mind finely tuned to the demands of county cricket, if support were to be rekindled and Somerset were to cease to be the subject of snide ridicule.

Much went right in that elusively heady 1958. Wight was at times batting like a dream; his exquisite timing brought him 175 against Surrey. McCool was cutting and pulling in great style. Geoff Lomax, who had come down from Lancashire, was opening the innings and reaching 1,000 runs for the first time. When Stephenson was unfit, Peter Eele was proving a very adequate deputy (and a good enough left-handed batsman to score a subsequent century for the county). Ken Palmer excelled with Dennis Silk in a win against Lancashire and was awarded his county cap. Ken Biddulph made the quiet kind of progress that shouldn't be discounted. Very much as Lobb's deputy, he took 40 wickets in 1958; then came 69 and 83 in the next two seasons. The pace bowler would tell the story of a meeting with Fred Trueman soon after joining Somerset. 'Nowt to worry about, Kenny. You'd get in that bloody team for your batting.'

There was also Langford, keen to demonstrate that he could spin the ball away from Bath. He did it with devastating effect this time at Weston, where the holiday-makers eagerly walked the few hundred yards up from the beach, to arc the ball in at will, just as prodigiously as Laker had a year or two earlier. Langford took 35 wickets in the three matches there, at a cost of 279 runs. His 116 wickets earned him much acclaim and stifled the reservations of those who claimed he lacked variety and sufficient tricks.

It wasn't all success under Tremlett by any means; he made mistakes. Some felt he had flaws of temperament and occasionally needed a sterner fibre. The fact is that he demonstrated, and very well indeed, that a professional could do the job. No longer was there a case for the county's starchier establishment figures to go on a vain treasure-hunt around the country to find an amateur with the right pedigree and at least a token willingness to pretend that we were still living in the twenties or thirties.

In the run-up to that 1958 summer, there were flickering signs of optimism. Malcolm Walker from Yorkshire held out deceptive hopes with a hundred against Essex. Lewis Pickles, from the same hotbed in the North, scored 1,000 runs in his first full season. Chris Greetham arrived, a dashing cover point and a good-looking batsman through the off side. He'd been a diamond sorter and a teacher, and – much more appealing to us journalists – a film extra. Tremlett knew how to get the best from him as a medium-paced bowler. Silk was certainly captaincy material and led the MCC teams in North America and New Zealand. But school life had to come first. As a batsman he was a fighter; as a fielder he was a short leg of sharp reflexes and courage. He was as prized as an after-dinner speaker as he was a county cricketer. Somerset would have liked to have been able to call on him far more often. There were seven first-class hundreds, only one alas for his county.

Graham Atkinson (yes, another Yorkshireman) scored his maiden century for Somerset in 1956 at the age of eighteen. It was the first of his twenty-one for the county. As an opening batsman he was always being tipped as a future Test player. That he failed is a matter of regret; so, in the minds of many supporters, was the fact that he left the county to play eventually for Lancashire for three more seasons. He was predominantly an on-side player, watchful and composed. Eight times for Somerset he passed 1,000 runs; it was 2,000 in 1961 and 1962. There were big stands with Virgin – the striking was apt to be better than the running between the wickets – Alley and Wight. He put on 300 with Wight for the third wicket against Glamorgan at Bath; this remained a record until beaten by Roebuck and Crowe in 1984.

Characters in the fraught fifties? Not so many, but one was Bryan Lobb. He smoked a pipe and good-natured sceptics were surprised that it ever reached his mouth because of his singular lack of co-ordination. It was evident in his fielding as he changed course a dozen times while the ball trickled straight to him at long-leg. He turned ungainliness into an art form. He was all arms and legs and gargantuan groans of anguish as he missed the ball. His batting was stunningly grotesque; the surprise was that bat and ball ever found a meeting point. But his bowling was a different proposition. The action wasn't quite classic, the skills were undeniable. He obtained swing into the bat, and bounce. In 1957 he became the county's first fast bowler since the war to take 100 wickets for the county – and Warwickshire, who let him go after one match, must have surveyed the statistic with retrospective surprise. His 369 wickets for Somerset were taken with an unassuming smile on his face.

'Lobby' was not averse to self-mockery. His judgement over a single or his general mobility between the wickets could be abysmal. He was once run out at Chesterfield, he admits, by deepish mid-on who overtook him ambling down the track from the bowler's end, and broke the wicket. That is a feat not easily achieved, even by a Somerset No 11.

Lobb was to be a schoolmaster, and no doubt a popular one. So was Tom Dickinson, who had a few games for Lancashire and a few more for Somerset about this time. My lasting impressions were of his distinct ability as a pace bowler and of his unconventional batting. More than once I saw him switch from left to right hand in the middle of an over – not to attempt the contentious reverse sweep but to deceive the fielders and show he could play the cover drive on both sides. They used to say he could also bowl with either hand.

Dickinson came originally from Parramatta, Australia, so it's as neat a moment as any to turn to the county's 'Digger' connection in those post-war years: John McMahon, Colin McCool and Bill Alley. No, that isn't all; but Greg Chappell and Kerry O'Keeffe can come a little later.

McMahon was first. He bowled left-arm slow, not always similarly. His length was sound and his intentions carried an Aussie competitiveness. By the time he got to Taunton he'd already played eighty-four matches for Surrey. He was a self-contained man who didn't need too much instruction; he took the ball and knew what was expected of it. In his second season for Somerset he spun out Kent at Yeovil with an 8-46 analysis. The next year was his best with more than 100 wickets. He still took 81 in 1957 but had gone by the end of the summer.

McCool was past forty when he had his first match for Somerset. He was a

Colin McCool is Somerset's acting captain and leads them on to the field for the visit of the South Africans to Taunton in 1960. (*Left to right*) Ken Biddulph, Roy Virgin, Peter Wight, Brian Langford, Peter Eele (partly hidden), Geoff Keith, Bill Alley, Alan Whitehead (hidden), McCool, Chris Greetham and Graham Atkinson

chunky, fair-skinned figure who had jaunty mannerisms with bat and ball. Off the field he was a quiet man, and it wasn't too surprising that he ended up a market gardener when he returned to Australia.

Somerset crowds have always liked a leg-spinner. It was true in the days of Braund and later when it came to the diminutive Cameron – before he lost the knack – and Lawrence. They liked to see McCool being given the ball. But in truth his value to the county was as a batsman. His 219 wickets for Somerset, over his five years, were expensively acquired. He could do beguiling things with the ball, though length and line seemed to become a decreasing consideration. There was nothing much wrong with either when he returned 8-74 against Notts.

As a batsman, he lifted Somerset. His wristy square cuts were as lethal as any in the game. He had the Australian's natural verve for hooking. He topped 1,000 runs each season and missed 2,000 by only 34 runs in 1956. His team-mates watched with envy the way he played the spinners. There are many innings to remember him by: the stand of 215 with Wight at Stourbridge; the two hundreds he so *nearly* made against his Australian pals at Taunton (90 and 116). We'll also remember the rapier sharpness of his reflexes as he stood in the slips, rather deeper than usual. His son, Russel, born in the county town, came over in 1982. The young man also bowled leg-spinners and the visit wasn't exclusively sentimental. Somerset were initially impressed; but he failed to take a wicket in his only senior match and wasn't retained.

William Edward Alley was thirty-eight when he had his first game for Somerset and nearly fifty when he had his last. He never stopped talking, never stopped pulling fours and sixes to mid-wicket and never ceased to thrill a crowd. He had the craggy features and broad-shouldered build of a prizefighter. And that was what he had once been, along with stints as a dance-hall bouncer, blacksmith's striker and boilermaker's mate (not necessarily in that order). He had been playing league cricket for nine years in Lancashire before coming down to Somerset. Not many in the West Country had heard of him when he arrived. He put that right in no time, as he advised opposing captains to populate, as thickly as they reasonably could, the leg-side boundary. Then he started going down on one knee to pull, hook or sweep mischievously between the fielders, or more often over their heads into the beer tent or some other appropriate resting place for the ball.

Alley himself worked up a thirst with a minimum of orthodoxy. But he had a marvellous eye and a sense of discrimination that should never be undervalued. His twenty-four hundreds for Somerset were in the main immensely entertaining. They were normally accompanied by badinage with suffering bowlers, admiring wicket keepers and mesmerised partners. He also spoke his mind, as at the time he made his abrupt and acerbic departure. But mostly it was humour and exciting cricket from this extrovert left-hander.

Somerset began by using him as an opening bat. He did sterling stuff with the wrong technique for the job. The county showed greater wisdom in awarding him his cap after only four matches. It wasn't just his batting; his bowling, rather faster than medium pace, was utterly reliable. Bill's accuracy was legendary and it's said no one ever saw him send down a bad ball. He could swing and seam it. Few batsmen could force the pace against him – and very few escaped if they cut uppishly in the direction of gully when he was fielding there. If you want chapter and verse for his philosophy of non-wastage as a bowler, go to Yeovil in 1960. Against Essex he bowled 93 deliveries in a tidy and vocal row without conceding a run.

But we must come to 1961. The season belonged to his convivial presence. The crease was his God-given territory. He occupied it with the mannerisms of a lusty, lovable black-sheep squire. There were none of the divisive trappings of the elevated landowner. Day after day he went striding out to the wicket as if on a rough shoot with a few of his disreputable aristocratic chums. He wasn't quite top-drawer – that was what everyone found so engaging. He'd cuss, chance his luck socially and reject most of the etiquette.

In 1961, whether as undisputed Squire of Somerset or mighty cricketer (who could probably have reorganised his life a little and played deservedly for Australia), Alley was in every headline. He scored 3,019 runs and came second in the national averages, behind Ken Barrington who compiled 1,000 fewer runs. By any standards – mostly beefy, unconventional ones – he was magnificent. In the May, when still well sweatered, he went up to Nuneaton and scored 221 not out. Many of them, it's true, came from that cherished arc of his, between mid-wicket and long-leg.

'Here, Bill, what's wrong with the off side?' the more brazen Warwickshire supporters would yell, in challenge rather than criticism. And he'd steer the next ball exquisitely between cover and extra with boundless aplomb – and a grin of ironic triumph to match.

He was forty-two at the time, though there was always a fascinating mystique about his age. In any case, he preferred boundaries to singles. 'Got to save me feet for the bowling', he'd say.

During early June, when he was at his most monopolistic, he hit 523 runs and was out only once. When Surrey came to Taunton, he scored 183 not out in the first innings and 134 not out in the second. His fellow Australians knew of his propensity for the leg side and several of them didn't rate him in any sense as Test-match material. Bill could will himself to make the occasional point; this he did without ceremony when the Tourists arrived in Somerset. He took them for 134 and 95. The Sydney patois, they do say, rumbled away joyfully down more than 22 yards of the wicket. His aggregate for the county alone (2,532 runs) was a Somerset record; so was his number of hundreds (eleven).

With so much dominant batting by Alley, aided and abetted by Graham Atkinson and Wight, it's remarkable that the county didn't finish higher than tenth. Yet runs alone were a felicitous bonus, especially as only a few years earlier Surrey had bowled them out for 36 and Hampshire for 37 in successive seasons.

Wight's best summer, glittering with lustrous stroke play, had been in 1960 – though it was in the previous June that with the magic of his wrists and that wondrous ability to hit the ball so well on the up, he hit an undefeated 222 off a Kent attack which in the end was standing back to applaud. The whisper persisted that he recoiled from really fast bowling. That was based on Trueman's success rate against him. Perhaps one can risk prosecution by confirming that Fiery Fred, not the most subtle of adversaries, was Wight's *bête noire*. Most of the evidence reveals just how adeptly the skilful West Indian dealt with pace.

There were seven centuries from him that season. One was against Cambridge; and we shouldn't let the match pass without comment. It was played on the most docile of Taunton wickets; neither side had a particularly strong bowling side. And there were *seven* hundreds. As *Wisden* noted: 'For the first time in cricket history, there were four separate three-figure opening partnerships in a match.'

Cambridge eventually won the extraordinary match by 6 wickets after being left to score 266 in just under three hours. The winning four came in the last over from Richard Bernard, later briefly with Gloucestershire but who, like the Somerset fast bowler Tony Pearson, another Cambridge man, put medicine before county cricket.

In the first innings, Atkinson, Virgin and Wight scored centuries in a total of 418-7 declared. Prideaux, Lewis and Willard responded similarly for

New Somerset coach George Lambert, the former Gloucestershire fast bowler, runs over the training schedule with skipper Maurice Tremlett. Behind them (*left to right*) are Geoff Lomax, Harold Stephenson, Bill Alley and Graham Tripp

Graham Atkinson   Roy Virgin   Chris Greetham

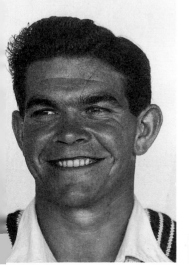  

the University (416-4 declared). Roger Prideaux went on to get a second hundred, this time striking his way on both sides of the wicket and figuring in a stand of 137 in eighty-one minutes with Tony Lewis.

Stephenson captained Somerset for five years in the early sixties. He had an affable personality and a pragmatic approach to leadership. His triumph was that he took the county to third and so nearly the championship in 1963. 'Steve' had by then an improved and more rounded bowling side with the arrival of Fred Rumsey; for a season or two before that he'd been leaning on Palmer and Langford. Rumsey, left-arm and decidedly quick, came on a special registration from Worcestershire, where neither his record nor his scope had been excessive.

In the West Country his impact was immediate. He had a suitably fearsome appearance as he approached the wicket on a pounding run-up. He was heavily built around the trunk; later the tummy broadened a little and the arm dropped correspondingly. Rumsey took 520 wickets for Somerset and played in five Tests. During his spell with the county he was a considerable asset. His hostility in his first season was something of a revelation and he finished with 102 wickets. Sharing the new ball with the newcomer, Palmer turned in some brilliant performances. There were green tracks that summer; he consistently found movement in taking a memorable 139 wickets. Only Derek Shackleton and Barry Knight took more.

Stephenson couldn't be seriously faulted tactically. He got the best out of his team. It wasn't always easy. Wight's batting was far more fragile; Alley couldn't bowl in the late matches because of a back injury; Virgin was only just getting used to cricket again after National Service. Right till the end there was realistic talk, all the same, of seeing the championship pennant fluttering over the Taunton ground for the first time. A defeat against Surrey and then the rain when they played Sussex dealt a double body blow.

The early sixties had brought a few changes in policy and personnel. A Gloucestershire man (perish the thought!), George Lambert, was brought in as coach and even for a few matches. Before him there had been Bill Andrews – during one of his intermittent periods in favour with the committee – and A. C. Shirreff, the former Squadron Leader who had captained Combined Services. After Cambridge, he'd played for both Hampshire and Kent. His third county 'posting', which included some duties as assistant secretary, was brief and, we suspect, none too happy. He was given only two matches for Somerset and never a bowl.

Mervyn Kitchen joined the playing staff. He looked like a young farmer and walked like a worldly, old sailor. He was a left-hander, vigilant and uncomplicated in defence, able to punch and pull when runs were needed. He'd been scoring plenty of such runs for Flax Bourton and was an emerging teenage hero around the lanes of his native Nailsea. There were to be seventeen hundreds and more than 15,000 runs before he took up umpiring.

Brian Roe used to open the innings with studied correctness. Three times he scored his 1,000 runs, four times he reached a century. He was a neat, diminutive figure ('so small that we felt we always wanted to mother him', matronly supporters used to say). Greetham continued to play with an aura of charm much to the liking of the home crowds. But Baig had sadly made his departure after only twenty-three matches, and that all-round journey-man from Lancashire, Lomax, had also gone. Lomax's methods were never spectacular; he did an adequate job for a time as an opening batsman and at medium pace his bowling was persevering rather than penetrative.

During the sixties, his namesake Ian Lomax came and went after half a dozen matches. Vincent Lindo came and went after a single appearance. Neither should be wholly discounted. Lomax was a towering Old Etonian with as much interest in racehorses, his own, as belting a cricket ball. He had a big farm in Wiltshire and a long-cherished wish to sample county cricket. His big, unsubtle hitting for the Minor Counties side was well known. On his own initiative he earned himself a chance for Somerset, though the romantic hopes of the gentleman farmer were never quite fulfilled.

Lindo was a Jamaican and everyone seems to have forgotten him. That's surprising. In 1963 he turned up for a trial, three years after making a nominal appearance for Notts. He was decidedly whippy in the nets and was put straight into the side for the match against the Pakistan Eaglets. The touring team of variable talent and enormous enthusiasm batted only once. They probably weren't too sorry, even if the young, gifted Mushtaq could stay unconcernedly for a two-hour century. Somerset's West Indian trialist was given the second new ball and in 21 deliveries he dismissed five batsmen at a cost of 1 run. His match figures were: 26.1-5-88-8. They still weren't apparently impressive enough to win him a contract.

That fixture against the Eaglets brought Stephenson's patient deputy as wicket keeper, Eele, his only first-class hundred. Not too much luck came his way in county cricket, evident again more than twenty years later when he lost his place on the umpires' list. Some of his colleagues felt he was decidedly unfortunate. But he was an introvert by nature and the system swung against him.

Another umpire, who met with much success during and after his Somerset days, was Ken Palmer. Some would argue that he deserved more than one Test match. It came then, partly out of convenience for the selectors, in the February of 1965. The England bowlers out in South Africa were toppling with stomach strains, recurrent soccer injuries and damaged heels. Palmer received the emergency call in Johannesburg where he was doing some coaching. He set off in a hurry for Port Elizabeth in time for the fifth Test – and was given the new ball. There's no Elysian postscript. He took 1-113 from 35 tiring overs in the first innings, 0-76 in the second. And, rather ungraciously, he was put at No 11 in the batting order.

Ken, joined by brother Roy in the Somerset side in the mid-sixties, was one of several talented West Country boys who came through more or less at the same time. As a bowler he had strength in the shoulders rather than height in the upstretched arms. He could keep hitting the seam. He could cut the ball off the wicket at a deceptive speed, at times too fast for casual, unsuspecting batsmen. In 1961 he was almost first in the country to the double; there were four occasions when he took 100 wickets in a season.

Langford remained consistent, spinning and not flighting, also getting his hard-earned 100 wickets. For a few seasons Geoff Hall was brought in to reinforce the seam attack. Somerset were, over a six-year period, daring to stay in the top half of the table. The players had smarted over some of those 'League of Nations' taunts. It didn't hurt so much if they were winning.

CHAPTER FIFTEEN

Pay Rebels, Changing Times

It would be dishonest to suggest that all was sweet harmony. The fact was that, however much it was shielded from the members, the dressing room didn't always hum with good humour. There were strained relationships at the time the county were contemplating a successor to Stephenson as captain.

'Steve' was bothered by a leg injury and had announced that he would be giving up at the end of 1964. Alley took over for part of that season and many assumed he would be officially appointed for the following summer. Some of the capped players were a good deal less than enthusiastic. They hadn't got on too well with Bill at various times during the year. Langford, for instance, had been dropped for the first time since he'd become a senior player. They held a meeting among themselves and, while having much admiration for Alley as a cricketer, made it clear that in some cases they wouldn't be staying if he became skipper. Their choice was Colin Atkinson.

There's an illogical and romantic view that county cricket is a game of incessant sunshine. A team lives and travels in close proximity. The jealousies and rivalries spring in the main from insecurity and a disparity of rewards. Players become taut, even neurotic, as form suffers. They grow in introspection and resentment as factions form and selectors' prejudices, as they see them, are manifested.

A view persisted among some of the more reactionary committee members at Taunton that players were paid to express themselves on the field and nowhere else. Andrews and one or two others were disparagingly labelled as barrack-room lawyers when they became quite vociferous about their rights soon after the war. Now here was another group of capped professionals having altogether too much to say. They happened to be spunky and, if necessary, spiky individuals. 'One or two of the players here are on a lot of money. We aren't getting our fair share. It's time the pay structure was levelled out', said players like Langford, Virgin, Atkinson, Palmer and Kitchen.

Headlines started to mushroom on the sports pages. There was daily talk of rebels and pay revolts. 'Dear me, all so unedifying', said senior officials one after the other. They just couldn't conceive that times were changing and that sport was becoming a tough, abrasive and highly commercial business.

The pros were much maligned. They were dubbed as militants and trouble makers, supposedly unconcerned for the county's financial plight. But they won – deservedly. The gap between their earnings and the pay packets of a few others was too great. The run-making of Virgin and Atkinson, the wicket-taking of Palmer and Langford had to be more generously rewarded. It was agreed that all capped players would in future be offered similar contracts.

Those late sixties, despite some sterling individual and collective feats by Somerset, were an edgy period. Graham Atkinson left, offered a one-year contract when he, and others, felt he was worth more. It was a great pity. He went without the captaincy, which justifiably might have been his at some stage, or even a benefit.

Successive balance sheets made depressing reading. The secretary, Richard Robinson, lost popularity by some of his public statements. He was called 'Mr Gloom' and took a battering in the correspondence columns. People, influenced by the pervading mood of pessimism, were murmuring that the county club might have to fold before long. Suggestions that it might be necessary to sell the Taunton ground brought an emotional retort from Bill Andrews, then on the executive committee. 'This is ridiculous talk – it would be like losing Lord's from the English cricket scene.'

All this led up to a particularly tense, fidgety meeting at Glastonbury, where a vote of no confidence in the principal officers was taken. The casualties were the chairman Bunty Longrigg, treasurer Rex Frost and secretary Robinson.

But we are jumping a year or two ahead. We must return to the cricket itself – and to the appointment of Colin Atkinson as captain in 1965.

I'd heard from Bunty that the players had lobbied for me. But the appointment still rather surprised me. There were better players, and plenty of players senior to me. Looking back, I feel I'd previously been made vice-captain for the wrong reason – because I was an amateur. It's a fact that I was never paid by Somerset. When I was captain, I was paid by Millfield and they in turn were paid by Somerset. It was a circular motion to retain my amateur status.

Atkinson had arrived to teach at Millfield in 1960 – with the intention that he would have the summer term off to play for the county, if asked. He'd been getting runs and wickets for Northumberland and Durham, and Stephenson, who used to play himself for Stockton-on-Tees, recommended him to Somerset. He was that rarity, a leg-spinner, who batted with resolve and fielded with sharp agility in the covers. For a year when doing research in psychology after studying for his degree, he played as a pro in Northumberland. 'You got a tenner for a match and ten bob for 5 wickets or 50 runs. There were advantages as a pro – you batted early, bowled early and fielded more or less where you wanted.'

At Millfield, under Jack Meyer initially — he was later to become headmaster — he taught English and Latin, and helped with the games. Soon he became a housemaster. On the field he was a great enthusiast with a basic shyness that masked a competitive nature. He was happiest of all when tossing up his leg-breaks and he was bitterly disappointed when arthritis affected his spinning finger in 1963; his county cricket career seemed to be over. As a compromise he led the 2nd XI in his holidays. Experimentally and with modest success he began to bowl seamers at medium pace.

Surprised Atkinson may have been to learn that he was wanted again, this time to lead the county side; but he was also delighted. He was a man who liked responsibility; he could make decisions and stand by them. Those hints of friction within the dressing room didn't delay his acceptance. 'Bill Alley? Perhaps he appeared more difficult than he was. All Bill wanted to do was bat, bowl or field in the gully. If he was doing one of these, he was happy. He liked a grumble and a swear. We used to wind him up. He might let go a few oaths in response and then everything was OK.'

The new captain accepted that he'd be handling 'a team full of idiosyncrasies'. The challenge of that rather appealed to him. 'Just imagine having Kenny Palmer and Fred Rumsey trying to work out from which end they wanted to bowl. Fred could be concerned that a blade of grass was the wrong colour. Perhaps he didn't look the perfect athlete in build but in full flight he was a very fine bowler.'

Atkinson had his own rigid ideas on the game. He believed vehemently that in a three-day match there should be a stipulated number of overs bowled in the last hour. 'I proposed it at a captains' meeting at Lord's and got laughed out of court. Brian Close was one of thirteen captains who voted against it. Ironically he lost his England job the following year because of an incident concerning the slow over rate.'

It was on that same Warwickshire ground that Atkinson rounded on Geoff Clayton, the wicket keeper who had been brought down from Lancashire to take over from Stephenson.

> It was a perfect wicket and Warwickshire were chasing a third-day target and looking as though they'd get them. We were holding the overs up to a reasonable level but Clayton's idea was to slow the play up quite a lot more. You couldn't bowl till the wicket keeper was in position and he was very deliberately taking his time. He wouldn't do what he was told. In the end I threatened to send him off and said that Roy Virgin would take over the gloves. He improved a bit . . .

The final over rate remained a contentious issue with the Somerset captain.

> We were playing Notts at Taunton. It was a belter of a wicket and they had a poor attack. Towards the end as we chased the target, Notts slowed things to what I felt was a terrible rate. I went in myself and asked the umpire if he could do something about the over rate. He had

a word with the captain but nothing happened. We failed to win. Just 2 more overs and we'd have done it. I was incensed – I didn't blame the captain any more than the system and the toothlessness of the umpires.

For a quiet man, amiable and civilised, his three years as skipper weren't absolutely free of controversy. Who will forget the Bank Holiday match at Bristol, where he ordered a crawl and positively no favours for Gloucester-shire? He incurred the unmitigated wrath of the home supporters; there were scenes of extreme anger. Seldom, if ever, has a visiting captain to the Nevil Road ground been subjected to so much ill will.

Atkinson, a sensitive person, must have hated it all. But years later his viewpoint hadn't changed or even softened.

We were in no position to win. Yet the crowd expected us to declare and give the opposition a chance to come out on top. We had played badly and, in effect, lost the match twice – yet we'd come back from the dead. I delayed my declaration and then made a token gesture. They hadn't a cat in hell's chance. They knew it and so did everyone else.

There was an unpublicised sequel involving Atkinson and Gloucestershire's captain John Mortimore. 'I was a bit miffed. John did a thing I didn't approve of. He spoke to the local press and was critical of me. Never in my life did I speak to the press and say I disapproved of an opposing captain's tactics. You tell him so, over a beer, that's the way to do it. I didn't like what he'd done and I told him so.'

Under the diffident, rather tense and sometimes schoolmasterly skipper, Somerset climbed to third in the championship in 1966 for the third time in their history. They also got to the final of the Gillette Cup the following year. The introduction of the one-day game had, of course, revolutionised attitudes and boosted balance sheets. The players, in Taunton and elsewhere, remained wary; they were reluctant to devalue their studiously acquired techniques and to subject themselves to ridicule with a desperate travesty of a shot. But the crowds were finding it hugely entertaining – and everyone agreed it was time Somerset appeared in cricket's heady cup final.

It was an event rather than a match. Raucous rural accents rattled the traditional decorum of Lord's. There was a crowd of 20,000; and, you suspected, far more open-necked shirts from Hatch Beauchamp and Huish Episcopi than MCC ties from St John's Wood, or even Dover and Canterbury. Some came in farming smocks. The atmosphere was heavy with rustic banter and the tang of apple juice. It was a carnival occasion, a day to strip Lord's of some of its fustier pomposity. There was some disapproval from the game's higher echelons. But surely this was good-natured parody and wholesome fun; it was also a cumulative celebration that Somerset had actually got somewhere at last.

After all that, they lost. Kent won by 32 runs but it was the best final so far. The match was tighter and more entertaining than seemed likely at lunch when Kent were cruising along at 129-1 after 34 overs. They finished with an unexceptional 193. Somerset had come back with a marvellous spell of 13 overs, during which they took 6 more wickets for only 21 runs. Alley, Ken Palmer and Rumsey bowled quite superbly. Roy Palmer also captured 3 wickets, though more expensively.

The scoring rate was a reasonable one and Peter Robinson proved a doughty opener. But the left-hander's assertive strokes weren't sustained by those who followed. Kent's bowlers tied them down after tea. Alley was a man who could have swung the bat – and the pendulum – back. He was beautifully taken at backward short leg; then there was an optimistic late flurry from Barwell and Burgess until, overcome by the anxieties of the moment, their judgement wavered and they found themselves haplessly at the same end. Kent deserved their win. Somerset were let down by their batting but there were no recriminations: they'd tasted the nectar of a Lord's final and they liked it.

The metaphor prompts a lighthearted memory from the semi-final at Old Trafford, where Somerset beat Lancashire by 100 runs. Herbert Sutcliffe was the adjudicator and he was chatting with Len Creed, a Somerset committee member later to be chairman.

'I've heard rather a lot about your so-called famous cider down there – I'd love to sample some.'

Creed, a one-time farmer-turned-bookmaker, knew that another devoted West Country supporter always carried a stone jar of the potent brew in his car. 'Go and get Mr Sutcliffe a drop, Guy.'

A tumbler was filled and passed to the adjudicator. ''Tis better when it's laced with gin', the great Yorkshire cricketer was assured. He showed a distinct partiality for such a palatable elixir and to the delight of his doting companions asked for a second glass.

'By this time wickets were tumbling,' recalls Creed. 'I looked at Herbert and he'd gone off, sound as a bell. But the match was now going very much Somerset's way. It was full of incident and good performances by the bowlers. I decided I'd better discreetly wake the adjudicator.'

The venerable Sutcliffe sat up with a start. He was probably a little embarrassed. 'Em, er, what's happening? Who's doing well?'

Len Creed, yet to win regional fame and a surfeit of free drinks on the strength of bringing Viv Richards to this country, responded with a deferential whisper. 'It looks very much like Kenny Palmer, Mr Sutcliffe.' And so it was, justifiably, when it came to the Man of the Match announcement.

Atkinson went back to schoolteaching when it came to 1968, without the Gillette Cup triumph that was so nearly his. His successor, for one year, was a self-effacing twenty-five-year-old law student who had just sat his finals. Roy Kerslake was a useful off-spinner and middle-order batsman but it simply wasn't in his nature to parade his skills when there were more experienced county cricketers around. Ever accident-prone, as he joked so often during and after his brief playing career, he was hurt before the season even started and it was midsummer before he assumed the full leadership. Two of his virtues were his fielding and the warmth of his personality.

It was a difficult season. Ken Palmer had both injury and illness, which was no way to celebrate one's testimonial year. Tony Clarkson, a talented Yorkshireman who opened the innings at times with some success, broke his leg and was missing for six weeks. One could sense that changes of personnel were imminent. Brooks, who had kept wicket for one summer, and Barwell were about to leave the county game. Rumsey was going, and so was Alley, who was less than enchanted with the offer of one-day cricket only in future. He'd scored 1,000 runs in his fiftieth year. Now he grumbled and left. It was good to see him back many times at Taunton, jocularly holding court in the bar, during his distinguished days as an umpire. And there was an embracing and apposite loudspeaker announcement – and prolonged applause – when some years later he made his final appearance as an umpire at the county headquarters.

Greetham had already left, of course, remembered in the Somerset records for his ninth wicket stand with Stephenson (183 at Weston); so had Clayton. The wicket keeper, small and independent, had eighty-five victims in 1965 and was almost as good as anyone in the country. He was once sent in as night-watchman, against Middlesex at the Imperial Ground, Bristol, and reached his maiden century. At Kidderminster he held six catches in an innings. It was a pity that he never quite integrated.

The administrative unease occasionally resulted in shafts of cynicism within the dressing room. But there was some sunshine, too, and the public were often oblivious to the murkier area of politics. Somerset even had two local lads, Kitchen and Virgin, doing consistent deeds at or near the top of the order. You could forget all that envious 'League of Nations' stuff now. Kitchen, bold and bandy-legged, scored five hundreds in 1968. Against Northants he carried his bat for 161. Old team-mates at Flax Bourton and other village grounds along the Bristol–Weston road were ecstatic.

Among the slow bowlers, Robinson, left-arm and accurate, supported Langford. He had a splendid match at Trent Bridge, where he took 7-10 in just over 17 overs. The wickets didn't always help him but he captured slightly fewer than 300 wickets – and scored three timely centuries. He was later to become a most conscientious coach.

Kerslake's successor was Langford, expected by many to be given the job twelve months earlier. He was in charge of a fragile side, which lacked new-ball aggression and middle-order batting solidarity. Somerset went back to the bottom of the table. Any diversions were welcome. At the Brislington Ground in Bristol a slim young man called Greg Chappell scored a sublime 128 not out against Surrey in the John Player League. It was seen on television and everyone still seems to talk about it. At Yeovil, in the same competition, Langford achieved the ultimate unbeatable feat: he bowled his 8 overs without conceding a run.

Chappell's hundred was the first ever scored in the Sunday League. But his fifty-two appearances for Somerset over two seasons – the county hoped in vain it would be longer – contained many treasured cameos. He had come here to sharpen up and refine his technique against seam on greenish English wickets. He went away a better player, poised to become one of the great international batsmen and to lead Australia. At Taunton he was a nineteen-year-old with an unquestionable stamp of confidence, completely assured and never arrogant. Burgess used to say: 'When Greg walked out to bat he reminded me by his bearing of a captain in the Guards.'

Chappell's innate sense of stroke play, like that of Richards or Martin Crowe afterwards, enthralled one with the preciseness of its timing. Kerslake was his first captain in England. They must have got on well, for Chappell was a witness when Kerslake was married. The ceremony was clearly organised on a tight schedule; it took place at ten in the morning, and the Somerset skipper was tossing up half an hour later.

The quiet Aussie was given his cap, of course. 'He got a wonderful century at Weston. I took his Somerset cap out in my pocket when it was my turn to bat and presented it to him at the wicket', said Kerslake. The county seldom did anything the formal or expected way.

Chappell had predetermined the direction his career should go. He knew when it was time to leave his digs at the Crown and Sceptre in Taunton (where he drank orange juice for most of the time) and to see what he could do at the highest level at home. He was grateful for what championship cricket here taught him technically; he was also probably pleased that Somerset told him to forget about his leg-spinners and to see what he could do, with swing and seam, at medium pace.

The seventies were approaching; things could only improve. Two left-handers, both nineteen and fair-haired, Brian Rose and Peter Denning, had made their entry. Derek Taylor, a wicket keeper, was on the way from Surrey. There was Allan Jones, an opening bowler renowned for his hostility and his grunting action, coming from Sussex, and Maurice Hill from Notts by way of Derby. There was a West Indian, Hallam Moseley, recommended by Gary Sobers no less, about to qualify. And at Lord's, two spectators discovered their joint affection for Somerset and decided it was about time a club for all the county's exiles was formed. In a matter of years the Somerset Wyverns had a thousand members and were soon giving much valued financial support to the county club.

The 1970 summer did bring some modest improvement. One had to wait till August, all the same, for much sign of success in the championship. But Virgin was successful all the season. As a batsman he reached a personal peak which must have put him very close to Test recognition. At the wicket he was a small, almost chunky figure. His footwork was trim, his timing through the covers was often flawless. There were seven hundreds from him in the championship, another in the Sunday League and yet another in the Gillette Cup. He was the first Englishman to reach 2,000 runs in championship cricket.

A £10,000 legacy offered a welcome glimmer or two of optimism for the treasurer as he prepared the annual accounts. Maybe it also brought encouragement to the new secretary, Jimmy James, recently returned from Africa. He stayed five years, full of enthusiasm as ever, before moving briefly to Lancashire and then, until his retirement in 1986, to Hampshire.

The significant newcomer was Tom Cartwright. He came from Warwickshire, to play 101 times and take 408 wickets for Somerset. He was a man of strong opinions and at times he crossed swords. Mike Brearley, writing about him in the county's centenary publication, said: 'Of all the cricketers I know, he comes closest to the ideal craftsman . . . He's a great thinker – and talker – about the game.'

Cartwright played in only five Tests; a grudging reward for someone who bowled at nagging medium-paced cunning better than any of his domestic contemporaries. The mistake was to call him a defensive bowler. He contained oppositions but he was always inviting batsmen to go after him. As a coach he revealed considerable technical knowledge, passing on his own secrets on how to swing and cut the ball. The parting was painful, though not publicly too acrimonious. He was on a one-year contract with a three-month notice clause. There were differences with the committee and views that didn't always coincide with those of the captain. Team selection once or twice became a contentious issue. Tom, sensitive and superficially dour, was suspended from his duties as coach and player. In 1971 he'd bowled quite beautifully to take 104 wickets. Now, three years later, he was struggling for fitness – and packing his bags.

Staying with the retrospectively spicy theme of controversy in the seventies, we should perhaps drop back a year or two – to what happened at Clarence Park. It was the occasion when irate spectators lowered the county flag to half-mast when it came to close of play. It was a drastic and, many would say, not unreasonable gesture. A holiday-maker and cricket lover was already striding out on to the square to speak to the umpires and players to register his public protest. Other demonstrators had persistently walked in front of the sightscreens. It was all very unseemly but, we suspect, found some sympathy with a number of the Somerset committee. Several senior members even came to the press caravan to express fairly unambiguous views about the way the match was being handled by their captain, Langford.

What had happened was that rain limited play to 77 overs over the first two days. Then, in front of a large, good-natured crowd, Burgess and Cartwright bowled brilliantly on a drying pitch to dismiss Worcestershire for 132, giving Somerset a lead of 51. There were four hours left; the spectators in festival mood felt they were entitled to some kind of imaginatively conceived finish. They got nothing of the sort. Somerset meandered to 145-6 at tea. The declaration never came. Hill and Taylor, presumably under orders, crawled most of all. The futile charade ended at 181-6. It was a negation of the spirit of cricket. There was much impulsive talk of memberships being cancelled. The county chairman, Lt-Col Goldney Grey, was left saying: 'Oh dear, we'll have to call a meeting – we don't want demonstrations like this ever again.'

Langford may not have been the most adroit skipper Somerset ever had.

When he took over early on, a few brave declarations went wrong. He became more cautious on the third days. But it should be appreciated that there were frequently patent playing limitations within the sides he handled. After that ill-judged travesty at Clarence Park, the amiable Langford gritted his teeth and accepted the censures. At the same time, he defended his action: 'I don't blame the crowd for being annoyed but it takes two teams to make a game when so much of the playing time has been lost through rain. Tom Graveney admitted to me that he had completely misread the wicket. Frankly I was never in a position to declare – the pitch was too good.'

Controversy carries a journalistic relish that the author finds hard to leave. And wasn't this, after all, the moment for Brian Close to turn up in the West Country? He was disaffected by the climate of his native Yorkshire and was ready to be talked into a change. At the Somerset headquarters he drank whisky rather than cider. There was a different attitude, a different fibre down at Taunton, and he sniffed sceptically. Soon he was leading the county. He made sure more catches were held in the field. He was inclined to chase the younger pros; a few of them resented it. Then, paradoxical as ever, he'd put his arm round their shoulders: 'I'm not a hard man – you've got it all wrong. I'm soft and sentimental.' And so he was over many things. But not out on the field, where he fielded at short leg and expected others to be equally brave; not when it came to hammering a cussed hundred against Surrey the day after he'd lost several teeth; not when it came to taking on Wilf Wooller. 'The unpleasant match' (so the records say) was in 1972. Somerset compiled 113-2 at pedestrian pace over 72 overs on the first day. Close adjusted the tempo with his own pugnacious century on the second. St Helens was in a thoroughly bad humour by the time the visiting captain made his delayed declaration at 3pm.

Wooller, never one to pussyfoot, was beside himself. He went with a purposeful heavy-breathing stride to the microphone and announced over the loudspeaker system that spectators could have their money back if they wished. It was the ultimate in reproach and humiliation. The breezes coming in off Swansea Bay were heavy with pungent accusation. Some said there was a highly charged no-go area between the dogmatic Wooller and the cussed Close. The umpires, Arthur Fagg and David Evans, agonised but felt obliged to report 'the voice of outraged Glamorgan' to Lord's for allegedly criticising them for not making a brisker start on the opening day.

Not a match to cherish – or was it? Close no doubt climbed into his car at the end with a veiled smile of deep satisfaction. Glamorgan were still bowled out twice, and lost by an innings.

Some believed Close would never settle with his new county, others that he wouldn't be fit enough. He actually hit five hundreds in his first season with them, one with monstrous meaning against his native side. He continued to play his beloved sweep, knowing that it was always likely to be his downfall. His best innings were those when he had to fight as only a Yorkshireman can. For all his protestations about the one-day game, his record in it was often a stirring one.

The Australian connection was maintained. John Inverarity nearly came, Kerry O'Keeffe did. O'Keeffe was a quickish leg-spinner with a high action and an ability to turn the ball from the off or produce some excellent top-spinners, At first he was under-bowled by Somerset, though he ended the summer with 74 wickets. The tall, tidy Taylor kept to him particularly well – it wasn't easy.

Cartwright was the mainstay of the bowlers. Roy Palmer had gone – remembered for several penetrative stints, a John Player hat-trick at Bristol with the last three balls, and that public reprimand for picking the seam at Bath, just as White had done without censure years before – and now Jones had an increasingly responsible role. His fielding was suspect and the crowd were inclined to tease him rather cruelly. But at his best he was a most underrated bowler. He proved it at Hove with 9-51.

Moseley had some back trouble but was in every sense a popular addition. He came in with a spring-heeled run, had a handsome action and swung the ball away. He also fielded with a Barbadian ebullience and his genial, equable personality equipped him for the role of an unofficial public relations officer. He was much liked around the circuit, especially by elderly mums and doting schoolchildren.

Graham 'Budgie' Burgess was another of those local lads with an agricultural physique. His medium-paced bowling was growing in wiles and wisdom all the time. There was more discipline in the batting, too. The maiden hundred came against Gloucestershire early in 1973. Eight days later he did it again, at Edgbaston.

Under Close, Somerset fluctuated in the table. His was always a very personalised style of leadership. It incorporated surprises and even a few eccentric judgements. It was the kind that occasionally invited criticism. But he took the county to fifth position in 1974, and fourth in 1977.

The 1974 summer was a memorable one. Somerset finished second to Leicestershire in the John Player League, two points behind. They reached the semi-finals of both the Benson and Hedges and Gillette Cups. Outright success was tantalisingly elusive but there was an aura of renewed stature. It was visible in the way the players carried themselves. Their buoyant wins were achieved for much of the time without the injured Cartwright, while Kitchen was also often unfit that season.

Enforced experiments in the batting order brought unexpected bonuses. Taylor, someone who minimised risks, turned into a reliable opener. Young Denning, with his distinctive straw-coloured hair and exquisite fielding, hit a memorable century off Surrey in the Gillette quarter-finals. Schoolmaster Bob Clapp went into the record books for his bowling on Sundays. And there were a couple of newcomers, their names making absolutely no impact when printed on the scorecards for the first time. Who, after all, were Vivian Richards and Ian Botham?

Richards had been brought back from Antigua, on the whim of bookmaker Creed. He qualified with historic Lansdown; then, less than consumed with self-confidence, he had to discover for himself whether he was good enough for county cricket. His debut was at Swansea in the Benson and Hedges competition. Close put him at No 4 and he scored 81 not out. At the captain's insistence, the players lined up to applaud him in. Creed, the hardened turf accountant, was in tears. Charlie Barnett gave Richards the gold award. Afterwards he said to everyone within earshot: 'Today we've seen a truly great player of the future.'

Botham, who came from Yeovil, had been on the Lord's groundstaff. He was only eighteen when he came into the side, mainly to take over from the injured Cartwright. At once he was an all-rounder of precocious appeal. He could move the ball away from the bat far more than you would expect for a player of his limited experience. And that clean, generous arc of the bat as he drove had riveting qualities.

In these years of the seventies, Stuart Wilkinson and the talented, well-proportioned Richard Cooper had briefly stayed. Dennis Breakwell, a slow left-arm bowler and wholehearted team-mate, had arrived from North-amptonshire, and Jim Parks from Sussex. Parks hadn't always been a wicket keeper, of course. His value to Somerset now was primarily as a high-order batsman, with some keeping in the one-day matches.

Quite rightly the 1975 season was a time for centenary celebrations. There were some stirring top-table speeches but the self-congratulations were a little muted. The previous year had been one of genuine playing success – yet the club had made a loss of nearly £11,000, and the bank overdraft was now up to £23,000. There was recurrent mention of ominous words like 'crisis' and 'survival'. Those earlier doom-laden sentiments of secretary Robinson seemed to take on a renewed relevance. Successive treasurers were now saying: 'We must place the finances of the club on a firmer footing or . . .' The missing verb, and it carried no sensationalism, was 'perish'.

Plans for redeveloping the county ground, to make use of its facilities throughout the year, were now seen as a matter of priority. A centenary-year appeal was launched. The Supporters' Club, just over twenty-one years old, generated increased interest. Harold Gimblett was prominent among the fund-raisers, initially with his own appeal. At a cricket dinner in Weston, he stunned his large audience with an unmitigated attack on all those who were failing to respond to the appeal. Then, impetuous as ever he was at the crease, Harold suddenly announced he was planning a sponsored walk from John O'Groats to Land's End. He hadn't even told his wife who was sitting next to him. It was a brave, romantic thought but utterly unrealistic. He wasn't fit enough and his doctors forbade it.

A sense of urgency had at last gripped Somerset after far too much complacency and amiable apathy. By 1978 the president, Colin Atkinson was initiating his 'pavilion appeal', backed by the new captain Brian Rose who went on record as saying:

The pavilion largely indicates the health of a club and if it is a good pavilion it can inspire pride and loyalty among the players . . . unfortunately, the one at Taunton gives a very bad impression in the

SOMERSET COUNTY CRICKET CLUB

Somerset v. Australians

Played at Bath on May 18th, 19th and 20th, 1977

Somerset won by seven wickets

The Australians won the toss and batted

Australians

		First Innings		Second Innings	
R. B. McCosker	..	c Botham b Garner	2	run out	2
C. S. Serjeant	..	st Taylor b Burgess	13	c Garner b Botham	50
*G. S. Chappell	..	b Garner	113	c Garner b Botham	39
G. J. Cosier	..	b Garner	44	c Taylor b Botham	2
K. D. Walters	..	c Denning b Burgess	23	b Botham	25
D. W. Hookes	..	b Botham	3	b Burgess	108
†R. W. Marsh	..	b Garner	3	b Garner	0
K. J. O'Keeffe	..	c Denning b Burgess	11	c Denning b Moseley	20
J. R. Thomson	..	b Burgess	0	c Botham b Garner	0
M. F. Malone	..	b Burgess	2	c Richards b Breakwell	17
G. Dymock	..	not out	0	not out	6
		Extras: 10b, 2w, 6nb	18	Extras: 15lb, 1w, 4nb	20
		Total ..	232	Total ..	289

Fall of wickets: 1-2, 2-57, 3-177, 4-197, 5-200, 6-204, 7-223, 8-223, 9-231

1-16, 2-18, 3-141, 4-172, 5-183, 6-214, 7-251, 8-252, 9-271

Bowling

	O	M	R	W	O	M	R	W
Garner	20	8	66	4	23	6	71	2
Moseley	16	5	52	0	17	6	55	1
Burgess	9.3	2	25	5	9	3	41	1
Botham	15	2	48	1	22	6	98	4
Breakwell	7	0	23	0	0.3	0	4	1

Somerset

B. C. Rose	..	not out	110	c Marsh b Thomson	27
P. W. Denning	..	c Marsh b Dymock	39	b Chappell	34
I. V. A. Richards	..	c Hookes b Malone	18	c Cosier b O'Keeffe	53
*D. B. Close	..	c McCosker b Malone	0		
D. Breakwell	..	c Chappell b O'Keeffe	23		
I. T. Botham	..	c McCosker b O'Keeffe	59	not out	39
P. A. Slocombe	..	not out	55	not out	8
†D. J. S. Taylor	..				
G. I. Burgess					
J. Garner					
H. R. Moseley					
		Extras: 4b, 6lb, 26nb	36	Extras: 4b, 3lb, 3w, 11nb	21
		Total for 5 wkts. dec.	340	Total for 3 wkts.	182

Fall of wickets: 1-81, 2-116, 3-117, 4-146, 5-228

1-50, 2-129, 3-129

Bowling

	O	M	R	W	O	M	R	W
Thomson	16	2	60	0	12	1	57	1
Dymock	17	7	48	1	5	0	25	0
Malone	22	4	70	2	9	2	18	0
O'Keeffe	35	15	114	2	5.1	0	32	1
Chappell	2	0	11	0	8	4	29	1
Walters	2	1	1	0				

* Captain   † Wicketkeeper   Umpires: H. D. Bird, T. W. Spencer

cricket world. There are poor facilities for the players. It's generally cold and damp and offers no proper viewing points to watch the game in a relaxed manner. There is little privacy and it is vital that this appeal succeeds.

Few would have disagreed with that – certainly not visiting players who referred to their changing room as 'the dungeon'. Taunton was looking seedy and shame-faced. It was time to think of the spectators as well as the players, time to restore some visible pride to accompany what everyone sensed was about to be the most exciting and assertive era in the county's history.

Faint hearts there still were, and hard-nosed businessmen on the committee who knew that the bad times, financially, were only yesterday or the day before. They saw the dangers of overstepping, blinded by an increasing climate, as they saw it, of hitherto unknown glamour and status. They noted the packed Sunday crowds but warned: 'Steady . . . steady . . . don't rush. It may not last. Spend cautiously.'

But Somerset had to gamble. They had to build a new pavilion to save their embarrassment. They had to embrace their members more. They had to encourage their sponsors. They had to function in the most vibrant and professional way, commensurate with the necessary bearing of a county club whose team had become the most discussed and often the most entertaining in the country.

Atkinson said:

I offered to be chairman of the appeal. It was an emotional reaction. The original cost was less than a quarter of a million and ended up more than £400,000. We've been paying off the bank at the rate of £50,000 a year. I feel we are into a reassuring financial pattern with the overdraft coming down all the time.

Additional work was done on seating, car parking and other overdue facilities. Executive blocks were built, to be hired out on an annual basis with notable success. But some continued to argue that the club were taking on too big a commitment too soon; they would have preferred Somerset to settle for a long-term strategy involving gradual improvements. There was indeed some sign of compromise when it came to a resolution to pull down the old Ridley Stand. The minute was rescinded at the next meeting.

We are jumping ahead. Let us return to the late seventies, where Close was coming to the end of his captaincy. His period of supervision had been eventful, always touched by polemics like the man himself. His North Country style of leadership was generally admired by the crowds in the West and for at least most of the time by the players under him. They were also inclined to exchange eloquent looks that ranged from doting to despair. When they moaned about the way he used them – or the way he criticised them – he was well out of earshot. There were as many stories about him at Taunton and Bath as ever there were about him at Bradford and Headingley.

More than half were true. Len Creed authenticates one: 'We were playing at Worcester and I'd accidentally locked myself out of my car at the close of play. Brian Close invited me and a colleague from Lansdown to have a lift in his car to a pub. A young Ian Botham was in the passenger seat.' Suddenly, in some consternation, Creed saw Close take both hands off the steering wheel – he was, of course, famed for his driving – and ask Botham whether he could see any blood on them.

'Em, no, skipper. Why?'

'Well, there should be. I saw you out on the field sliding around on your ass. Back in the dressing room, I picked up your bloody boots and rubbed my hands along where the studs should have been.' Close was making a point in his own severe and graphic way. He was suggesting a change of footwear for the following day.

In 1976, to the joy of his Somerset devotees, Close was selected to play in the first three Tests against the West Indians at the age of forty-five. The following season he retired after twenty-nine years of first-class cricket. His testimonial brought him £35,000. He had begun the regeneration process at Somerset and for some years his highly personalised influence would still be detected.

Five times he scored 1,000 runs for the county and then in his last season led them to fourth position. When the Australians came to Bath in the May of 1977, he was out for a duck – but it was the memorable climax of his seven years with Somerset. The Aussies were beaten by 7 wickets. It was the first time the Tourists had lost to Somerset in twenty-two meetings, going back to 1893.

Only a few days before the fixture the Bath pitch was flooded (not for the first time) and there was realistic talk of switching the match to Taunton. But then the sun came out and more than 1,000 runs were scored. The author was mesmerised from the first till the last ball. Two former Somerset players, Chappell and O'Keeffe, were playing for the Australians. As captain, Chappell went in at No 3 and scored 99 before lunch. There are so many lasting memories: of a gangling, seemingly languorous newcomer of mountainous height and tender-hearted nature, Joel Garner, who took a wicket in his first over; of some lovely bowling by him and Burgess; of Rose's unbeaten hundred; and Botham's boyish aggression . . . and of Hookes' hundred in 81 balls.

It was a match of charm and much entertainment. Spoilsport Australians from an older generation might have liked a little more restraint and discipline from a few of their players. But Chappell determined the mood – to match the weather. It was the only time the Australians lost a three-day match that summer. They won a good deal of friendship instead.

These years of the seventies were throwing up a clutch of promising young players, many of them with local roots. Phil Slocombe had come in during 1975, scoring a neatly composed hundred on his third championship appearance and going on to his 1,000 runs. He was chosen for the MCC against the Australians and his name was already a long-range tip for Test-match status. The standard of his fielding, especially in the covers and outfield, never wavered but the undisputed early promise was not wholly sustained. He looked at his best in 1978 when he twice carried his bat. He had the footwork to play the slow bowling well but some technical flaws were never quite eradicated. Towards the end of his nine-year career he changed his attractive stance, to the surprise of many – and he hoped in vain for more regular selection.

There were also Vic Marks and Peter Roebuck, Oxford classical and Cambridge legal, Blundells and Millfield, of farming and academic stock respectively. Marks was the all-rounder, the off-spinner who was to bowl for England. He was whimsical and easy-going; he also had a neat turn of phrase, though not in the literate class of Roebuck, liberally and aptly described as 'studious' in appearance. Roebuck's maiden century came during the extraordinarily prolific Weston Festival of 1977, when both Rose and Richards scored double centuries and more than 2,000 runs were accumulated, often entertainingly, from the two matches against Northants and Surrey.

We can also conveniently pair Colin Dredge and Keith Jennings. Dredge, from Frome, had a big heart and a bad action; few better epitomised the spirit of Somerset cricket and he was to demonstrate his value, whether as a gritty back-up seam bowler or, as occasionally needed, as the prized possessor of the new ball. Jennings turned in some proficient spells at medium pace, especially in the one-day matches.

All this time, no one could possibly have better represented the quintessence of the engrained Somerset approach, however, than 'Budgie' Burgess from Glastonbury. He had scored his first two hundreds within days of each other. But he simply wasn't the kind to start building a column of county records. He endearingly dispensed the good with the bad, an exquisite off-drive to the fence with an appalling whack down an opponent's throat. Colleagues liked him because he could still be a modest match winner; they liked him just as much for his loyalty and unselfish attitude to team affairs. He could swing the ball both ways at will, on the sworn words of wicket keeper Taylor; he could belt quick runs with much style – and muscle. The temperament suggested a stroll with his mates down to the George and Pilgrim on a Sunday night rather than a demanding physical commitment in the pursuit of county cricket. In a memorable phrase, Eric Hill said that some of Burgess's fielding reminded him of 'a courtly canter'. He was, all the same, a fine one-day cricketer and always seemed to be figuring in (and at times winning) unbearably tight finishes.

It was an era when the dressing room chirped with local accents, give or take the stray Caribbean cadence. Denning's belonged irrefutably to Chewton Mendip, where dad had kept the butcher's shop and bowled to Peter on the back lawn. Maybe self-preservation and courage were important then. Later, at Taunton in 1977, against Gloucestershire, he drove and pulled and 'carved' his way to a hundred in each innings. Only a few weeks before he'd badly broken his jaw.

Breakwell's voice was a Staffordshire one. But he had a West Country sense of humour, maybe acquired in the days when he shared a self-catering club flat with Botham and Richards. Apart from his bowling, he could make punchy, distinctive shots, and was thrilled with his sole century, against the New Zealanders in 1978.

The county's wicket keeping remained in safe, unfussy hands. Taylor fully deserved his Test trial in 1976; he had led Somerset five times when Close wasn't fit or available. He always stood up to Cartwright and had some dazzling legside stumpings to show for it. Cartwright used to say: 'I wouldn't swap him if I had the pick of the whole country – I can't remember him putting down a catch off me.'

Botham and Richards had brought Somerset an aura of stardom. It was new for Somerset – and gave them an intoxicating excitement. The sheer precocity of Botham was a large part of his appeal. He went for his shots, he lived dangerously. His cricket was often naïve, or defiant. He worked on his own suspect theories as he bowled too many short-pitched balls, or kept hooking over-ambitiously. But he was an all-rounder of exceptional talents. In 1977 he played twice against the Australians and twice took 5 wickets in an innings. His England future was assured: here was a strong, self-confident, instinctive cricketer who could swing the ball away towards his line of poised slips, and who could rivet the spectators by his intrepid inclination to take on the fast bowlers as well as the slow ones. His first hundred for Somerset had come against Notts in 1976 and people were saying: 'He's the best all-rounder we've had since Arthur Wellard.'

He was soon parading an enormous versatility of talent and was, of course, a better batsman than Arthur, though both had a penchant for sixes. In no time, Botham would be starting to dominate whole columns of the record books. But, like all men of instinct, the pattern would inevitably be inconstant.

And meanwhile there was Richards. He had matured in a season of county cricket and was almost instantly a West Indian Test batsman, standing four-square with his legendary heroes, Worrell, Weekes and Walcott. Here was uncoached genius. The footwork and timing were impeccable, and what he called the God-given eyesight. He could unfurl a silken cover boundary of Hammond's calibre. His lofted drives and hooks were more effortlessly savage than anything a West Country crowd had ever seen before. And, oh joy, there was not the merest grain of automation in his style. At the wicket he would suddenly err like any other mortal. Greatness is all the sweeter with the balance of fallibility. For both Somerset and the West Indies, we saw impish pleasure on his face as he improvised. He invited revisions in the coaching manuals as he directed balls on his off-stump through the mid-wicket area. He still made it look supremely graceful though old-fogey bystanders, bound by convention, shuddered in reproach (or was it envy?).

By the end of the seventies he'd scored twenty-six centuries in the first-class game alone. They included two doubles for his country, at Trent Bridge and the Oval, and four for Somerset – against Yorkshire at Harrogate in

1975, and against Gloucestershire, Sussex and Surrey, all in 1977. His personality through this heady phase was much to the liking of the home crowds. He was unassuming and accessible. There were a few flashes of extreme anger, too, caused once or twice by insensitive racial taunts or by extreme self-criticism when he felt he had given his wicket away needlessly. Half the team were in tears after Somerset had failed to clinch the Sunday League title in 1978. Richards, frustrated beyond control and angry at the way he had changed his mind to give a simple catch, smashed his Jumbo bat into a hundred pieces against the stone floor.

Brian Rose had been made captain in 1978. He wasn't everyone's choice; there were other candidates. Certainly in his early days as a county cricketer he wasn't obvious captaincy material. For their part, Somerset seemed to hesitate about his long-term value and he went off to qualify as a teacher. In fact, the county's lack of faith in him was surprising. He was a tall left-hander, who struck the ball particularly well off the front foot; he would also clip the ball off his pads with some style. At Weston, where he'd lived for all but the first few days of his life, he hit 205 against Northants. He became an authoritative opening bat. Once at Taunton he took 3 wickets in 4 balls and the pundits were saying he should have bowled more.

Alec Bedser came down to the West Country, ostensibly to check on Botham. He went back enthusing about Rose who made his Test debut on the 1977–8 tour of Pakistan and New Zealand.

But would he make a good skipper? He was very much a private person, inclined to keep his thoughts to himself. He did his thinking – and he was an intelligent man – out on the golf course or when he tended his garden. He knew a great deal about both begonias and cover drives. His friends saw him puffing away on his cigar and wondered what sort of a leader he would prove.

Rose did the job for six years and for much of that time made a genuine success of it. He was good on tactics and had no great difficulty adjusting from three- to one-day cricket. If there were minor divisions in the dressing room they were kept discreetly out of the public view. Under him, Somerset had their best and dizziest summers. He had great international cricketers playing in his team. No one outside the dressing room will ever know how easy or difficult that was. But in the days when Somerset were the most talked-about, glamorous and televised county club in England, Rose was in charge – and he has every justifiable reason to bask in that astonishing wave of regional acclaim.

As a first-class cricketer, he took an unusual number of painful blows. The one that hurt most was psychological. It concerned the infamous Benson and Hedges zonal match with Worcestershire in May 1979. Somerset were thrown out of the competition in an official ruling that in sweeping condemnation was unprecedented. The reverberations threatened to shatter the county's morale. Many saw it as the day of the county's greatest shame. Loyal supporters spluttered: 'It's the vengeance of the establishment.' But they rather suspected it was more than that.

In a mathematical ruse of great complexity, Somerset reasoned that they could guarantee a quarter-final place for themselves by declaring after just 7 balls. It didn't matter that Worcestershire would win: Somerset would still qualify on striking rate, assessed by dividing the number of balls bowled by the number of wickets taken.

This pathetic, token match lasted twenty minutes. The spectators were outraged and so were the Worcestershire officials who refunded admission money. So were Glamorgan who stood to suffer. So were the other counties, Lord's, newspaper columnists, florid-cheeked retired colonels and ordinary cricket lovers. So were sponsors who were pumping in cash, supposedly for matches to be played in a normal fashion.

The Test and County Cricket Board, not always renowned for speed of action, this time moved in swift summary justice. Somerset were dismissed with ignominy from the competition; of all the counties, only Derbyshire opposed the ban.

'The Board unanimously condemned Somerset's action as being totally against the spirit of the game.' It was reported that Colin Atkinson, president of Somerset, had addressed the TCCB meeting and had said that the declaration after only one run had been scored was 'indefensible and deeply regretted'.

The whole affair was profoundly embarrassing for many of the county committee. There were fears, actually unfounded, that membership would suffer. West Country supporters were uneasy and divided. Some were troubled by what they saw as an open cynicism for the game and an arrogant indifference to the paying public. Others remained undeviatingly loyal, pointing out the fundamental fact that no rule had been broken.

Is it possible to look back more dispassionately at this distance? Rose, a man of measured deliberations and integrity, carried the heavy burden of responsibility. He was castigated on all sides. The experience left him more defensive; he steadfastly refused to talk about the incident. His friends said he was bitterly affected by the volume of animosity. Seven years later, he told me:

> We talked it over for a long time, back in the hotel when it was pouring with rain, and then again when we got to the ground. We were virtually unanimous, though it had to be my ultimate decision as captain. What we did was within the rules and I still have no regrets. It was the right thing for us to do, although many people probably won't agree. From the initial reaction of our officials, I feel they may have misjudged the mood of the team – and, in fact, that of the Somerset public. Not all the public may have agreed with what was done but they stood behind us and that was most gratifying. We'd lost out once or twice on a cruel technicality and didn't want to do so again. Now, we thought, perhaps it was our turn to win on a technicality.

Roy Kerslake, the chairman of Somerset's cricket committee and of the club itself then, was at Worcester with the players on that fateful morning.

I hesitated but in the end said I'd support the team whatever their decision. I was probably influenced by the fact that Brian had spoken on the phone to Donald Carr, secretary of the TCCB, who had confirmed that there was nothing in the rules to prevent what we proposed to do. Later I felt it was maybe wrong for the game of cricket and I offered to resign from the chairmanship.

Atkinson said:

It was the wrong thing to do. At the same time, I had some sympathy for the captain and the team. A captain's job is to get the team into the next round within the regulations. In the event I regret what happened but my heart doesn't make me feel that what they did was essentially or intentionally anti-cricket. There have always been things, throughout the history of the game, to raise eyebrows.

Somerset were despised. There was appalling publicity and the press made us pariahs. There wasn't much cricket going on in the days that followed and it seemed to me the papers had nothing else to write about. People went right over the top in condemning us – and so did the other counties. Emotions were running high. I suggested to some of the other counties that they were acting as a kind of kangaroo court. It would have helped if the meeting could have been delayed till feelings had cooled. But it wasn't possible to wait because of the next round of the competition coming up. And everyone was baying for blood. I think we should have had our knuckles rapped and fined – kicking us out was an over-reaction.

What the president discovered was a group of professional cricketers, incensed and 'feeling hard done by'. In the face of the savage media and hierarchical comment, the players' attitude hardened rather than mellowed.

The author's belief is that the misjudged ploy was generated by a chance remark in the dressing room as the whole team pondered the surest way of getting into the quarter-finals. It was sometimes said that one trouble with Somerset was that the team had too high an IQ. Excessively clever notions also need to be rationalised in a more detached environment than a changing room.

Surely Lord's could have been far more assertive once they had wind of what Rose and his players intended to do. It remains only to say that Atkinson rang Worcestershire, expressed his apologies and offered to play the match again the next day or the day after that. The suggestion was rejected.

Somerset's players incurred the wrath of a cricketing nation, the fair-minded as well as the pious and hypocritical, in a manner that was unprecedented in the history of county cricket. They closed ranks, saying little but conceding no ground. Some of them wondered privately if they had gone too far. Almost all of them, maybe in naïvety, were considerably surprised by the amount of fury directed at them. If there had been one dissenting voice within the dressing room it was Derek Taylor's, but he hadn't spoken out with too much emphatic force during the elongated discussions.

None of them knew for certain what to expect when it came to returning to Taunton for the Sunday match against Hampshire. If the home crowd also turned on them, they realised they'd be demoralised. The players stepped from their cars and hurried into the changing rooms. But the Somerset supporters arrived in their thousands to cheer. They hadn't all approved of what had happened but here they were now, presenting a wave of unforgettable loyalty when it was most needed.

'We're with you, Rosey – now go on and win something for us.' Everyone sensed that a conquest, infuriatingly elusive for too long, was near at last.

CHAPTER SIXTEEN
Glory and Glitter

One-day cricket, where there was more slogging than blocking – and not so much time to ponder the niceties of the game's sophisticated technique – had always endeared itself to Taunton's cricketing public. By the late seventies receipts at John Player matches were double those at many other counties. Ground records were being broken at Bath and Weston. Vocal support was strong; so, rather too much so at times, was the proof of the generously consumed cider. The atmosphere, wrapped up in rustic good nature, was for the most part a felicitous fillip to the team and something to be envied by every opposition. Just occasionally, in the uglier mood of our changing sporting times, there was bad behaviour and the necessity of legal action. It didn't look good when it was seen on television.

Rose, gratified at the warmth of the support, promised that he would do his best to arrange imminently for a title to come to Somerset. In 1976, they'd actually lost by one run off the final ball in the Sunday League. Then in 1977, when they rather fancied their prospects in the Gillette Cup, there had been that absurd 15 over match with Middlesex in the semi-final at Lord's. The players had patiently waited for six days for the weather to improve. Somerset, in a state of unparalleled panic, had all gone for 59: three of the team run out and three more out to full tosses. Middlesex won at 61-4; say no more.

There was worse frustration to come: defeat in the Gillette Cup final and the all-important Sunday League game, on successive days in September 1978. Somerset had been favourites to beat Sussex, yet lost by 5 wickets. Botham's 80 wasn't enough; nor was all the vocal support, up from the West Country – or the supernatural implication on the banners that 'Richards walks on scrumpy'. In anguish, feeling that the Somerset spectators had been let down, the West Indian hurled his loser's medal on to the floor of the changing rooms.

But there was still the next day. Back at Taunton, Somerset needed only to tie with Essex. The sun shone, the atmosphere with a crowd of 10,000 was electric, and they lost again, this time by 2 runs. Back in the pavilion the players slumped on the benches. They were silent, lost in their tortured thoughts. Half of them were crying. They made a token appearance in front of the crowd who were calling sympathetically for them; then the players bolted the door of their changing room and slumped once more on the benches. There was one acrid question they were all asking in their eloquent silence: 'Shall we ever win any bloody thing?'

They did, of course. On the last two days of the 1979 season, they beat Northants in the final of the Gillette Cup and, as Kent faltered at home to Middlesex, Somerset beat Notts to gain the John Player League title, too. It was the first time in 104 years that the county had picked up any major trophy.

On the Saturday at Lord's, before a capacity crowd, Somerset scored 269-8 and won by 45 runs. Their debt to the West Indians, Richards and Garner, was immense. Richards was at the wicket by the seventh over and stayed till the last. His 117 was, by his most expansive standards, a *controlled* gem. And Garner, 'Big Bird', all 6ft 8in of him, took 6-29. Once Cook had been run out and Lamb sweetly stumped, it had to be Somerset's triumph. The economy of Jennings' and Botham's bowling shouldn't be ignored; nor Rose's useful runs at the start of the day.

Then it came to Sunday, at Trent Bridge. Would Somerset's 185-8, helped by Roebuck's half-century, be sufficient? The surprise was that they won by 56 runs. Only Robinson and Rice resisted; 7 wickets tumbled for 46, mostly to Garner, Botham and Dredge, though Richards delivered 7 overs of intelligent modesty.

It was a weekend to cherish, for both romantics and historians. The Benson and Hedges expulsion was forgotten. So were those succeeding decades of folly and failure. Perhaps it was an illusion but one gained the impression that people, players and cricket lovers far away from the region, were pleased for Somerset. Status that only came with the possession of pennants had been overdue.

The 1979 summer had been full of bountiful deeds. Test-match calls had depleted the county side and would do so increasingly in the coming years: it was part of the price of new-found stardom. Somerset, fielding a weakened team, lost the last match of the championship season – and it brought to an end an extraordinary sequence of twenty-three matches without defeat. The club has never had an unbeaten run to compare with it.

The sentimentalists were sorry to note that venues like Glastonbury, Yeovil and the Imperial Ground, Bristol were now missing from the fixture lists. There were even dark rumours that Bath and Weston might be in jeopardy before too long. But Somerset surged into the eighties with a self-confident step.

In 1980, Rose went back to Worcester where no doubt his ears were burning; his bat was gripped with a commendable resolve. He made a century in each innings. It was also the season when he played in three Tests against the West Indians, under his county vice-captain, Botham. Somerset's pattern of high scoring had been set in May when they had reached 534-6 in 100 overs at the expense of hapless bowlers like Graveney – who surely deserved to be brought on before the total had passed 300 – Partridge, Brain, Wilkins and even Procter. Botham turned in one of his famous innings of muscular magnificence, taking 184 minutes for his 228. The author found himself complementing groundstaff and other doting spectators in retrieving the ball from distant car parks and the groundsman's cabbage patch. Some of the sixes reached the Tone and floated downstream with the fish, for ever out of sight if not mind. That day, Botham's partnership of 310 with Denning was a new record for the fourth wicket, beating that of Richards and Roebuck three years before. Denning made 98. 'For most of the time I just sat on me bat and watched "Both" get on with it', he said with typical modesty.

Garner and Richards were away playing for their country. Rose was ill for a time and Botham went down with back trouble. But there were compensations. Nigel Popplewell got his maiden hundred for them. He'd landed a contract on the strength of scoring half his side's runs when Cambridge were all out for 98 at Bath the season before. The spectators took to him: his jokey, classless ways, his self-mockery, his value as a team-man, even though a detached view suggested his fielding at short leg was better than his medium-pace bowling.

Jeremy Lloyds, that same year, took 11 wickets against Worcestershire at Weston. He had demonstrated that he could turn the ball; many suspected that he was just as capable a batsman, probably at his best as an opener. He had a run there for Somerset and fashioned several neat innings. But the county already had an accomplished off-break bowler in Marks, and as a batsman Lloyds was inclined to fall from favour. In 1985 he chose to switch to Gloucestershire where he discovered the scope was greater.

Moseley, able to play again, was bowling as well as ever. Only the sheer profusion of pacemen from the West Indies denied him a Test or two. He wasn't quite as fast now but he could curve the ball away from the bat – and keep going as long as he was asked, beaming shyly as he returned after his latest over to the applauding spectators on the long-leg fence. Another West Indian, Hugh Gore from Antigua, recommended by Richards, was here for the season and bowled accurately at left-arm medium pace. An additional Somerset player on a one-year contract was Sunil Gavaskar.

In different circumstances, with different rules of registration, he'd have been welcome for many more years. He wrapped up against the early-summer cold and sat reading his paperbacks between innings. We don't imagine he warmed to the crash-bang necessities of the Sunday League or, at times, the remorseless itinerary demanded of county cricketers. He was popular with the Somerset team and much admired by the young players.

The quality was unquestionable; he left behind several innings of rare charm by which we can remember him. He came as the temporary stand-in for Richards, a master in his own right, and it was apposite that he should leave with 155 not out against Yorkshire. There was a hint that he might return to Taunton but it would not have been practicable. Martin Crowe was to be the new overseas player, available to come in when Richards and Garner weren't available.

Surely there's a controversy of some sort to list in that same season. Indeed there is. Somerset were playing at Bristol and the scores were level when it came to the last ball. Roebuck and Dredge paused and then chased in signs of jubilation for a leg-bye. But the umpire, Ken Palmer, was shaking his head. 'I'd already called "Over" so you're out of luck', he told the batsmen. And he a Somerset man, too.

Peter May, president of the MCC, came to open the new headquarters pavilion in the May of 1981, during the match with the Australians. The design met with much approval, if not with that of one of *The Times* cricket correspondents. It was an appropriate year to launch a new phase. Somerset came third in the championship, second in the John Player competition and won the Benson and Hedges Cup for the first time.

Surrey were very much outplayed. They made 194-8, of which Roger Knight alone provided some substance with 92. Somerset got the runs in the forty-fifth over, to win by 7 wickets. It seemed almost a formality that Richards should score 132 not out. He began with seemly if untypical restraint, a gratifying approach after both Rose and Denning had gone by the third over.

If Richards, peerless among his contemporaries when it came to making stylish and ferocious hitting compatible, was the match winner against Surrey, then Garner was not so far behind. His bowling figures were 11-5-14-5. Everyone in the first-class game now acknowledged that he was the most difficult fast bowler to score runs off. Yet it wasn't just his pace: it was the bounce he obtained, his devastating use of the yorker, the problems of picking up the flight of the ball quickly as he released it from that prodigious height. His arm always looked as high as the pavilion clock.

The Ex-Somerset County Cricketers' Association was formed in 1982. Members, and officials of the county club, in this group are: (*Back, left to right*) Graham Burgess, Tony Brown, Brian Langford, Mike Latham, Dennis Breakwell, John Gardner, Dennis Silk, Geoff Lomax, Eric Hill, Terry Barwell, Lewis Pickles, Bryan Lobb, Ken Biddulph. (*Centre*) Peter Robinson, Max Jeffrey, Les Angell, Roy Smith, Graham Atkinson, David Kitson, Ken Day, Graham Tripp, Peter Eele. (*Front*) Trevor Jones, John Barnwell (Secretary), Dickie Burrough, Michael Hill (county chairman), Jake Seamer, Norman Mitchell-Innes, Cecil Buttle, George Woodhouse.

Somerset were marvellously represented when it came to the fifth Test match at Leeds in 1980 and photographer Ken Kelly brought them together to capture this piece of county history. The two Test umpires were Ken Palmer (*left*) and Bill Alley. The four Somerset players taking part in the match were Viv Richards, Brian Rose, Joel Garner and Ian Botham

During Somerset's golden years, Richards and Garner in tandem, batsman and bowler, both lethal and languid, gave the county a majesty and an authority which they had never possessed before – and may never possess again. They were also genial individuals without the tiresome trappings of fame. Their Caribbean personae, with Richards' fallibility as well as his instinctive grandeur of batsmanship, was embraced by a mesmerised Taunton public. They used to say: 'He could have played for no other county but Somerset.'

The vastness of their talents was apt to dwarf the workaday exertions of lesser mortals. But we should still pluck from 1981 the way Denning battled to 98 when Underwood had what for him was an ideal wicket – or the way at Bath Rose and Roebuck, both injured, went out to save the match against Gloucestershire; or Lloyds' maiden hundred against a Lancashire side which included Michael Holding.

The dramatic emergence of Somerset, in the face of history, as one of the country's most dominant sides – viewed alongside big local crowds, the obsessive commercialism within the game and a discernible shifting of balance between players and officials in most clubs – brought inevitable problems. Committee members and one or two officials were becoming just a little restive. What had started as a whisper was gaining vocal momentum.

'The players are getting too powerful. Soon they'll be running the club.'

More than a few people were becoming quite paranoiac about player-power. Their much-voiced concern sprang in a few cases from self-interest and dubious motives and as such might be discounted.

But it was a fact that a widening gap was growing, about this time, between players and committee. It probably suited some of the cricketers – they didn't want to be pestered by 'amateur' committee members who, as the players saw it, had taken an egotistical delight in getting themselves elected. The argument was occasionally valid, more often unfair. Certainly there was an uneasy lack of communication and some mutual suspicion.

The players took Roy Kerslake, as chairman of the cricket committee, to their bosom. He was their Father Confessor, a kindly considerate man who gave them legal advice and retained close personal friendships with many of them. Some senior members were jealous of the relationship he had with the players. He stood down at one stage and was persuaded to come back.

There was also the extraordinary case of Peter 'Jock' McCombe, a tubby, good-natured Glaswegian who admitted he was star-struck. Just as he had once idolised George Best, now he turned his attention to Richards and later Botham as well. The county gave him a nebulous title of players' liaison officer; in effect he was the baggage man and often the confidant. He carried the messages and collected the groceries. Some, in the language of abrasive fiction, saw him as a 'heavy', the minder of the superstars. He did shield his heroes from untimely journalists and even committee members, but it was only his physique that was heavy. Jock, who hadn't even seen a cricket match until he arrived in Somerset, was, as the obituaries said, 'a harassed, kind, unpretentious man'.

Amid the rumblings of excessive player-power, McCombe's was a name that recurred in the edgy conversations. 'He's closer to the team than we are – it isn't right.' Jock was rather embarrassed by the stage whispers. The senior players had determined his role. He carried it out with diligence and extreme loyalty. There were tentative attempts to manoeuvre him out of the job. The players would never have allowed it.

He died aged forty-six in 1984, while he was staying at Richards' home in Antigua. The West Indian asked to be excused from the next one-day Test and brought the body back to England. Every pew was filled for the funeral service in Taunton. McCombe's good friend Roy Kerslake read the lesson. Four of the players bore the coffin. Every member of the team, every leading official of the club was present. This once unskilled labourer died a celebrity and a much-loved figure. Some on the fringe of the committee probably never understood why.

The balance of power within a successful club can be a sensitive subject. The Somerset president Colin Atkinson, questioned by the author, said:

> It did bother me at one stage. But I'm not criticising the players – I think there are usually reasons why they want more power. When relationships break down, there are two parties involved. Perhaps we didn't have it right by a long way and it could be argued that we haven't got it absolutely right now. Players are inclined to think committees are just there to criticise them. They aren't; they are just enthusiasts. In most sports, players look on the administrators as a necessary evil.

What should also be appreciated is that the Somerset team, full of whims, foibles and exceptional personal deeds, had by now taken on a new mental fibre. It was reflected in the team talks before the big games, and by the appointment of Dennis Waight, a mightily compact Aussie as physiotherapist. His own muscles were built up during his days as a swimming instructor, rugby-league player and hard-swinging amateur boxer. 'Half of you can't touch your toes', he joked (or maybe he wasn't joking) when he arrived at Taunton. He introduced rigorous early-morning exercise sessions that earned him looks of affected hostility and the nickname 'Sluggo'. His reputation as an earthy, conscientious advocate of uncompromised fitness had been established in his handling of the West Indies Test team. Now he was fast getting rid of the creaking joints and the flaccid midriffs at Somerset.

In short, Somerset were more professional. The television lens seemed to follow them wherever they went. They were the most dynamic team, at least for much of the time, in the whole of England. They savoured it, realistic enough to sense that it might not last. There was a tendency to cosset and pamper them; the fawning increased. Within the dressing room, life was good – especially if you weren't on the fringe of the team, nor got irritated by the internal politics.

During 1982 Botham made the Taunton boundary appear ludicrously minute as he hit a hundred off 56 balls from a helpless range of Warwickshire bowlers. A few months earlier, playing for England against Central Zone of India, the hundred came off 48 balls. Comparisons were made with Jessop, though it was their scoring rate rather than their style which had something in common. Botham had already proved himself one of the game's timeless entertainers and match winners. But there was much more to come, with bat and ball, on the field and off.

Roebuck was now opening the innings; Lloyds was taking prized wickets and scoring a hundred in each innings at Northampton, a feat which won him his cap but didn't lead to a long-term future with the county all the same; Taylor went out on a high note. Back in 1976 this most efficient wicket keeper had claimed eight dismissals in a match at Cardiff. Now he created a new record for one-day cricket with eight *catches* against Oxford and Cambridge in the Benson and Hedges competition. This was to be his last season with Somerset before moving to a new career in Australia. Trevor Gard, tidy and unshowy, would now be given the chance for which he'd waited patiently. He walked with a big stride for one so small, never without his cap. He was a village boy, useful with his 12 bore and, it was claimed, proficient with his ferrets.

Were there other potential first-team players around? Mark Davis, a left-arm seam bowler from Kilve, was looking a distinct prospect; so was Nigel Felton, an engaging left-hander and likely opener, from Millfield. About this same time a sixteen-year-old, Gary Palmer, son of Ken, emerged. He was seen then as a genuine all-rounder, rather better as a quickish bowler.

An engagement in the finals of something or other was becoming a pleasant habit. Somerset went back to Lord's to defend the Benson and Hedges title – and won again. Notts were put in to bat, were all out for 130 in just over 50 overs, and lost a one-sided match by 9 wickets. Randall and Rice, on whom Notts leaned, were both bowled by Marks who, largely on the strength of that, won the gold award. No one begrudged him it, even if Garner took 3-13. The equable Marks had, by intelligence and some improvisation, turned himself into an excellent one-day cricketer – as England discovered. He was overtly cheerful and serene as a Chinnock sunset; in the corner of the dressing room he chain-smoked with feverish concern for what might be happening out there.

At that Lord's match all the Somerset bowling was commendable, not least that of Moseley in his belated and only final. Then half-centuries by Roebuck and, inevitably, Richards carried them home in just over 33 overs.

The maligned Weston square, slandered and libelled over the years with varying degrees of validity, was relaid at the end of the season. In August Somerset had lost by an innings to Middlesex. They lasted for only sixty-five minutes when they batted a second time. The openers, Roebuck, who had grafted for 67 overs on the first day, and Lloyds, were the only ones to reach double figures. Hughes and Cowans obtained lift almost at will. The Somerset total was 57; all 10 wickets went down in an embarrassing 46 deliveries.

All of which fuelled the old argument that Clarence Park should be diplomatically dropped from the list of venues. This, in turn, brought a sturdy rejoiner from faithful local members and loyal sponsors. 'You can't rely on the wicket, the facilities are poor and there's a lack of privacy', chorused the players. 'It makes economic sense to use the excellent facilities at Taunton for as many matches as possible', came the voices of seconders, thundering over the Mendips from headquarters.

The long-term future of the outside venues remains a delicate issue as this book is being written. Those local committee members at Weston and Bath, who have worked so hard to sustain the sponsorship and retain their festivals, say: 'Think of the public relations aspect – don't alienate your supporters who live away from Taunton.'

Bath's square was also relaid. There were so many memories there, against the backcloth of all those churches and the Abbey, and the Georgian crescents tucked into the hillsides. It seemed unthinkable to many that the Recreation Ground, whatever its failings, could be lost at some time. And how could one lose Weston, where the holiday-makers come up from the beach to watch, where good-hearted drunks were known to fall out of the conifers, where Geoff Lomax had got an unlikely hat-trick and where Peter May had with Lock and Laker drunk locally brewed elderberry wine to celebrate another championship title for Surrey?

Somerset dipped to tenth in the table when it came to 1983. Some of the reasons are easy to find. There were injuries; four players were involved in the World Cup. But there were still record receipts and membership – and a record eighth wicket stand at Leicester (172). Richards made 216, Botham 152. It should never be forgotten that Botham, known to his friends as 'Beefy' – he limited friendship when it came to the Fourth Estate – can excel in adversity. At Leicester he went in at No 9 because he was unwell. It was hard to convince reputable bowlers like Roberts, Taylor, Cook and Steele of his state of health.

At Bath, where Gloucestershire were the visitors, the early-morning atmosphere was ecclesiastical and decorous; that was until Popplewell went to the wicket with a brisk stride, encouraged by the suggestion that he should score some quick runs. Brought up in a legal household, he liked to take advice and act on it precisely. In forty-one minutes, he swung, drove, swept and pulled his way to a hundred. Graveney and Dudleston invited him to keep going, in the spirit of the match and with the hope of creating a result. It still wasn't the fastest century of the summer. That was achieved by O'Shaughnessy (thirty-five minutes) in an absurd romp for Lancashire against Leicestershire.

That was the strength of Popplewell. With a boyish enthusiasm he'd mould to the demands of the team. He was happiest of all when it meant going for his shots, including his beloved square cut. The evening before his frantically composed century, Popplewell went on a hilarious cruise with team-mates and friends down the Avon. At one stage, as a diversion to the bacchic activities on board, he allowed himself to be pushed into the water.

He was quite sober but not averse to the occasional extrovert jape. His exhibition of the butterfly stroke met with much acclaim. Wet clothes and a late night brought no ill effects. He was on time next morning, unlike the author. It was a loss to Somerset, and a surprise to many, when he gave up county cricket at the end of 1985 for some law studies.

He played his part in the run-up to the NatWest final in 1983. His was a vital stand with Botham in the memorable semi-final against Middlesex. Both sides finished on 222 but Somerset went through because they had lost fewer wickets. Botham, calm, responsible, calculative, was still there at the end with 96 not out; he had batted for 205 minutes and some would make out a case that it was his finest innings.

Back to Lord's for the final against Kent, Somerset won by 24 runs to sustain their era of triumph. The groans reverberated all the way up the M4 and M5 when Richards (51) was out the last ball before lunch. The light was poor, the movement from Dilley was off-putting. But Popplewell and Marks cajoled the score to 193. Kent tried in vain to keep up with the asking rate. Garner's bowling was once more too deadly, Gard's leg-side stumpings were too agile, and the dependable Marks was around for 3 opportune wickets, as well as another Man of the Match award.

Somerset had been forced to call on four different captains that year. One of them was Botham, who now in 1984 took over officially from Rose. He liked doing the job and at times did it very well. Much of the time he was away playing for England; domestically it was his benefit year and was worth more than £90,000 to him.

It was the summer when Martin Crowe, a mature, accomplished twenty-one-year-old New Zealander, turned up to play for Somerset. He took a few weeks to get used to our wickets. Then he scored just under 1,900 runs, complemented by 44 wickets. Richards was on tour here with the West Indians and Crowe took his place in such a way that, aesthetically and statistically, Somerset didn't suffer. That is the greatest compliment that one can pay the New Zealander.

He came to Taunton as the result of a chance remark during a radio commentary. The county chairman, Michael Hill, was travelling with his wife to watch the 1983 Test at Trent Bridge. 'We were running late so I switched on the car radio to see how the match was going. The New Zealand commentator happened to say that Martin was looking for a county so that he could play some cricket here.' At lunch, the Somerset chairman found himself sitting next to the New Zealand manager and broached the subject. 'I'll bring him across to you for a chat.' And that was the prelude to an enthusiastic exchange of letters, followed by Crowe's nostalgic entry to the county scene. It was nostalgic because he, the correctness of his feet, eager stroke play and the almost flawless manner he chiselled one innings after another, belonged to another age, golden and chivalrous. He reminded some of the young Chappell who had arrived in the West sixteen years earlier. But it wasn't simply that he made his runs so well; he had a presence that was attractive. His approach to cricket was as enthusiastic as it was academic. He

Tony Brown, the Somerset secretary, welcomes Martin Crowe to the county ground

built a valuable rapport with the younger players and observers noted his distinct leadership qualities. But the 'overseas' rule meant that he would have to withdraw when the West Indians returned to the county.

In that one season, Crowe hit six hundreds. His best was against Leicestershire when he scored 190, and with Roebuck (128) created a new county record for the third wicket. It was a quite magnificent partnership. Somerset needed 341 in 87 overs – and the first 2 wickets had gone for 3 runs. They still won by 6 wickets.

Roebuck blossomed in his own right during 1984. He'd been criticised for falling short too often, just when a big score seemed in prospect. He tried to extend his repertoire of strokes, and to stay. It was something of a double success: he reaped 1,700 runs and seven centuries from all first-class matches. His method would never be dynamic; it would always be an exercise of intellectual challenge. On the reassuring form of that season, it was hard to make a firm adjudication on which was the better, his batting or his writing.

Marks, the vice-captain, had no intention to be outdone by his old chum. He turned in an 8 wicket bowling performance against Kent. Even more to his impish delight, no doubt, he surprised his dressing-room intimates with three championship hundreds towards the end of the year. Their composition was much admired, too. He reached 1,000 runs for the first time – and cut down on his smoking.

There were farewells to be said. The big-hearted Moseley left rather more abruptly than was necessary. Denning went because his work was done and

Lloyds because he thought Gloucestershire might have more use for him. Slocombe, who had promised so much, decided to leave, and so did Hugh Wilson, a big fast bowler who must have felt somewhat aggrieved when the likeable but almost forgotten Breakwell was played instead of him in an aberration of team selection for the NatWest quarter-final match with Kent.

Julian Wyatt, another farmer's son to join Somerset, batted with courage against the West Indian fast bowlers. He was also in an opening stand of 246 with Roebuck when Yorkshire came to Taunton. It became evident that he would have the edge over Richard Ollis, an upright left-hander who was once stranded on 99 not out against Gloucestershire, for whom Graveney stage-managed an extra over to give the batsman the chance of his maiden century. Likewise, among the bowlers, Davis at this stage seemed to have the edge over Palmer. Davis sorted out some technical shortcomings and then took 66 well-earned wickets before he was injured. He found it very difficult indeed over the next two seasons to build on that haul. Palmer's progress, too, stumbled.

The 1985 season was a painful paradox. Everything should have gone right; very little did. The playing record was an unmitigated disaster. There was one win only in the championship and the county finished bottom. Morale suffered, despite a few brave faces and plenty of brave performances. Some of the younger players looked in vain for motivation. Membership was down, though not to the extent of causing alarm. The buzz of excitement around the boundary, an uplifting musical accompaniment for the past seven or eight years, was less noticeable.

One or two of the team performances carried almost an air of resignation. When there was public criticism, senior players would respond defensively: 'What else do you expect? We've never had the chance of a settled side.' It was a valid point. Botham was available for only eleven championship matches. He took 11 wickets for Somerset – and that was no return from an England bowler. Garner was repeatedly bothered by a knee injury. The seam back-up was fragile and frequently inadequate. There was a cruelness in the way the injuries multiplied: Dredge, Rose, Wyatt, Roebuck, Gard were all missing from the side, some for long periods.

Stephen Booth, the slow left-arm bowler who had come down from Yorkshire and first played with some promise as a nineteen-year-old two summers before, now took 4 Australian wickets. Many thought Richard Coombs – based at first on his excellent 5-58 against Middlesex at Weston – looked the better prospect. He was taller and a few years older than Booth and was ready to give cricket a go once his university studies were over. At that same Weston Festival, Jonathan Atkinson, son of the president, took everyone by surprise with a fine debut against Northants, just after his seventeenth birthday. He arrived at the ground not even knowing he was playing; his name wasn't on the scorecard. Nepotism had nothing to do with it, though his proud parents watched in trepidation from the sponsor's tent. Young Atkinson was clearly in on merit. Tall, slim, rushed into his flannels too quickly to be nervous he hit three sixes and eleven fours in both a daring and composed innings of 79. His partner, Botham, was there to encourage him – and to lead the applause.

But for the problems of finding eleven fit players for each successive match, Atkinson might not have had that early chance. It also worked in favour of Richard Harden, a tidy and mature-looking nineteen-year-old who scored a hundred against Cambridge University. Richard Hayward, once briefly with Middlesex and Hampshire, was another century-maker in that fixture. He'd been flown to England in a hurry from New Zealand to bolster a sagging team, many of whose batsmen were spending their days prone and powerless in the treatment room.

The glaring contradiction of Somerset's dispiriting season of 1985 came with the mountainous individual feats. There were eighteen centuries, nine of them from the peerless Richards. When Warwickshire came to Taunton in the June, he was feeling particularly weary after a late-night journey home from Leeds. You wouldn't have known: he went in to bat, sparred for a couple of overs and then made 322.

Young Paul Bail had just gone off, hit on the head – and Felton was out first ball. There was never a prelude that visibly disconcerted Richards. He stayed around for just under five hours. In that time some of the bowling, notably by Small, was very good. Richards was on a different plane of achievement altogether. There was far too much artistry ever to call it a slog. The Warwickshire fielders described it variously as controlled brutality, unabated butchery and, from one opponent less inclined to blood-red imagery, 'the kind of batting genius I pray I compete against never again in my suddenly very inadequate career.'

Those who missed the innings pretended they were there. The author was lucky enough to be in the press box and to share a lengthy, quite emotional, sojourn with the great West Indian later that evening in the almost deserted, equipment-strewn dressing room. Richards talked about religion, about Rastafarian friends with whom he'd once gone to school and about loyalty – from choice – but hardly at all about cricket.

We can't allow the same omission. Earlier in the day, his first hundred came in 112 minutes (105 balls), his second hundred in 88 minutes (76) and his third in 76 minutes (63). The pattern was obvious. One kept thinking of Bill Andrews' famous words after standing awe-struck on the Clarence Park boundary as Richards playfully chipped one of his double centuries. 'That lovely bugger is going to score a thousand runs one of these days!' At tea, Brian Langford told Richards that he could beat Gimblett's record innings of 310. Maybe someone even whispered in his ear that MacLaren had scored 424 on this same ground. Neither statistic would have impressed him. It was only the game's historians, he used to say, who were interested in figures.

Botham remained an enigma during the summer. He had a new agent, there was exaggerated talk of a showbusiness career and there was some sartorial eccentricity from him, allied to marketing considerations. Some of his mates couldn't quite fathom which direction, professionally, he was going. His batting could still be thunderously thrilling. There were eighty sixes by him, a dozen of them coming in an innings at Edgbaston. It was a world record, in the 'Beefy' tradition, – team-mate Wellard previously held the record with a mere sixty-six. An envious opponent was heard to say: 'He's the only bloke I know who can get sixes at will off mishits.'

The superb, outrageous batting feats were chronicled on the sports pages with the ecstatic ring of schoolboy fiction. They were heroic, tinged with the liberties of unreality. His five hundreds included the fastest of the season, that bewildering onslaught at Birmingham, where 94 of the runs came off boundaries. He needed just 26 scoring strokes. His disdainful regard for the Warwickshire bowlers was equalled by his consideration for the scorers. He kept their job – and their entries – simple, just as long as they could write quickly and were strong on arithmetic.

No one will ever quite work out how, in a summer of such personal dynamism, Somerset ended up with sheepish discomfiture on the bottom. This was also the year, after all, when Popplewell went out with a stirring 172 at Southend. Nearer home, at Bath, Marks, marvelling in his mischief, had already bowled Somerset to an isolated innings win over Lancashire. The off-spinner, ever honest, would accept the shortcomings of some of the Lancashire batting. But his 8-17 was something to be cherished, a reward for long, willing, masochistic stints on third days when runs were on offer and bowling averages were sacrificed in the interest of the team.

And on into 1986, with a new captain. Botham had already decided to sign for one more season instead of two. Then his resignation from the captaincy was announced in the tabloid, for which he was contracted, before the county were told. Later that same October day, he turned up at a much publicised and highly theatrical meeting at the county ground. There seemed to be more journalists and camera crews around than members. At the news conference that followed, under the TV lights, it was hard to say who looked more tense and nervous, Botham or Atkinson. The resigning skipper, reading from his prepared statement, said he didn't feel he could devote enough time to doing the job adequately. He was succinct and showed no inclination to answer supplementary questions. Then the club president ended the speculation by announcing that Roebuck would be the successor.

There'd been a reasonable case for Marks and less so for Richards. But Roebuck, still not yet thirty, had strong support. He had done the job a few times very well indeed, with a more dashing style than his circumspect batting might have implied. He was, in addition, the kind of person who responded to mental challenges. Early signs were encouraging. His answers to journalists' questions were thoughtful and refreshingly free of cliché. The hopes, from committee room and boundary seats, were that he'd help to generate a new resolve.

Richards, who had just hit the fastest Test century on record on his native St John's Ground in Antigua, had hardly got back to Taunton before he was ready to maintain the mood. His hundred off Glamorgan came from 48 balls. Greg Thomas, a fledgling Test bowler returned from the Caribbean, gave away 51 runs in 4 overs. Richards scored 49 of them; in a stand of 115 with Roebuck, the mesmeric West Indian made 102.

Never to be outdone for too long by his close friend, Botham was soon winning games with last-over sixes and looking reassuringly relaxed. It had been a bad winter for him. Not much had gone his way during the West Indies tour. The runs had been elusive, the bowling expensive and the headlines lurid. There were allegations of drug-taking and bedroom pranks. Some of the stories, by circulation-conscious tabloids, had a familiar spurious appearance; some seemed to have more than an element of truth. He'd also parted company, not unexpectedly, with his agent.

Earlier in the year he had won much acclaim for his marathon walk in aid of leukaemia research. That feat of stamina alas led to other allegations and questions from the police. From Botham the denials continued – and the writs for libel from his solicitor apparently multiplied. But suddenly he took almost everyone by surprise when in the course of a three-page spread in a Sunday paper he admitted he'd been smoking pot in the past. It read like the latest bewildering twist in the Life and Times of Ian Terence Botham.

The saga appeared to go on with a bewildering, self-destructive fervour. Botham's loyal admirers shifted the argument and directed their scorn on the merciless media. Others, who had thrilled to his great talents on the field, were saddened and at times appalled by mounting indiscretions. 'Whatever kind of standard is he setting for the young who idolise him'? was a recurrent lament. There had already been one conviction for drugs possession, followed by pious shrieks of dismay from the public and talk of severe reprimands. Later, after Botham's confessions in print, the TCCB imposed an unprecedented ban; this ruled out any first class cricket during the June and July of 1986 – 'for bringing the game into disrepute', 'prejudicing the interests of cricket' and other listed misdemeanours. The ban was a punishment, partly designed to affect his Test match earnings. Somerset argued in vain that they were being unfairly penalised in the process. Botham himself, now with a new agent and new ideas said to incorporate a possible future in Australia, went off to fish and forget, and be nearer his family. He was always sounder in judgement over a run than a pungent word: he turned up at a stag dinner in Manchester and his so-called satirical observations on the Test selectors and contemporary cricketers only added to the crude self-inflicted wounds. And all this had happened when he was two wickets short of Dennis Lillee's Test world record of 355.

Ian Botham has been one of cricket's greatest all-rounders and it has been a privilege to watch and wonder. He has brought fame and infamy to Somerset. Often he has looked stronger than the county. But he has also undeniably loved Somerset, enticing thousands of additional spectators to Taunton, Bath and Weston, to savour his instinctive, glittering entertainment. Not many players, in the whole history of the game, have possessed his prodigious natural gifts. He's highly marketable, highly quotable and, a man of surprising complexity, highly strung. He's flawed – and he knows it. The sweeping paradoxes of his nature will never disappear.

He will remain likeable, irritating and contemptuous of many conventional standards. The headlines are likely to continue long after this book is published.

Back to cricketing matters. Somerset now had a new batsman, the capable South African left-hander Jon Hardy, from Hampshire, and a new bowler, Nick Taylor, who had already tried in vain to make some sort of impact with Yorkshire and Surrey. Richard Bartlett, just out of Taunton School, had made a most promising hundred on his debut against Oxford. Roebuck achieved a double century at Trent Bridge, and Marks 14 wickets at Sophia Gardens, partly bowling into a gale.

There remained a loyalty of support that many other counties envied. It was reflected in the continued enthusiasm of the district committees, the backing of the Supporters' Club and the Wyverns. Most people seemed relieved that the dear old (and much maligned) pavilion had won its reprieve. The evocative wooden structure, not up to safety standards, wouldn't lose its façade after all. Despite trying times with the weather over several recent seasons, the intimate ground was looking as good as ever. As head groundsman, Gordon Prosser, who had taken over from the conscientious Don Price, deserved much credit for that.

It was only right that Somerset, the most potently emergent county in England over the past ten years, should now provide a national tour manager. Tony Brown, a successful county captain and then secretary-manager with Gloucestershire, had moved to Taunton to take over as secretary in 1983. Before long he was managing with wisdom and diplomatic skill the politically fraught tour of India.

The long-term future of county cricket, as we know it, remains a matter of unconvincing optimism. There are too many ominous questions, many of them to do with sponsorship, economic realities and changing social patterns. It could be difficult for Somerset as some of the greatest players in their history leave. Can life be anything but anti-climatic after the wondrous deeds of Richards, Garner and Botham?

At the end of the 1986 season, the decision not to offer new contracts to the illustrious West Indians brought varying reactions of disbelief, dismay, and inevitable cries of disloyalty directed at the cricket committee, as well as some support. It must have been an agonising choice, balancing the achievements of Richards and Garner against the skills of Crowe, nearly lost to another county. This kind of torment, caused by the subject of overseas registrations, is not unknown. "Long-term realism" is not always compatible with sentimental gratitude. Richards and Garner, for their part, felt they had been let down.

In more than a hundred years of first-class cricket, Somerset have survived such emotional issues as this, floods, flaccid management and an intermittent threat of bankruptcy. All we ask now, in cheerful resilience – and to justify the title of the book – is that the sun continues to shine, the sixes still bounce reverentially off the tombstones in St James's churchyard . . . and that the apple juice keeps its especial West Country fizz.

Statistical Supplement

OFFICIALS

Year	President	Year	Secretary
1891–1915	Hon. Sir Spencer Ponsonby-Fane, B.T.	1908–1910	H. E. Murray Anderdon
1916–1922	H. E. Murray Anderdon	1911–12	G. Fowler
1923	A. E. Newton	1913–19	R. Brooks-King
1924	The Marquis of Bath, K.G.	1920–22	S. M. J. Woods
1925	Lt.-Col. Sir Dennis F. Boles, B.T.	1923–31	A. F. Davey
1926	Col. H. M. Ridley	1932–36	J. Daniell
1927	Rev. Preb. A. P. Wickham	1937–49	Brig. E. H. Lancaster
1928	Col. H. M. Ridley	1950	N. J. C. Daniell
1929	L. C. H. Palairet	1950–55	Air Vic-Marshall M. L. Taylor
1930	V. T. Hill	1955–69	R. Robinson
1931-32	Major A. G. Barrett	1970–75	A. K. James
1933	Lt.-Col. W. O. Gibbs	1975–79	R. G. Stevens
1934–35	Lt.-Col. Sir Dennis Boles, B.T.	1979–82	D. G. Seward
1936	The Duke of Somerset	1982–	A. S. Brown
1937–46	R. C. N. Palairet		Chairman
1947–49	J. Daniell		Until 1952 the President of the Club
1950–53	Major G. E. Longrigg		also acted as Chairman.
1954–60	The Bishop of Bath & Wells	1952–53	Major G. E. Longrigg
1961	J. C. White	1954–59	A. H. Southwood
1962–65	W. T. Greswell	1960–69	E. F. Longrigg
1966–67	Lord Hylton	1969–71	Lt.-Col. G. C. G. Grey
1968–71	E. F. Longrigg	1972–73	C. R. M. Atkinson
1971–76	R. V. Showering	1974–76	H. W. Hoskins
1976–	C. R. M. Atkinson	1977–78	L. G. Creed
	Secretary	1979	R. C. Kerslake
1891–94	Jointly: T. Spencer, H. E. Murray Anderdon	1979–82	J. M. Jeffrey
1895–1907	Jointly: H. E. Murray Anderdon, S. M. J. Woods	1983–	M. F. Hill

BATSMEN

Batsmen with 10,000 or more Runs in Somerset career

Batsman	Runs	Average	Years
H. Gimblett	21,142	36.96	1935–54
P. B. Wight	16,695	32.75	1953–65
W. E. Alley	16,644	30.48	1957–68
R. T. Virgin	15,458	28.52	1957–72
F. S. Lee	15,252	27.99	1929–47
M. J. Kitchen	15,213	26.41	1960–79
M. F. Tremlett	15,195	25.93	1947–60
G. Atkinson	14,468	32.08	1954–66
L. C. H. Palairet	13,851	35.79	1891–1909
I. V. A. Richards	13,524	50.46	1974–85
A. Young	13,081	25.40	1911–33
S. M. J. Woods	12,637	25.07	1891–1910
H. W. Stephenson	12,473	20.02	1948–64
E. Robson	12,439	17.67	1895–1923
L. C. Braund	12,209	25.38	1899–1920
P. W. Denning	11,559	28.68	1969–84
B. C. Rose	11,498	32.95	1969–85
A. W. Wellard	11,432	19.34	1927–50
J. C. White	11,375	18.77	1909–37
H. F. T. Buse	10,623	22.69	1929–53
P. R. Johnson	10,201	25.83	1901–27
P. M. Roebuck	10,109	36.36	1974–86

First Class Centuries Scored for Somerset:

49 H. Gimblett	7 H. F. T. Buse	G. G. Tordoff	1 W. T. Greswell
43 I. V. A. Richards	P. A. Slocombe	3 J. G. Wyatt	R. J. Harden
27 L. C. H. Palairet	H. W. Stephenson	2 M. P. Bajana	R. E. Hayward
P. B. Wight	M. M. Walford	C. A. Bernard	V. T. Hill
24 W. E. Alley	6 M. D. Crowe	B. L. Bisgood	G. Hunt
23 F. S. Lee	J. W. Lee	G. I. Burgess	B. C. Hylton-Stewart
22 R. T. Virgin	A. E. S. Rippon	A. Clarkson	W. Hyman
21 G. Atkinson	J. C. White	M. Coope	J. A. S. Jackson
B. C. Rose	5 C. H. M. Greetham	S. M. Gavaskar	A. T. M. Jones
19 S. M. J. Woods	5 J. W. Lloyds	W. C. Hedley	G. R. Langdale
17 P. R. Johnson	E. Robson	J. G. Lomax	W. T. Luckes
M. J. Kitchen	4 H. D. Burrough	R. J. O. Meyer	F. M. McRae
16 J. C. W. MacBryan	F. A. Phillips	R. C. N. Palairet	H. Martyn
15 M. F. Tremlett	4 N. F. M. Popplewell	K. E. Palmer	J. M. Parks
14 I. T. Botham	B. Roe	A. D. E. Rippon	O. G. Radcliffe
13 L. C. Braund	W. N. Roe	A. W. Wellard	E. Sainsbury
D. B. Close	D. J. S. Taylor	1 F. L. Angell	O. M. Samson
P. M. Roebuck	3 J. H. Cameron	D. Breakwell	D. R. W. Silk
12 M. D. Lyon	G. S. Chappell	T. W. Cartwright	R. Smith
C. L. McCool	3 N. A. Felton	J. B. Challen	R. P. Spurway
11 A. Young	H. T. Hewett	G. Clayton	H. T. Stanley
10 E. F. Longrigg	J. Lawrence	S. G. U. Considine	F. W. Terry
9 C. C. C. Case	V. J. Marks	G. F. Earle	M. Walker
A. E. Lewis	N. S. Mitchell-Innes	P. J. Eele	H. E. Watts
8 J. Daniell	P. J. Robinson	G. Fowler	G. E. S. Woodhouse
P. W. Denning	S. S. Rogers	W. H. Fowler	

Most Centuries in a Season:
- 10 – W. E. Alley in 1961
- 9 – I. V. A. Richards in 1985
- 7 – F. S. Lee in 1938
- 7 – H. Gimblett in 1946
- 7 – R. T. Virgin in 1970
- 7 – I. V. A. Richards in 1977 and 1981
- 7 – P. M. Roebuck in 1984

Most Runs off One Over:
- 31 (666661) A. W. Wellard off F. E. Woolley Somerset v Kent at Wells in 1938
- 30 (.66666) A. W. Wellard off T. R. Armstrong Somerset v Derbyshire at Wells in 1936
- 30 (466626) Zaheer Abbas off D. Breakwell Gloucestershire v Somerset at Taunton in 1979
- 30 (4(4)6646L) I. T. Botham off P. A. Smith Somerset v Warwickshire at Taunton in 1982
- 28 (444646) G. L. Jessop off J. C. Braund Gloucestershire v Somerset at Bristol in 1904
- 28 (666.46) H. L. Hazell off H. Verity Somerset v Yorkshire at Bath in 1936

Fastest 50: 15 minutes G. F. Earle 59 v Gloucestershire at Taunton in 1929

Fastest 100s:
- 41 minutes N. F. M. Popplewell 143 (62 mins.) v Gloucestershire at Bath in 1983 9×6, 17×4
- 49 minutes, 50 balls I. T. Botham 138* (66 mins, 65 balls) v Warwickshire at Edgbaston in 1985 12×6, 13×4
- 52 minutes I. T. Botham 131* (52 mins 56 balls) v Warwickshire at Taunton in 1982 10×6, 12×4
- 58 minutes, 48 balls I. V. A. Richards 102 v Glamorgan at Taunton in 1986 6×6, 12×4
- 63 minutes H. Gimblett 123 (79 mins) v Essex at Frome in 1935 3×6, 17×4

Fastst 200s:
- 135 minutes S. M. J. Woods 215 (150 mins) v Sussex at Hove in 1895
- 165 minutes I. T. Botham 228 (186 mins) v Gloucestershire at Taunton in 1980 10×6, 27×4

Fastest 300s: 276 minutes (244 balls) I. V. A. Richards 322 (294 mins, 258 balls) v Warwickshire at Taunton in 1985 8×6, 42×4

Most Sixes in an Innings:
- 12 – I. T. Botham 138* v Warwickshire at Edgbaston in 1985
- 10 – I. T. Botham 228 v Gloucestershire at Taunton in 1980
- – I. T. Botham 131 v Warwickshire at Taunton in 1982
- – I. T. Botham 134 v Northants at W-s-M in 1985
- – I. V. A. Richards 186 v Hampshire at Taunton in 1985
- 9 – H. Gimblett 141 v Hampshire at Wells in 1937
- – I. V. A. Richards 189 v Lancashire at Southport in 1977
- – N. F. M. Popplewell 143 v Gloucestershire at Bath in 1983 (see above)

Sixes Hit off Consecutive Balls in Same Over:
- 5 – A. W. Wellard off T. R. Armstrong v Derbyshire at Wells in 1936
- – A. W. Wellard of F. E. Woolley v Kent at Wells in 1938

Record Wicket Partnerships:

*1st wicket	346	H. T. Hewett (201) and L. C. H. Palairet (146) v Yorkshire at Taunton in 1892
	273*	N. A. Felton (156*) and P. M. Roebuck (102*) v Hampshire at Taunton in 1986
	258	A. E. Lewis (120) and L. C. H. Palairet (194) v Sussex at Taunton in 1901
	246	J. G. Wyatt (87) and P. M. Roebuck (145) v Yorkshire at Taunton in 1984
	245	B. C. Rose (133) and P. A. Slocombe (103*) v Gloucestershire at Taunton in 1979
	245	J. G. Wyatt (145) and P. M. Roebuck (123*) v Oxford University at The Parks in 1985
	243	N. F. M. Popplewell (172) and P. M. Roebuck (69) v Essex at Southend in 1985
	234	J. W. Lee (109) and F. S. Lee (140) v Essex at Leyton in 1932
2nd wicket	290	J. C. W. MacBryan (132) and M. D. Lyon (219) v Derbyshire at Buxton in 1924
	262	R. T. Virgin (162) and M. J. Kitchen (189) v Pakistanis at Taunton in 1967
	251	J. C. W. MacBryan (148) and A. Young (125*) v Glamorgan at Taunton in 1923
	249	L. C. H. Palairet (154) and R. C. N. Palairet (156) v Sussex at Taunton in 1896
	219	G. Atkinson (115) and P. B. Wight (167*) v Sussex at Eastbourne in 1961
	200	H. Gimblett (146) and G. G. Tordoff (89) v Derbyshire at Taunton in 1952
3rd wicket	319	P. M. Roebuck (128) and M. D. Crowe (190) v Leicestershire at Taunton in 1984
	300	G. Atkinson (190) and P. B. Wight (155*) v Glamorgan at Bath in 1960
	297	P. B. Wight (125) and W. E. Alley (183*) v Surrey at Taunton in 1961
	262	L. C. H. Palairet (161) and C. A. Bernard (122) v Hampshire at Southampton in 1900
	249	N. F. M. Popplewell (133) and M. D. Crowe (125) v Middlesex at Bath in 1984
	239	I. V. A. Richards (170) and P. M. Roebuck (101) v Gloucestershire at Bristol in 1980
	238	F. S. Lee (115) and H. F. T. Buse (132) v Northamptonshire at Kettering in 1938
4th wicket	310	I. T. Botham (228) and P. W. Denning (98) v Gloucestershire at Taunton in 1980
	251	I. V. A. Richards (204) and P. M. Roebuck (112) v Surrey at Weston-super-Mare in 1977
	226	D. J. S. Taylor (179) and D. B. Close (96) v Glamorgan at Swansea in 1974
	206	I. T. Botham (167*) and G. I. Burgess (78) v Nottinghamshire at Trent Bridge in 1976
	200	H. Gimblett (231) and G. E. S. Woodhouse (70) v Middlesex at Taunton in 1946
	199*	S. M. J. Woods (124*) and L. C. Braund (105*) v Hampshire at Southampton in 1908
5th wicket	235	J. C. White (113) and C. C. C. Case (122) v Gloucestershire at Taunton in 1927
	227	I. V. A. Richards (217*) and D. B. Close (91) v Yorkshire at Harrogate in 1975
	222	P. A. Slocombe (78) and B. C. Rose (173*) v Gloucestershire at Bristol in 1982
	221	D. B. Close (138*) and P. A. Slocombe (102) v Gloucestershire at Bristol in 1975
6th wicket	265	W. E. Alley (156) and K. E. Palmer (125*) v Northamptonshire at Northampton in 1961
	196	M. F. Tremlett (100) and P. B. Wight (162) v Middlesex at Bath in 1959
	187*	P. M. Roebuck (131*) and D. Breakwell (100*) v New Zealanders at Taunton in 1978
	183	V. J. Marks (134) and J. W. Lloyds (113*) v Worcestershire at Weston-super-Mare in 1984
	177	H. W. Stephenson (100) and J. G. Lomax (99) v Cambridge University at Taunton in 1956
	174	S. M. J. Woods (146) and J. T. Daniell (107) v Lancashire at Taunton in 1899
7th wicket	240	S. M. J. Woods (144) and V. T. Hill (116) v Kent at Taunton in 1898
	189	J. C. White (142) and R. A. Ingle (101) v Hampshire at Southampton in 1935
	182	S. S. Rogers (101) and H. W. Stephenson (82) v Northamptonshire at Frome in 1950
	177	I. T. Botham (134) and J. C. M. Atkinson (79) v Northamptonshire at Weston-super-Mare in 1985
	162*	M. M. Walford (141*) and H. F. T. Buse (59*) v Indians at Taunton in 1946
8th wicket	172	I. V. A. Richards (216) and I. T. Botham (152) v Leicestershire at Leicester in 1983
	163	M. D. Crowe (113) and J. W. Lloyds (73*) v Lancashire at Bath in 1984
	153*	I. V. A. Richards (181*) and C. H. Dredge (34*) v Pakistan at Taunton in 1982
	143*	E. F. Longrigg (187*) and C. J. P. Barnwell (49*) v Gloucestershire at Bristol in 1938
	124	A. E. Lewis (201*) and Hon. M. R. H. M. Herbert (55) v Kent at Taunton in 1909
	122	D. Breakwell (58) and J. Garner (90) v Gloucestershire at Bath in 1981
	121	R. Smith (58) and J. Lawrence (111) v Essex at Taunton in 1952
9th wicket	183	C. H. Greetham (141) and H. W. Stephenson (80) v Leicestershire at Weston-super-Mare in 1963
	179*	N. F. M. Popplewell (135*) and D. Breakwell (73*) v Kent at Taunton in 1980
	146	W. T. Luckes (90*) and A. T. M. Jones (106) v Leicestershire at Leicester in 1938
	133	J. Lawrence (103*) and W. E. Dean (21) v India at Taunton in 1952
*10th wicket	143	J. J. Bridges (99*) and H. Gibbs (41) v Essex at Weston-super-Mare in 1919
	139	P. R. Johnson (117*) and R. C. Robertson-Glasgow (49) v Surrey at The Oval in 1926
	112	J. W. Lee (135*) and W. T. Luckes (59) v Kent at Taunton in 1934
	110*	A. G. Marshall (30*) and G. Hunt (80*) v Hampshire at Taunton in 1930
	92	H. L. Hazell (43) and H. T. F. Buse (58*) v Gloucestershire at Bristol in 1946

Highest Individual Innings for Somerset

322	I. V. A. Richards	Warwickshire	Taunton	1985
310	H. Gimblett	Sussex	Eastbourne	1948
292	L. C. H. Palairet	Hampshire	Southampton	1896
264	M. M. Walford	Hampshire	Weston-super-Mare	1947
257	L. C. Braund	Worcestershire	Worcester	1913
241*	I. V. A. Richards	Gloucestershire	Bristol	1977
231	H. Gimblett	Middlesex	Taunton	1946
228	I. T. Botham	Gloucestershire	Taunton	1980
222*	P. B. Wight	Kent	Taunton	1959
221*	W. E. Alley	Warwickshire	Nuneaton	1961
221*	P. M. Roebuck	Nottinghamshire	Trent Bridge	1986
219	M. D. Lyon	Derbyshire	Buxton	1924

2000 Runs in a Season with averages in brackets
(a) for Somerset (b) Championship Matches (c) All F-C Matches

		(a)	(b)	(c)
1938	F. S. Lee	2019 (44.86)	2015 (46.86)	2019 (44.86)
1949	H. Gimblett	2063 (43.89)	1839 (42.76)	2093 (43.60)
1951	M. F. Tremlett	2071 (37.65)	2018 (38.80)	2101 (35.61)
1952	H. Gimblett	2134 (39.51)	2068 (39.76)	2134 (39.51)
1960	P. B. Wight	2316 (41.35)	2086 (40.11)	2375 (41.67)
1961	W. E. Alley	2761 (58.74)	2532 (56.26)	3019 (56.96)
1961	G. Atkinson	2005 (38.56)	1892 (37.84)	2078 (37.10)
1962	G. Atkinson	2035 (36.33)	1951 (35.47)	2075 (35.77)
1962	P. B. Wight	2030 (44.13)	1853 (43.06)	2030 (44.13)
1970	R. T. Virgin	2223 (47.29)	2223 (47.29)	2220 (47.29)
1977	I. V. A. Richards	2161 (65.48)	2090 (67.41)	2161 (65.48)

Century in Each Innings: 1908 P. R. Johnson 164 and 131 v Middlesex at Taunton
1925 J. Daniell 174* and 108 v Essex at Taunton. Carried Bat. Aged 46
1928 R. A. Ingle 117 and 100* v Middlesex at Taunton
1938 F. S. Lee 109* and 107 v Worcestershire at Worcester. Carried Bat. Last man out
1949 H. Gimblett 115 and 127* v Hampshire at Taunton
1952 H. Gimblett 146 and 116 v Derbyshire at Taunton
1961 W. E. Alley 183* and 134* v Surrey at Taunton
1965 R. T. Virgin 124 and 125* v Warwickshire at Edgbaston
1977 P. W. Denning 122 and 107 v Gloucestershire at Taunton
1980 B. C. Rose 124 and 150* v Worcestershire at Worcester
1982 J. W. Lloyds 132* and 102* v Northamptonshire at Northampton

Highest Innings Totals: *For* 675-9d v Hampshire at Bath in 1924
630 v Yorkshire at Leeds in 1901
592 v Yorkshire at Taunton in 1892
584-8 v Sussex at Eastbourne in 1948
566-5d (in 100 overs) v Warwickshire at Taunton in 1985
561 v Lancashire at Bath in 1901
560-8d v Sussex at Taunton in 1901
554 v Sussex at Taunton in 1899
545 v Worcestershire at Taunton in 1906
545-9d v Hampshire at Taunton in 1930

Lowest Innings Totals: *For* 25 v Gloucestershire at Bristol in 1947
29 and 51 v Lancashire at Old Trafford in 1882
31 v Gloucestershire at Bristol in 1931
31 v Lancashire at Old Trafford in 1894
33 v Lancashire at Liverpool in 1908
35 v Yorkshire at Bath in 1898
35 and 44 v Middlesex at Lords in 1899
35 v Derbyshire at Derby in 1935
36 v Surrey at Weston-super-Mare in 1955
37 v Hampshire at Taunton in 1955
37 v Hampshire at Bournemouth in 1956
37 and 37 v Surrey at The Oval in 1891

BOWLERS

Bowlers with 500 or more Wickets in Somerset career

Bowler	Wickets	Average
J. C. White	2167	18.02
A. W. Wellard	1517	24.32
B. A. Langford	1390	24.89
E. Robson	1122	26.60
H. L. Hazell	957	23.97
E. J. Tyler	865	22.29
K. E. Palmer	837	21.11
J. Lawrence	791	24.88
W. H. R. Andrews	750	23.38
W. E. Alley	738	22.04
J. Bridges	684	25.63
L. C. Braund	684	27.98
H. F. T. Buse	657	28.77
B. Cranfield	563	24.61
S. M. J. Woods	556	24.12
H. R. Moseley	547	24.10
F. E. Rumsey	520	19.79
A. E. Lewis	513	23.18
V. J. Marks	505	31.65

Most Wickets in a Season

A. W. Wellard	169	19.24
J. C. White	150	15.17
J. C. White	147	15.07
J. C. White	147	15.32
J. C. White	144	15.12
A. W. Wellard	143	18.22
A. W. Wellard	140	23.71

Most Maiden Overs in Succession:

H. L. Hazell 17 (105 balls) v
  Gloucestershire at Taunton in 1949
W. E. Alley 14 (93 balls) v Essex at
  Yeovil in 1960

100 or more Wickets in a Season

Bowler	No. of Times
J. C. White	14
A. W. Wellard	8
W. H. R. Andrews	4
B. A. Langford	4
K. E. Palmer	3
B. Cranfield	2
H. L. Hazell	2
J. Lawrence	2
F. E. Rumsey	2
E. J. Tyler	1
L. C. Braund	1
W. T. Greswell	1
E. P. Robinson	1
J. W. McMahon	1
B. Lobb	1
W. E. Alley	1
T. W. Cartwright	1

Players Achieving the 'Double'. Somerset Matches Only

Player	No. of Times
J. C. White	2
A. W. Wellard	2
W. H. R. Andrews	2
K. E. Palmer	1
W. E. Alley	1

FIELDING

Most Catches in a Career

No.	Player	Year	No.	Player	Year
381	J. C. White	1909–37	233	H. Gimblett	1935–54
355	L. C. Braund	1899–1920	226	B. A. Langford	1953–74
344	A. W. Wellard	1927–50	213	L. C. H. Palairet	1891–1909
308	R. T. Virgin	1957–72	211	A. Young	1911–33
267	W. E. Alley	1957–68	209	J. Daniell	1898–1927
259	J. Lawrence	1946–55	209	P. B. Wight	1953–65
253	E. Robson	1895–1923	206	J. G. Lomax	1954–62
249	H. L. Hazell	1929–52	205	S. M. J. Woods	1891–1910
241	M. F. Tremlett	1947–60			

Most Dismissals in a Career by a Wicket-keeper

No.	Ct.	St.	Wicket-keeper	Years
1007	698	309	H. W. Stephenson	1948–64
827	568	241	W. T. Luckes	1924–49
661	587	74	D. J. S. Taylor	1970–82
415	297	118	A. E. Newton	1891–1914
242	209	33	G. Clayton	1965–68
188	133	55	H. Chidgey	1900–21
179	146	33	T. Gard	1976–85

COMPETITIONS RECORD

County Championship Matches

John Player Special League

Year	Position	Year	Position	Year	Position
1891	5=	1924	8	1959	12
1892	3	1925	15	1960	14
1893	8	1926	14	1961	10
1894	6	1927	14	1962	6
1895	8=	1928	14	1963	3
1896	11	1929	15	1964	8
1897	11	1930	13=	1965	7
1898	13=	1931	13	1966	3
1899	13=	1932	7	1967	8
1900	11	1933	11	1968	12
1901	12=	1934	15	1969	17
1902	7	1935	14	1970	13
1903	10	1936	7	1971	7
1904	12	1937	13	1972	11
1905	15	1938	7	1973	10
1906	11=	1939	14	1974	5
1907	14	1946	4	1975	12
1908	16	1947	11=	1976	7
1909	11	1948	12	1977	4
1910	16	1949	9	1978	5
1911	16	1950	7=	1979	8
1912	14	1951	14	1980	5
1913	16	1952	17	1981	3
1914	15	1953	17	1982	6
1919	5=	1954	17	1983	10
1920	10	1955	17	1984	7
1921	10	1956	15	1985	17
1922	10	1957	8		
1923	9	1958	3		

Year	Position
1969	16
1970	15
1971	5
1972	7=
1973	11
1974	2
1975	14
1976	2=
1977	9=
1978	2
1979	1
1980	2
1981	2
1982	9
1983	2
1984	13
1985	10

Benson & Hedges Cup Record – Highlights: Semi-finalists 1974, 1978
Winning finalists 1981 (beat Surrey), 1982 (beat Notts)

Gillette Cup Record: Semi-finalists 1966, 1970, 1974, 1977
Finalists 1967 (lost to Kent)
1978 (lost to Sussex)
1979 (beat Northants)

Nat West Trophy Record: Finalists 1983 (beat Kent)

LIMITED OVERS (JOHN PLAYER SPECIAL LEAGUE 1969–85)

Highest Total For: 286–7 (38 overs) v Hampshire at Taunton in 1981
270–4 v Gloucester at Bristol Imperial in 1975
Against: 288–5 (40 over) by Hampshire at Weston-super-Mare in 1975

Lowest Total For: 58 (18.2 overs) v Essex at Chelmsford in 1977
Against: 72 (19 overs) by Nottinghamshire at Bath in 1982

Runs in Career: 4565 (av. 27.50) P. W. Denning 1969–84
4363 (av. 39.66) I. V. A. Richards 1974–85
3367 (av. 26.10) B. C. Rose 1969–85

Runs in Season: 578 (av. 52.55) I. V. A. Richards 1975
545 (av. 41.92) I. V. A. Richards 1977

Most Sixes in Career: 131 I. V. Richards (1974–85)
100 I. T. Botham (1973–85)

Most Sixes in a Season: 26 I. V. A. Richards 1977 (League Record)
19 D. B. Close 1974

Most Sixes in an Innings: 8 D. B. Close v Yorkshire at Bath 1978

Most Runs in an Over: 34 (7 ball over) I. V. A. Richards off D. A. Graveney (Glos.) at Taunton 1972

218

Most Wickets in a Career: 222 (av. 20.24) H. R. Moseley 1971–82
172 (av. 24.62) G. I. Burgess 1969–80

Most Wickets in a Season: 34 (av. 13.18) R. J. Clapp 1974 (League Record)
27 (av. 12.52) J. Garner 1982

Best Bowling Performances For: 6–24 I. V. A. Richards v Lancashire at Old Trafford in 1983
6–25 G. I. Burgess v. Glamorgan at Glastonbury in 1972
6–34 A. A. Jones v Essex at Westcliff-on-Sea in 1971
Against: 7–39 (inc. Hat-Trick) A. Hodgson for Northants at Northampton 1976
6–29 B. P. Hughes for Lancashire at Old Trafford in 1977
6–36 A. G. Nicholson for Yorkshire at Bramall Lane in 1972

Hat-Tricks: R. Palmer v Gloucestershire at Bristol in 1970
I. V. A. Richards v Essex at Chelmsford in 1982

Economical Bowling: 8–8–0–0 B. A. Langford v Essex at Yeovil in 1969 (League Record)
8–6–5–1 T. W. Cartwright v Essex at Chelmsford in 1973

Most Catches in a Career: 68 P. W. Denning 1969–84
57 I. V. A. Richards 1974–85

Most Catches in a Season: 11 I. V. A. Richards 1978
9 C. H. Dredge 1980

Most Catches in a Match: 4 P. J. Robinson v Worcestershire at Worcester 1971

Most Dismissals in a Career: 177 (33st/144c) D. J. S. Taylor 1970–82

Most Dismissals in a Season: 24 (5st/19c) D. J. S. Taylor 1981

Most Dismissals in a Match: 4 (1st/3c) D. J. S. Taylor v Lancashire and Essex 1972
4 (4c) D. J. S. Taylor v Notts 1978

Most Appearances: 191 P. W. Denning 1969–84
183 D. J. S. Taylor 1970–82

Highest Individual Innings For: 131 D. B. Close v Yorkshire at Bath 1974
128* G. S. Chappell v Surrey at Bridlington 1969
(First T.V. Century + First League Century)
128 D. B. Close v Gloucestershire at Bristol 1974
126* I. V. A. Richards v Gloucestershire at Bristol Imperial 1975
123* R. T. Virgin v Surrey at The Oval 1970
Against: 142 B. W. Luckhurst for Kent at Weston-super-Mare 1970

Highest Partnerships: 179 5th wkt. I. V. A. Richards (93) + I. T. Botham (106) v Hampshire at Taunton 1980
170* 2nd wkt. R. T. Virgin (42*) + G. S. Chappell (128*) v Surrey at Bridlington 1969
164 2nd wkt. B. C. Rose (62) + I. V. A. Richards (104) v Derbyshire at Taunton 1977

SOMERSET'S TEST CRICKETERS

	Years	Name	Tests		Years	Name	Tests
1	For *England*				1977/8–80/81	B. C. Rose	9
	1888–89	A. J. Fothergill	2		1982–83/84	V. J. Marks	6
	1894–95	L. H. Gay	1	2	For *Australia*		
	1895–96	S. M. J. Woods	3		1888	S. M. J. Woods	3
		E. J. Tyler	1		1945/46–49/50	C. L. McCool	14
	1901/2–07/08	L. C. Braund	23		1970/71	G. S. Chappell	87
	1902	L. C. H. Palairet	2		1970/71/77	K. J. O'Keeffe	24
	1893–97/98	T. Richardson	14	3	For *West Indies*		
	1921–30/31	J. C. White	15		1939	J. H. Cameron	2
	1924	J. C. M. MacBryan	1		1974/75–85/86	I. V. A. Richards	82
	1935	N. S. Mitchell-Innes	1		1976/77–85/86	J. Garner	56
	1936–39	H. Gimblett	3	4	For *New Zealand*		
	1937–38	A. W. Wellard	2		1929/30–31	T. C. Lowry	7
	1947–48	M. F. Tremlett	3		1981/82–85/86	M. D. Crowe	29
	1964–65	F. E. Rumsey	5	5	For *Pakistan*		
		T. W. Cartwright	5		1952/53–57/58	Khan Mohammad	13
	1954–67/68	J. M. Parks	46	6	For *India*		
	1949–76	D. B. Close	22		1959–66/67	A. A. Baig	10
	1964–65	K. E. Palmer	1		1970/71–86	S. M. Gavaskar	115
	1977–85/86	I. T. Botham	84				

CAPTAINS

1882–84	S. C. Newton	1949	G. E. S. Woodhouse
1885	E. Sainsbury	1950–52	S. S. Rogers
1891–93	H. T. Hewett	1953–54	B. G. Brocklehurst
1894–1906	S. M. J. Woods	1955	G. G. Tordeff
1907	L. C. H. Palairet	1956–59	M. F. Tremlett
1908–12	J. Daniell	1960–64	H. W. Stephenson
1913–14	E. S. M. Poyntz	–64	W. E. Alley – Acting Captain
1919–26	J. Daniell	1965–67	C. R. M. Atkinson
1927–31	J. C. White	1968	R. C. Kerslake
1932–37	R. A. Ingle	1969–71	B. A. Langford
1938–46	E. F. Lougrigg	1972–77	D. B. Close
1947	R. J. O. Meyer	1978–83	B. C. Rose
1948	N. S. Mitchell-Innes	1984–85	I. T. Botham
	G. E. S. Woodhouse	1986–	P. M. Roebuck
	J. W. Seamer		

Somerset team group 1986. *Back row, left to right,* Rainer Blitz, Nigel Felton, Richard Bartlett, Stephen Booth, Richard Harden, Jon Hardy, Nick Taylor, Robert Coombs, Murray Turner, Gary Palmer, Mark Davis, Julian Wyatt. *Front row,* Colin Dredge, Vic Marks, Viv Richards, Peter Roebuck (captain), Brian Rose, Ian Botham, Peter Robinson (coach), Trevor Gard, Dennis Waight (physiotherapist)

Index